St. Andrews University Publications, Issue 4

You are holding a reproduction of an original work that is in the public domain in the United States of America, and possibly other countries. You may freely copy and distribute this work as no entity (individual or corporate) has a copyright on the body of the work. This book may contain prior copyright references, and library stamps (as most of these works were scanned from library copies). These have been scanned and retained as part of the historical artifact.

This book may have occasional imperfections such as missing or blurred pages, poor pictures, errant marks, etc. that were either part of the original artifact, or were introduced by the scanning process. We believe this work is culturally important, and despite the imperfections, have elected to bring it back into print as part of our continuing commitment to the preservation of printed works worldwide. We appreciate your understanding of the imperfections in the preservation process, and hope you enjoy this valuable book.

CONTENTS.

I. **Colloquialisms. The Concords.** 1. Elasticity of O. Lat. Syntax, e.g. First Supine, *quominus*. 2. Plautus' colloquial Latin. 3. No Graecisms in Plautus. 4. Constructio ad Sensum, e.g. *refert* and *interest*. 5. Concord of Gender. 6. Concord of Number. 7. Plural of Abstract Nouns. 8. Attraction of Antecedent to Relative. 9. Of Rel. to Antecedent. 10. Change of Subject. 11. Pleonasm. pp. 1—10

II. **The Cases of the Noun.** 1. Cases without Prepositions. 2. Nominative. 3. Genitive competing with Abl. 4. Gen. of Respect. 5. No Greek Gen. in Plautus. 6. Gen. of Exclamation. 7. Gen. with *potior*, etc. 8. Gen. with *vereor*, etc. 9. Adjectival Gen. 10. *lucri facere*, etc. 11. *dotis dare*, etc. 12. *scelus viri*, etc. 13. Partitive Gen. 14. Gen. of Plenty and Want. 15. Gen. with *dignus*. 16. Gen. of Price. 17. Objective Gen. 18. Possessive Gen. 19. Predicative Dative. 20. Dat. of Purpose. 21. *arraboni dare*, etc. 22. Dat. for *ad* with Acc. 23. Dat. Commodi. 24. Possessive Dat. 25. Verbs with Dat., *curo*, etc. 26. Dat. with Adjectives. 27. Dat. of Capacity. 28. *nomen est mihi Gaio*, etc. 29. Locative-suffix. 30. History of Loc. 31. *viciniae*, etc. 32. Loc. and Abl. 33. *adveniens domi*. 34. *in Lemno*, etc. 35. Cognate Accusative. 36. Adverbial Acc. 37. Acc. of Time. 38. Acc. of Space. 39. Acc. of Motion. 40. Acc. with *dignus esse*, *perditus esse* and Intrans. Verbs. 41. Acc. with Verbal Noun. 42. *te novi qualis sis*, etc. 43. Acc. with Compound Verbs. 44. Verbs with Acc., *parco*, etc. 45. Acc. with *fungor*, etc. 46. Acc. with *ultro*, etc. 47. Acc. of Exclamation. 48. Acc. with Verb suppressed. 49. Acc. with *indutus*. 50. Construction of *instruo, impertio*. 51. Double Acc. 52. Vocative. 53. Ablative. 54. Abl. of Motion. 55. Abl. of Provenience. 56. *opus est, usus est*. 57. Abl. with *facio, vescor*, etc. 58. Adverbial Abl. 59. Abl. Absolute. 60. Abl. of Price. 61. Abl. of Cause. 62. Abl. of Description. 63. Abl. of Time. 64. Abl. of Place. 65. Abl. of Difference. 66. Abl. of Comparison. 67. Abl. with *dignus* and *decorus*. 68. Abl. of Plenty and Want. 69. Abl. of Respect. 70. Verbs with Abl., *prohibeo, caveo*, etc. pp. 10—37

III. **The Adjective.** 1. Noun for Adj., Adj. for Adv., etc. 2. Comparative, *certior fieri, potior f.*, etc. 3. *nequam, frugi (bonae)*, etc. 4. *unus, mille*. pp. 37—40

IV. **The Pronoun.** 1. Personal. 2. Possessive. 3. *quis . . quisquam, qui . . is*, etc. 4. *quisquis, quivis, quilubet*, etc. 5. *quae tua est prudentia*. 6. *qui; quin* for *isne qui*. 7. *is* for repeated *qui*. 8. *quis* Indef. 9. *quisquam, quispiam*. 10. *quisnam, ecquid*, 11. *quot calendis*. 12. *homo* for *is*. 13. *hic, iste, ille*. 14. *is*. 15. *is* for Reflexive Pron.

CONTENTS.

16. *ille* and *hic* for *is*. 17. *ego*, etc. . . . *is*. 18. *is* pleonastically added, *illud quidem*. 19. *is* for *ob id*, etc. 20. Pronominal Adverbs for Cases of Pronouns. 21. Pleonasm, e.g. *nemo homo*. 22. Deictic use of Pron. 23. *ipse*. 24. *idem*. 25. *quisque* and *quisquis*. 26. *alter*. 27. *ambo*. 28. *nullus*, etc. 29. *tantus*. pp. 40—52

V. **The Verb.** 1. Impersonal Passive. 2. Auxiliary Verbs. 3. Deponents. 4. Middle Voice, Active for Middle. 5. Frequentative Verbs. 6. *coeptus est*, etc., with Passive. 7. Omission of Verb. 8. Omission of *sum*. 9. *lubido est* for *lubet*, etc. 10. Sequence of Tenses. 11. Present Tense. 12. Pres. Inf. 13. Imperfect. 14. Imperf. Subj. 15. Future. 16. *amabo*. 17. Future Perfect. 18. *faxo*, etc. 19. Perfect. 20. *amatus sum* and *fui*. 21. Perf. Subj. 22. Pluperfect. 23. Pluperf. Subj. 24. Subjunctive and Optative. 25. Subj. for Imperative. 26. Subj. for Future. 27. Subj. in Dependent Clauses. 28. Parataxis. Indirect Questions. 29. Subj. by Attraction. 30. Subj. and Ind. in Dependent Clauses. 31. Indefinite use of 2 Sing. Subj. 32. Imperative. 33. Infinitive for Verbal Noun. 34. Acc. and Inf. 35. Verbs with Inf. 36. Verbal Phrases with Inf. 37. Inf. of Purpose. 38. Inf. of Exclamation. 39. Historical Inf. 40. Fut. Inf. Act. 41. Fut. Inf. Pass. 42. Supine. 43. Gerund and Gerundive. 44. Participle Pres. with *sum*. 45. Perf. Part. Pass. 46. Fut. Part. Act. 47. Part. for Noun.

pp. 52—79

VI. **The Adverb.** 1. Adv. with *esse*. 2. Adv. for Adj. 3. Qualifying Adverbs. 4. Comparison of Adv. 5. Construction of *fortasse*, etc.

pp. 79—81

VII. **The Preposition.** 1. Prep. and Adv., Tmesis, Postposition. 2. List of noteworthy Prepositions. pp. 81—92

VIII. **The Conjunction.** 1. Position of enclitic Conj. 2. List of noteworthy Conjunctions. 3. Causal. 4. Concessive. 5. Conditional. 6. Copulative. Asyndeton. 7. Interrogative. 8. Negative. 9. Prohibitive. 10. Temporal. pp. 92—137

IX. **The Interjection.** pp. 137—138

SYNTAX OF PLAUTUS.

I. COLLOQUIALISMS. THE CONCORDS.

1. The rules of Latin Syntax which prevailed in the classical period, e.g. that *quamquam* and temporal *quom* govern the Ind., *quamvis* and causal *quom* the Subj., so often fail us in reading Plautus, that Plautine Latin at first sight appears to be regardless of rules. This appearance is partly due to the fact that Latin Syntax obeys the Darwinian law of the 'survival of the fittest.' Out of a great variety of constructions possible in the time of Plautus, only one or two favoured types have survived to the classical period. While Plautus, for example, puts the Verbal Noun in *-tus* to a variety of uses, e.g. *spectatum eo, spectatu redeo, pulcher spectatui, facile factu*, etc., two of these, *spectatum eo* and *facile factu*, survived the struggle for existence and became the First and the Second Supine. Again we find in early writers *quo* Abl. Neut. used with *magis* in affirmative, with *minus* in negative sense, and accompanied by the Ind. when a fact is stated, by the Subj. when an intention, e.g. Ter. Phorm. 877 immo etiam dabo quo magis credas, Eun. 737 quo intellexi minus, Andr. 197 fallaciae ... quo (nuptiae) fiant minus. Out of all this variety emerges in class. Lat. the conjunction *quominus* governing the Subj. and associated with Verbs of hindering. It is partly due also to the colloquial character of Plautine Latin; and before taking up the details of Plautine Syntax, it will be well to consider how far colloquialisms interfere with a strictly grammatical expression in his plays.

2. Since Aelius Stilo declared that the Muses, if they had spoken Latin, would have used the Latin of Plautus, and since Cicero expresses his admiration for the old-fashioned language of a Roman matron by saying that it reminded him of Plautus and Naevius (de Or. 3, 45), we must see in his plays, not vulgar Latin, but the every-day talk of the educated Romans of his time. How far he permits himself on occasion to reproduce the vulgarisms of uneducated speakers is a question that has not yet been investigated;

but I greatly doubt that the investigation would shew that this or that departure from a rule of classical Latin Syntax was found only in the utterances of slaves or of characters like Ballio in the Pseudolus. We have indeed the express testimony of an ancient writer that *non salveo* in Truc. 259 is a piece of bad Latin, suited to the character who uses it:

AS. salve. TR. sat mihi est tuae salutis. nil moror. non salveo.

But the surly slave, Truculentus, from whom the play is named, is a unique type in Plautus' Comedies. He is a Roman 'Mrs. Malaprop,' who is credited with mutilated forms of words like *rabo* (v. 688) for *arrabo*, *osculentia* (v. 675) for *obsequentia* (with a suggestion of *osculum*), etc.; so that one can make no general inference from this particular case [a].

3. Nor can we suppose that Graecisms were employed by Plautus, as by the Augustan poets (e.g. Hor. desine mollium tandem querelarum), to embellish his style. This is out of keeping with the colloquial tone of Comedy. (On Pers. 385 non tu nunc hominum mores vides? see **VI, 2**; on Asin. 634 quas hodie adulescens Diabolus ipsi daturus dixit, see **V, 34**; on the Gen. of Respect, e.g. Rud. 213 incerta sum consili, **II, 5**, and of Exclamation, e.g. Most. 912 mercimoni lepidi! **II, 6**.)

4. We must then regard the Syntax of Plautus, as well as his vocabulary and the arrangement [b] of his sentences (and, I would add, his Prosody, e.g. *Philippus, volŭptatem, volŭptas mea*) as a faithful representation of the cultured every-day speech of his time. Of course every-day speech does not follow the strict laws of the logical expression of thought. What is known in our Grammars as 'Constructio ad Sensum' plays a great part in it. This 'Constructio ad Sensum' is a powerful agent in the development of

---

[a] See however Donatus on Ter. Phorm. 249, Eun. 432, 792, etc., and compare my note on p. 48 of No. III. of this Series.

[b] The elasticity of the dialogue metres allowed a fairly exact reproduction of every-day speech, except occasionally at the end of a line. Thus, while *causā, gratiā* are always preceded, not followed by their Gen., Adj., or Pron., we find occasionally at the end of a line *causa mea, causa tua*. The poetical ornament of alliteration may also interfere. (See F. Leo: Bemerkungen ueber plautinische Wortstellung, Göttingen, 1895.) The distorted arrangement which is normal in adjurations, e.g. Bacch. 905 per te, ere, obsecro deos immortales, apparently reflects every-day speech. Also an arrangement like *tua Bromia ancilla* 'your slave-girl B.' (See **IV, 2**.)

ntax in Latin and in all languages. For example, the notion
'concern' 'interest' was in Early Latin expressed by *refert*,
ich, I think, is most naturally explained as *re* (Abl.) (with the
ise of class. Lat. *ex re;* cf. Capt. 296 tua re feceris, and see my
te on this line) and *fert* 'it tends ' (cf. via fert ad urbem, Ter.
idr. 188 dum tempus ad eam rem tulit), 'it tends with (Engl.
)') my interest.' In course of time (later than Plautus and
:rence) the verb *interesse* came to be used in this sense, and
oceeded to take the same construction as *refert*, viz. *meā interest*.

amples from Plautus are :—
Pers. 70 ubi quadrupulator quempiam (Acc.) iniexit manum
= comprehenderit), tantidem ille illi (Dat.) rursus iniciat manum,
uc. 762 postid ego te manum iniciam quadrupuli, venefica; Asin.
nunc verba in pauca conferam (= breviter exponam) quid te
lim; Bacch. 161 ecquid in mentem est tibi (= meministi) patrem
)i esse?; Pers. 66 animus induci (= credi) potest eum esse civem
fidelem et bonum; Capt. 579 nunc iste te ludos facit (= deludit;
. II, 25), Aul. 253 quem senecta aetate ludos facias, Rud. 900
.m nunc et operam ludos dat (*v.l.* facit) et retia; Rud. 791 si te
in ludos pessumos dimisero.
On the use of an Acc. with *depereo, demorior,* and even *amore
rditus sum*, all three being equivalents of *deamo,* see **II, 40.**

5. The Concords are often violated in colloquial speech. Since
autus habitually uses the Fem. Adj. with *res* as the equivalent of
e Neut. Adj. used substantively (e.g. *mala res* and *malum, parva
s* and *par(v)um*), he allows in e.g. Merc. 337 quidquid est quam
m (= quod) agere occepi, Stich. 82 quom nihil quam ob rem
= ob quod) id faciam meruisse arbitror. From the Adj. *muliebris*
elicited a (suppressed) *mulieres* in Mil. 186 profecto ut nequoquam
: ingenio degrediatur muliebri, *earumque* artem et disciplinam
)tineat colere; similarly with *proletarius* in Mil. 753 proletario
rmone nunc quidem, hospes, utere; nam *i* solent ... dicere;
id with *erilis* in Pers. 193 scio fide hercle erili ut soleat impudi-
tia opprobrari, nec subigi *queantur* umquam ut pro ea fide habeant
dicem.

The Neut. Plur. and Neut. Sing. of Adj. and Pron. are so
.terchangeable in Plautus (e.g. *mira sunt* and *mirum* (*est*),
'III, 2, 'si'), that we need not wonder at the loose construction

of Poen. 913 A. vale et haec cura clanculum ut sint dicta. B. non dictumst (= dicta sunt). vale; cf. Poen. 542 per iocum itidem dictum (dicta *Bentley*) habeto quae nos tibi respondimus, Mil. 699 haec atque huius (horum *Ritschl*) similia alia damna multa mulierum me uxore prohibent, mihi quae huius similis sermones sera[n]t. In contrast with a 'Concord' like *mea Selenium* Cist. 631 (cf. Poen. prol. 17 scortum exoletum ne quis (quod *Ital.*) in proscaenio sedeat) may be noticed the common phrase *quod amas* (= amica) 'object of affection' (cf. Trin. 1160 postremo quod vis non duces ('marry'), nisi illud (i.e. the dowry) quod non vis feres). Like Virgil's *triste lupus stabulis* is the construction of Poen. 238 modus omnibus rebus, soror, optimum est habitu; cf. Mil. 685 nam bona uxor suave ductu est (suavest, *i.e.* -is est, ductu *alii*); and like Virgil's *hoc opus, hic labor est* is a phrase like *ea* (= id) *stultitiast* Pseud. 576. And a Neut. Pron. is often loosely used with reference to a preceding Noun, as in Trin. 405 minas quadraginta ... quid factumst eo? ('that sum of money'), Capt. 898 A. aeternum tibi dapinabo victum, si vera autumas. B. unde id? (= eum), Trin. 595 ager ... sed id si alienatur, Bacch. 125 A. non hic placet mi ornatus. B. nemo ergo tibi haec apparavit, cf. Rud. 215 algor, error, pavor, me omnia tenent. The use of the Acc. with the Inf. violates the Concord of Case in lines like Asin. 642 vobis est suave amantibus complexos fabulari, Cas. 89 non mihi licere meam rem me solum ... loqui!, Amph. 181 mihi in mentem fuit dis advenientem gratias ... agere.

6. The Concord of Number is violated in the O. Lat. phrases *praesente nobis*, e.g. Amph. 400, *absente nobis*, e.g. Ter. Eun. 649, the Abl. Sing. *praesente, absente* having apparently become a stereotyped form, much as *qui*, Abl., or rather Instr., Sing. of the Relative Pronoun (3 Decl.) became a stereotyped 'whereby,' e.g. Rud. 1110 ubi sunt signa qui parentes noscere haec possit suos, quibuscum periit parva Athenis?, Ter. Andr. 511 multa concurrunt simul, Qui coniecturam hanc nunc facio (so with *quo* in Poen. 905 omnia memoras quo id facilius fiat; from which has come the use of *quo* for *ut* with a comparative following; see **VIII**, 2). We have often a Sing. Verb with two Subjects, e.g. Pseud. 1097 epistula atque imago me certum facit, Mil. 225 qua cibatus commeatusque ad te et legiones tuas tuto possit pervenire, Ter. Adelph. 340 tum fama et gnatae vita in dubium veniet; and occasionally in O. Lat. we get a Plural Verb with 'A cum B,' e.g. Ter. Heaut.

473 Syrus cum illo vostro consusurrant (cf. Cato Orat. 51 si sponsionem fecissent Gellius cum Turio, Claud. Quadrig. 85 sagittarius cum funditore utrimque summo studio spargunt fortissime), a construction with which we may connect a line like Most. 560 sed Philolachetis servom eccum Tranium, qui mihi neque faenus neque sortem argenti danunt (cf. Amph. 731 cur igitur praedicas te heri me vidisse, qui hac noctu in portum advecti sumus?). Slightly irregular too is Naev. trag. 40 egone an ille iniurie facimus?

A Plural Verb is common not only with *uterque*, e.g. Curc. 187 uterque insaniunt, *alius alium*, e.g. Curc. 378 habent hunc morem plerique argentarii, ut alius alium poscant, reddant nemini, *quisque*, e.g. filios suos quisque visunt, Poen. 107 omnis meretrices, ubi quisque (Fem.) habitant, invĕnit, *uter* and *neuter*, e.g. Men. 779 loquere uter meruistis culpam, Men. 785 neuter ad me iretis, but also with *quisquam*, e.g. Amph. 1071 neque nostrum quisquam sensimus, Pers. 56 nam numquam quisquam meorum maiorum fuit, quin parasitando paverint ventris suos, Men. 192 ut superior sis mihi quam quisquam qui impetrant, Ter. Andr. 627, and very often with *aliquis* in commands like *aperite aliquis* Merc. 131, etc., exite huc aliquis Epid. 399, Accius 425 Oeneum aliquis cette in conspectum. And a collective Noun like *pars* often takes a Plur. Verb, e.g. Most. 114 sed magna pars morem hunc induxerunt, Truc. 105 fit pol hoc et pars spectatorum scitis pol haec vos me haud mentiri; cf. Poen. 619 sed quid huc tantum hominum incedunt? and even Epid. 213 tum meretricum numerus tantus, quantum in urbe omni fuit, obviam ornatae occurrebant. *Est* 'il y a' is suggested by Pers. 137 sicut istic leno non sex menses Megaribus huc est quom commigravit, but *menses* is Acc., as we see from Aul. prol. 4 hanc domum iam multos annos est quom possideo et colo, and corresponds to an Adverb of Time like *diu* in e.g. Amph. 302 iam diu est quom ventri victum non datis, *dudum* in e.g. Trin. 1010; with Nom., *sunt* is used, e.g. Most. 470 septem menses sunt quom . . . tetulit; and editors change *est* of the MSS. (*A n. l.*) to *em* in Pseud. 245 mane, est conloqui qui volunt te, since we have elsewhere *sunt qui*, e.g. Pseud. 462 sunt quae te volumus percontari. A change from a Sing. to a Plur. Verb is seen in phrases with *age*, e.g. Cas. 488 age modo, fabricamini, Stich. 221 logos ridiculos vendo; age, licemini. The same change of Number in a Noun is seen in the two divisions of a sentence like Trin. 237 numquam Amor quemquam nisi cupidum hominem postulat se in plagas conicere; eos petit, eos sectatur (cf. Curc. 494, Mil. 887, 993) and is often found with a Relative like *quisquis* and its Antecedent, e.g. Poen. 505 qui, quidquid agit, properat omnia (cf. Rud. 1140, Trin. 1168), Men. 560 ubi vir compilet clanculum quidquid domist atque ea ad amicam deferat; cf. Ter. Heaut. 393.

7. Another type of change from Plural to Singular is seen in lines like Ter. Heaut. 483 sqq., Eun. 225 sqq., Phorm. 241 sqq. Lastly we may mention under this heading the colloquial use of the Plural of Abstract Nouns, e.g. Merc. 794 at te, vicine, di deaeque perduint, cum tua amica cumque amationibus. (For more examples see Langen 'Beiträge,' pp. 103 sqq.) The colloquial use, so frequent in Plautus, of *gaudia* Plur. for *gaudium* Sing. produced in Late Latin the First Decl. form *gaudia*, whence Ital. gioja, French joie, etc.

8. The relation of Relative to Antecedent has some peculiar features in O. Lat., which must be stated at some length. (For fuller details, see Bach: 'de attractione quae dicitur inversa apud scriptores latinos,' Strasburg, 1888.) We often find the Antecedent recurring in the Relative Clause, e.g. Epid. 41 est causa, qua causa simul mecum ire veritust, Rud. 997 quo colore est, hoc colore capiuntur pauxilluli, Aul. 574 ego te hodie reddam madidum, si vivo, probe, tibi quoi decretum est bibere aquam, Merc. 1015 immo dicamus senibus legem censeo priusquam abeamus, qua se lege teneant contentique sint. This repetition is suitable to legal precision and is often found in laws, e.g. Lex Agrar. quaestores eo iure ea lege viatores . . . sublegunto, quo iure qua lege quaestores . . . sublegerunt.

But when the Antecedent is mentioned only once, it is, curiously enough, in the Relative Clause, rather than in the Main Clause, that Plautus seems to prefer to place it. When it stands in the Relative Clause, it is naturally attracted to the Case of the Relative; and so we have that peculiar feature of O. Lat. the 'Attraction of the Antecedent to the Relative' (imitated in Virgil's *urbem quam statuo, vestra est*). It seems very strange that in a line like Amph. 1009 Naucratem quem convenire volui, in navi non erat, Plautus should prefer *Naucratem* to *Naucrates;* but that is evidently the favoured mode of expression with him.

As other examples of Attraction may be cited :—

> Cas. 975 quid fecisti scipione (-nem *MSS.*) aut quod habuisti pallium?
> Mil. 155 hic illest lepidus quem dixi senem.
> Mil. 598 ne uspiam insidiae sient concilium (= concilio) quod habere volumus.
> Curc. 419 istum quem quaeris ego sum (cf. Epid. 448).
> Ter. Andr. prol. 3 populo ut placerent quas fecisset fabulas.
> Cist. 61 indidem (= ibidem) unde oritur facito ut facias stultitiam sepelibilem (cf. Caecilius 266 venire illi (= eo) ubi sitast sapientia).

and as examples of Plautus' predilection for the Relative clause:

> Curc. 433 ut ei detur quam istic emi virginem . . . et aurum et vestem.
> Capt. 179 nisi qui meliorem adferet
> quae mihi atque amicis placeat condicio magis.
> Truc. 275 pignus da ni ligneae haec sint quas habes Victorias.
> Pers. 373 dicat quod quisque volt.

With this importance attached to the Relative Clause we may connect the very frequent omission of the Antecedent, e.g. Amph. 652 omnia adsunt bona, (*sc.* ei) quem penest virtus, Capt. 574 quem patrem (*sc.* eius), qui servus est?, Curc. 581 ego illam reddidi, (*sc.* ei) qui argentum a te attulit, Mil. 355 cedo vel decem; edocebo minime malas ut sint malae, (*sc.* eo) mihi solae quod superfit, Bacch. 991 A. eugae litteras minutas! B. (*sc.* ei) qui quidem videat parum; verum, (*sc.* ei) qui satis videat, grandes satis sunt, Cas. 427 quid opus est, (*sc.* ei) qui sic mortuus? But *is* is often used, even when the Subject has been placed in the Relative Clause, e.g. Most. 250 mulier quae se suamque aetatem spernit, speculo ei usust, Trin. 137 ille qui mandavit, eum exturbasti ex aedibus, Trin. 985 quia illum quem ementitu's, is ego sum ipsus Charmides; cf. Most. 315 nam illi ubi fui, ind(e) effugi foras.

We find the same phenomena in other dependent Clauses; (1) the repetition of the Antecedent, e.g. Bacch. 442 quom patrem adeas postulatum, puero sic dicit pater, Cas. 393 nunc tu, Cleustrata, ne a me memores malitiose de hac re factum aut suspices, tibi permitto, which is the true explanation of the apparent use of *hic, iste, ille* for *is* in lines like Mil. 1083 si hic pridie natus foret quam illest, hic haberet regnum in caelo, Pseud. 430 nam istaec quae tibi renuntiantur . . . fors fuat an istaec dicta sint mendacia, Mil.

1053 nisi tu illi fers suppetias, iam illa animum despondebit, Aul. 656 hunc si amitto, hic abierit, Mil. 275 hic illam vidit osculantem, quantum hunc audivi loqui (contrast, e.g. Mil. 352 sed ego hoc quod ago, id me agere oportet, Poen. 644 hunc chlamydatum quem vides, ei Mars iratust); (2) the attraction of the Antecedent, e.g. Trin. 423 pater (= patri) quom peregre veniet, in portast locus, Cist. 592 vir tuus (= virum tuum) si veniet, iube domi opperirier; even when a Rel. Pron. plays the part of Antecedent, e.g. Bacch. 128 qui (= quem) si decem habeas linguas, mutum esse addecet, Rud. 972 quos (= qui) quom capio, ... mei sunt.

The ordinary treatment of Relative and Antecedent prevails in Plautus when the Rel. is in Gen., Dat. or Abl. Case or is accompanied by a Preposition or is in Acc. Case before an Inf., e.g. Capt. 113 maiores (*sc.* catenas) quibus sunt iuncti, demito, Capt. 573 nam ille quidem, quem tu esse hunc memoras, hodie hinc abiit Alidem; also when the Rel. Clause does not come first in the sentence, e.g. Amph. 546 nunc te, nox, quae me mansisti, mitto, ut concedas die.

9. Of the attraction of the Relative to the Antecedent (like Horace's iudice quo nosti populo) there is apparently an example in Terence, Heaut. 87 A. scire hoc vis? B. hac quidem causa qua dixi tibi; but not in Plautus; for in Cas. 932 inde foras tacitus profugiens exeo ⟨hoc⟩ ornatu quo vides, we can easily supply 'me exeuntem' (See R. Foerster 'die Casusangleichung des Relativpronomens im Lateinischen' in the Jahrbücher class. Philologie, Suppl. xxvii, pp. 170 sqq.).

10. The peculiar treatment of the Relative Clause in Plautus is probably rather a feature of Early Latin than of colloquial Latin. To the carelessness of every-day speech we may refer irregularities of construction like the following: Change of Subject, e.g. Capt. 266 nunc senex est in tostrina, nunc iam cultros attinet, Stich. 5 de nostris factis noscimus, quarum viri hinc absunt, quorumque nos negotiis absentum ... sollicitae ... sumus semper, Amph. 566, 587, Rud. 291, and other changes of construction, e.g. Pseud. 421 atque id iam pridem sensi et subolebat mihi, Pseud. 1183 quin tu mulierem mi emittis aut redde argentum (cf. Asin. 254 quin tu abs te socordiam omnem reice et segnitiem amove, atque ad ingenium vetus vorsutum te recipis tuum?). So violent a change as to be quite ungrammatical is seen in Men. prol. 64 ingressus fluvium

rapidum ab urbe haud longule, rapidus raptori pueri subduxit pedes, Poen. 659 tu, si te di amant, agere tuam rem occasiost (cf. Epid. 77 te cupio perire mecum benevolens cum benevolente), and the use of *ut opinor* with the construction of *opinor* in Ter. Adelph. 648 ut opinor eas non nosse te (cf. Cic. Rep. 1, 58 and ὡς οἶμαι, etc., in Greek) and *ut aibat* with the construction of *aibat* in Ter. Phorm. 480 ut aibat de eius consilio sese velle facere. Besides Anacoluthon, we find naturally Aposiopesis in the Dramatists' imitation of talk, e.g. Truc. 504 (for other examples see Niemeyer ' Plautinische Studien ' p. 3).

These may serve for the present as samples of Plautus' colloquialisms. Others, e.g. the use of the Abl. Abs. of the Subject of the Sentence (**II, 59**), Parataxis (**V, 28**), *suus sibi* for *suus ipsius* (**IV, 2**), will be mentioned at their proper place.

11. Redundancy of expression, so marked a feature of Plautus' style, may be classed with these colloquialisms, for undoubtedly it reflects every-day speech. Like the repetition of the Antecedent is e.g. Pseud. 960 hoc est sextum a porta proxumum angiportum; in id angiportum me devorti iusserat, Rud. 1310 ecquid meministi in vidulo qui periit quid ibi infuerit, Bacch. 821 tantist quantist fungus putidus, Most. 527 tu, ut occepisti, tantum quantum quis fuge, Bacch. 767 tam frictum ego illum reddam quam frictum est cicer, Asin. 435 neque eo esse servum in aedibus eri qui sit pluris quam illest, Mil. 21 peiuriorem hoc hominem si quis viderit, aut gloriarum pleniorem quam illic est. Pleonasms like *multi saepe* Mil. 885, etc., *propere celeriter* Rud. 1323, *priusquam—prius* Pseud. 885, *postquam—post* Trin. 417, *una simul* Most. 1037 etc., *universus totus* Trin. 171, *omnis totus* frag. 120, *hic hodie dies* Epid. 157 etc., *ergo igitur* Trin. 756 etc., *etiam quoque* Pseud. 122 etc. occur on every page. (On *nemo homo*, see **IV, 21**; on the double Negative, **VIII, 8**; on *magis* with Comparative, **III, 2**; for statistics of Terence's use of Pleonasm, E. Johnston : de sermone Terentiano quaestiones duae. Königsberg, 1905). They evidently come direct from every-day talk, in which emphasis is sought by repetition and laboured statement, e.g. Rud. 896 ne quid significem quidpiam mulierculis (cf. Vid. 67, Mil. 431 ; and see **IV, 3**, below), Amph. 159 nec quisquam sit quin me omnes esse dignum deputent, Pers. 53 veterem atque antiquum quaestum maiorum meum servo atque obtineo et magna cum cura colo. Two different forms of expression are jumbled together in lines like Rud. 587 praeter animi quam lubuit sententiam, Epid. 625 e tuis verbis meum futurum corium pulcrum praedicas.

We have a two-sided remark apparently in Pseud. 1044 Quid tu intus, quaeso, desedisti quam diu?, like the exclamation in Ter. Heaut. 363 persuadere illi, quae solet quos spernere! A few may possibly be put down to the 'non astrictus soccus' of Plautus, e.g. the recurrence of *ut* (in different senses) in Mil. 70 sqq. or of *arbitror* in Stich. 82 sq quom nil quam ob rem id faciam meruisse arbitror. minime, nolo turbas; sed hoc mihi optumum factu esse arbitror, or even of *aio* in Most. 1027 sq. te velle uxorem aiebat tuo nato dare, ideo aedificare hic velle aiebat in tuis, Rud. 561 sq. nocte hac aiunt proxuma se iactatas atque eiectas hodie esse aiunt e mari; although this last does indeed seem to echo every-day talk (like our 'says he, .. says he'). (For other examples of repetition, e.g. ut .. ut Capt. 248, mihi .. mihi Aul. 551, me .. me Curc. 577, Most. 202, see Rauterberg, 'Quaestiones Plautinae.' Wilhelmshaven (progr.), 1883). The heaping up of Assonances like Capt. 358, quod bonis bene fit beneficium, is a deliberate rhetorical ornament which all the early Dramatists, except Terence, assume, and even Terence in his Prologues (see Leo: Analecta Plautina II. Göttingen, 1898).

II. THE CASES OF THE NOUN.

1. The Latin of Plautus' time stands at a stage between the very early period, when the use of Prepositions to give force and precision to the meaning of the Cases was not much in evidence, and the classical period; just as classical Latin itself stands at an earlier stage than the encroachment of the Prepositions even on such cases as the Genitive and Dative[c]. The primitive expression, e.g. *salio monte* 'leap from the mountain,' became first *desilio monte*, and finally *salio (desilio) de monte*. Plautine Latin may be said to be coincident with the transition from the second to the third type of expression. For its unclassical uses of a prepositionless case are usually found after a Compound Verb, e.g. Amph. 207 abituros agro, Cas. 307 gladium incumbam; although we find a few survivals of the primitive type, especially stereotyped phrases like *foro*

[c] The germs of this appear at an early stage, e.g. Cato Agr. Cult. 158 addito de perna frustum, 70, 2, de ea potione unicuique bovi dato; cf. Pseud. 1164 dimidium de praeda, Capt. 1019 (see below, on *ad* Prep.).

fugiunt Pers. 435, *saxo saliat* Trin. 265, *i malam crucem* (*rem*) beside *i in malam crucem* (*rem*) 'go and be hanged,' as in legal Latin the stereotyped phrase *tribu movere* survived long after Plautus' time, and in both colloquial and literary Latin the quasi-adverbial *rus ire, domo ire*, etc.[d] *Invado*, used of a disease, takes the Acc. (Trin. 28, Asin. 55), otherwise *in* and Acc. (Bacch. 711, Asin. 908, Epid. 670). Just as the meaning of a Case was eked out by the addition of a cognate Preposition, *salio de monte, salio ex monte* (or *desilio, exsilio*), etc., so was the meaning of an Adverb. Plautine Latin is rich in Adverbial compounds like *in-ibi, inter-ibi*, etc., e.g. Pers. 125 marsuppium habeat, inibi (= in eo) paulum praesidi, Pers. 165 interibi (= inter eas res) ego puerum volo mittere ad amicam meam.

2. **Nominative.** Under this heading may be mentioned a type of Parataxis, which consists in using two words in Apposition, instead of subordinating the one to the other. A good example of this characteristically O. Lat. usage is Capt. 232 nam fere maxuma pars morem hunc homines habent, with *maxuma pars, homines* instead of *maxuma pars hominum*. The same notion could be expressed by the Adverbial Accusative (see 36), *homines maxumam partem*. Not far removed from this is the O. Lat. phrase *plerique omnes* (e.g. Trin. 29) instead of 'plerique, ne dicam omnes' or the like. Some ancient editors put a comma between *plerique* and *omnes*. On 'id genus' (homines), etc., not found in Plaut. or Ter., see 36; on the pleonastic use of *is* with the Subject of the sentence, IV, 18; and on the use of the Nom. for the Voc., see below, 52.

3. **Genitive** (A. W. Blomquist : de Genetivi apud Plautum usu, Helsingfors, 1892).

In Greek the Gen. has absorbed the Abl. In Plautus the Gen.

---

[d] The quasi-adverbial nature of these words even in Plautus' time is seen from his use of a Preposition when an attribute is employed, e.g. in domo istac Curc. 208, in patriam domum Stich. 507, ad alienam domum Rud. 116, so that in Ennius trag. 281 V., domum paternamne anne ad Peliae filias, it may be right to construe *ad* ἀπὸ κοινοῦ. When the attribute is a Poss. Pron., the usage varies, e.g. *domi nostrae* Men. 359, Most. 874, Poen. 838, but *in nostra domo* Cas. 620, Pseud. 84 (cf. Truc. 262 nostrae domi *P*, in nostra domo *A*); *domos abeamus nostras* Poen. 814, but *in nostram domum* Amph. 409, Capt. 911, Trin. 382. (The reading *ab domo* is doubtful in Aul. 105, Epid. 681; cf. Stich. 523). Of course *proxuma vicinia* 'next door' (cf. 54) and *mala crux* are rather word-groups than Nouns qualified by an Attribute.

and Abl. have the same function in sentences like : Men. 901 me complevit flagiti et formidinis (Gen.) and Cist. 127 me complevi flore Liberi (Abl.); Cist. 165 paternum servum sui participat consili (Gen.) and Mil. 263 non potuit quin sermone suo aliquem familiarium participaverit de amica erili (Abl.); Mil. 1033 quia tis (Gen.) egeat, quia te (Abl.) careat; Vidul. 42 cibique minimi (Gen.) maxumaque industria (Abl.); Pseud. 1196 quem ego hominem nullius coloris novi (Gen.) and Rud. 997 quo colore est (Abl.). (For other types of the concurrence of Gen. and Abl. see below, 4, 15, 16).

4. A characteristically Plautine Genitive is what is usually called the Gen. of 'Respect,' e.g. Amph. 105 quam liber harum rerum multarum siet; Pseud. 746 A. ecquid argutust? B. malorum facinorum saepissime. We should express this by the Preposition 'in,' 'easy-going in these matters,' 'talented in villainy.' This notion of 'in,' 'in respect of' is expressed by the Abl. in sentences like Bacch. 268 adulterare eum aiebat rebus ceteris; Capt. 1025 compedibus quaeso ut tibi sit levior filius atque huic gravior servus. Sometimes the 'Gen. of Respect' and the 'Objective Gen.' (e.g. fugitans litium Ter. Phorm. 623) are hardly distinguishable; thus in Asin. 855-7 si huius rei me mendacem inveneris . . . amantem uxoris maxume, it seems unreasonable to separate the functions of the two Genitives. Cf. Capt. 264 quarum rerum te falsiloquum mihi esse nolo. The Plautine Gen. with *credo* is called in some Grammars a 'Gen. of Respect,' in others a 'Partitive Gen.', e.g. Asin. 459 quoi omnium rerum ipsus semper credit; Truc. 307 numquam edepol mihi quisquam homo mortalis posthac duarum rerum creduit. We find it also with *fidem habeo* in Pers. 785 quia ei fidem non habui argenti, which favours the title 'Gen. of Respect'; but the occasional addition of *quicquam*, *quid* associates it with the 'Partitive Gen.,' Asin. 854 neque divini neque mi humani posthac quicquam accreduas; Poen. 466 quid ei divini aut humani aequomst credere? Other Verbs with the Gen. that may be mentioned in this connexion are *fallor*, Epid. 239 nec satis exaudibam, nec sermonis fallebar tamen; also Verbs of incriminating, convicting, penalizing (like *furti accusare*, *capitis damnare*), e.g. Bacch. 696 quem mendaci prendit manufesto modo, Truc. 132 manufesto mendaci, mala, teneo te, Poen. 737 homo furti sese adstringet, Poen. 1337 iniuriarum multo induci (-dici?) satius est,

Most. 1099 apud iudicem hunc argenti condemnabo, Truc. 762 postid ego te manum iniciam quadrupuli, Mil. 371 quem pol ego capitis perdam. Cf. Poen. 184 dupli tibi, auri et hominis, fur leno siet. With *insimulo*, the crime usually stands in Gen., but we find Acc. in Amph. 859 collibitum siet meo viro sic me insimulare falso facinus tam malum (cf. Amph. 820, etc.). In the phrase *animi sanus, laetus*, etc., the Loc. is usually recognized. But we find in Plautus, e.g. Epid. 138 desipiebam mentis, quom illa scripta mittebam tibi, where *mentis* is clearly Gen., although in Trin. 454 satin tu's sanus mentis aut animi tui?, the emendation has been proposed, *tu sanus menti's*.

5. Some of the Plautine 'Genitives of Respect' would, if found in an Augustan poet, be called Graecisms, e.g. Rud. 213 hac an illac eam incerta sum consili (cf. Ter. Phorm. 578 quod quidem me factum consili incertum facit; Ennius trag. 142 V. suarum rerum incerti). But the imitation of a Greek construction [a] is as suitable for the literary style of Augustan poetry as it is unsuitable for the every-day language of Plautus. Their Italic origin is proved by their occurrence in other dialects, e.g. (Oscan) manum aserum eizazunc egmazum 'manum asserere earum rerum.' Similarly the use (especially in Tacitus) of the Gen. of the Gerund and Gerundive to express purpose, e.g. Tac. Ann. 2, 59 Germanicus Aegyptum proficiscitur cognoscendae antiquitatis, is found in Umbrian, e.g. ocrer peihaner 'arcis piandae.' It is therefore a native construction, and, although not found in Plautus, is once used by Terence, Adelph. 270 ne id adsentandi magis quam quo habeam gratum facere existumes. (On Rud. 247 me laborum levas, see below, 14).

6. The Gen. of Exclamation is another Plautine usage which is often, but probably in error, ascribed to the influence of Greek. Examples are very rare: Most. 912 di immortales, mercimoni lepidi!, Truc. 409 o mercis malae! In Mil. 1223 there is no need to change *o fortunata muliĕr es* of the MSS. into *o fortunatae mulieris*. The Acc. usually has this function in Plautus and always in Terence, e.g. Ter. Phorm. 134 iocularem audaciam! (see below, 47).

7. Nor can we ascribe to Greek influence (cf. ἄρχειν τινός, μεμνῆσθαί τινος) the Gen. with *potior, memini, obliviscor* (in Ter. Eun. 306

---

[a] The Gen. in Capt. 825 non ego nunc parasitus sum, sed regum rex regalior, Ennius trag. 56 V. mater optumarum multo mulier melior mulierum, is the Partitive Gen. But there is a mixture of two ideas. (See above, I, 10.)

oblitus sum mei; in Plaut. only with Acc. of thing, e.g. Cas. 104 non sum oblitus officium meum ; cf. Livius Andronicus Odyss. 4 te oblitus sum). From Cas. 112 hercle me suspendio, quam tu eius potior fias, satiust mortuum, we might infer that *potiri* took the Gen. because it was the equivalent of *potis* (cf. Greek πόσις ' lord ') *fieri ;* and the same explanation has been offered of *oblivisci, reminisci, meminisse*, the equivalents of *oblitus, memor, esse.* The treatment of these three Verbs (cf. *venit mihi in mentem*, also *commonere* Rud. 743 mearum me absens miseriarum commones) scarcely differs from the classical usage (for details see Babcock in Cornell Studies xiv, 1901); but the Plautine use of *potiri* calls for remark. *Potire* (Active), ' to put in possession of' (good or bad things), takes Acc. of person and Gen. of thing, e.g. Amph. 178 eum nunc potivit pater servitutis ; *potiri* (Passive), ' to fall into the power of,' takes Gen., e.g. Capt. 92 postquam meus rex est potitus hostium ; *potiri* (Deponent), ' to make oneself master of,' ' to obtain,' takes Acc., e.g. Rud. 190 laborem hunc potiri, Ter. Adelph. 876 hic potītur gaudia (see below, **45**), and sometimes Abl., e.g. Pseud. 1071 si ille hodie illa sit potitus muliere, Ter. Phorm. 830 curavi propria ut Phaedria poteretur.

8. The Verbs *miseret, taedet, pudet*, etc., govern the Gen. in Plautus' time, as they do later; also *fastidire*, e.g. Aul. 245 abiit .. fastidit mei, Turpilius 103, Titinius 94, Lucilius 293, 654 Ma. fastidire Agamemnonis, but the MSS. shew the Dat. in Stich. 334 mihin (mein *edd.*) fastidis?; also *cupere*, e.g. Mil. 963 quae cupiunt tui (but also Acc, e.g. Mil. 1050 quae te cupit). *Studeo*, which we shall find (**44**, below) to be used with the Acc. as well as the Dat., appears with the Gen. in Caecilius 201 qui te nec amet nec studeat tui. Could we have a better example of the elasticity of Early Latin Syntax and of the danger of altering the traditional text of Plautus when an abnormal construction is exhibited ? Of *vereor* with Gen. we have many examples in the Dramatists, e.g. Ter. Phorm. 971 neque huius sis veritus feminae primariae, Afranius 302 veretur tui (cf. 31, 99), and (Impersonal) Atta 7 nilne te populi veretur, qui vociferere in via?, Pacuvius 182 Tyndareo fieri contumeliam, cuius a te veretur maxume? Cf. *metuens sui* Turpilius 157.

9. The Genitive has often the function of an Adj., e.g. Mil. 502 nisi mihi supplicium virgarum de te datur (cf. v. 511 nisi mihi supplicium stimuleum de te datur). This Gen. of Description or Quality may stand alongside of an Adj., e.g. Men. 269 ego autem homo iracundus, animi perditi. That the same function is exercised by the Abl. has been already remarked, e.g. Mil. 10 fortem atque fortunatum et forma regia (see below, 62); although *cuiusmodi* (with *eiusmodi*, etc.) is never replaced by *quomodo*, which is, as in classical Latin, appropriate to Verbs. Noteworthy is Most. 81 paucorum mensum sunt relictae reliquiae, Ter. Heaut. 909 decem dierum vix mi est familia; also Most. 782 magni sunt oneris, quidquid imponas, vehunt; Aul. 325 trium litterarum homo (i.e. F U R).

10. The type of Genitive represented by *lucri facere*, a type variously explained in Grammars as 'Gen. of Material' and 'Partitive Gen.,' is much affected by Plautus. Here are some examples: *lucri facere*, e.g. Most. 354 ecquis homo est qui facere argenti cupiat aliquantum lucri?; Bacch. 859 nihil est lucri quod me hodie facere mavelim; Poen. 771 me esse hos trecentos Philippos facturum lucri; *sumpti facere*, Cas. 425 et praeter operam restim sumpti fecerim; Trin. 250 quod ebibit, quod comest, quod facit sumpti; *compendi facere*, e.g. Most. 60 orationis operam compendi face; Pseud. 1141 operam fac compendi quaerere; Asin. 307 verbivelitationem fieri compendi volo. The phrase *damni facere* occurs only in a context which admits of *damni* being a Partitive Gen., Merc. 421 multo edepol, si quid faciendumst, facere damni mavolo; Bacch. 1032 quam propter tantum damni feci et flagiti (cf. Pseud. 440); Asin. 182 neque ille scit quid det, quid damni faciat. We find also the Acc. in these phrases; *lucrum facere* (when used absolutely), e.g. Truc. 426 lucrum hercle videor facere mi, voluptas mea, ubi quippiam me poscis; *sumptum facere* (when used absolutely), e.g Asin. 217 necesse est facere sumptum, qui quaerit lucrum; Bacch. 98 et operam dare mi et ad eam operam facere sumptum de tuo; *compendium facere* (with Gen.), e.g. Stich. 194 ut faciam praeconis compendium, 'to dispense with an auctioneer'; Rud. 180 errationis fecerit compendium, 'will make short work of wandering.' We find also *ponere (addere, conferre) ad compendium*, e.g. Cas. 517 id ponito ad compendium.

11. From this Gen. it seems but a step to the Gen. *praesidi* in Poen. 670 trecentos nummos Philippos portat praesidi, *peculi* in Cas. 258 cui homini hodie peculi nummus non est plumbeus, and the Gen. *dotis* in phrases like Pers. 394 dabuntur dotis tibi inde

sescenti logi, Cist. 562 unde tibi talenta magna viginti pater det dotis, Trin. 1158 spondeo, et mille auri Philippum dotis (cf. Truc. 845 sex talenta magna dotis demam pro ista inscitia). We find the Acc. *dotem* in Trin. 509 eum (sc. agrum) dabo dotem sorori, Trin. 1143 aurum . . quod darem tuae gnatae dotem.

And from this Gen. again it is not far to that curious use of the Gen. of the Gerund seen in Poen. 34 (matronae) domum sermones fabulandi conferant, Mil. 637 ut apud te exemplum experiundi habeas.

Some find a Gen., some a Loc. in the phrase *boni consulere* 'to regard in a favourable light,' Truc. 429 quicquid attulerit, boni consulas.

12. To the type *scelus viri* (e.g. Curc. 614, Pers. 192) belong *flagitium hominis*, e.g. Asin. 473, *monstrum mulieris* Poen. 273, *deliciae pueri*, e.g. Pers. 204, and *frustum pueri* Pers. 848. Not unlike them is the Partitive Gen. in Poen. 856 apage? nescio quid viri sis, Amph. 576 (cf. Poen. 92) quid hoc sit hominis?, Cist. 605, etc., quid istuc est verbi?

13. The Partitive Gen. is as greatly affected by Plautus as by Cicero. He even prefers *hoc negoti* to *hoc negotium* in Trin. 578 (cf. Mil. 956) dic hoc negoti quomodo actumst; cf. Amph. 172 non reputat laboris quid sit 'what a trouble it is,' Amph. 421 signi dic quid est, Amph. 463 hoc operis, Aul. 370 rapacidarum ubi tantum siet in aedibus. *Quid rerum* is a common phrase, e.g. Aul. 54 ne me observare possis quid rerum geram, Pers. 513 Persae quid rerum gerant; and *ubi terrarum, nusquam gentium*, etc., are as frequent in Plautus' time as they are later (cf. *interea loci* 'meanwhile,' *postid locorum* 'afterwards'; *minime gentium* Merc. 419, Poen. 690). Of other Adverbs with the Gen. may be noticed *adfatim* (lit. 'up to satiety'; cf. fatigo), e.g. Mil. 980 tibi divitiarum adfatimst, Cist. 231 aliorum adfatim est qui faciant; *largiter*, e.g. Rud. 1188 credo edepol ego illic inesse argenti et auri largiter, Rud. 1315 largiter mercedis indipiscar. Along with *parum* (i.e. parvum, Neut. Sing.) we find its equivalent, *parva res* (cf. I, 5), Amph. 633 satin parva res est voluptatum in vita? Cf. Cist. 777 gaudeo tibi mea opera liberorum esse amplius. Plautus apparently uses both *copiae est* and *copia est, operae est* and (in Merc. 286) *opera est*, e.g. Merc. 990 ut aliter facias non est copiae, Cas. 810 illo morbo quo dirumpi cupio non est copiae (-ae *A*, -a *P*); Capt. 216 quom quae volumus nos copiast, Mil. 1041 multae idem istuc cupiunt quibus copia

non est; Truc. 883 operae mi ubi erit, ad te venero, Merc. 286 dicam si videam tibi esse operam aut otium.

This use of the Gen. is pushed to an extreme in phrases like Poen. 641 (after *quid boni,* v. 640) boni de nostro tibi nec ferimus nec damus, Most. 1018 (after *quod negoti,* v. 1017) mecum ut ille hic gesserit, dum tu hinc abes, negoti?, Ter. Phorm. 709 ante brumam autem novi negoti incipere! Noteworthy too is Ter. Eun. 408 A. immo sic homost, perpaucorum hominum. B. immo nullorum arbitror, si tecum vivit.

14. The 'Partitive' Gen. with *largiter, adfatim* borders on the 'Gen. of Plenty and Want.' Here, as we have seen, the Abl. competes with the Gen. (cf. Amph. 170 laboris expers, Asin. 43 expers metu; Bacch. 849 exheres vitae, Most. 234 exheres bonis), although different words seem to shew a predilection for the one Case or the other. Thus *plenus* is found 24 times with Gen. but only once with Abl., Merc. 881 caelum ut est splendore plenum!; *careo* with the Gen. does not occur (by accident?) in the extant plays of Plautus, but is found once in Terence, Heaut. 400 tui carendum quod erat; *cumulatus* takes Gen. in Aul. 825 scelerum cumulatissume (cf. Caecilius 61 homo ineptitudinis cumulatus); *levare* in Rud. 247 ut me omnium iam laborum levas!; *onustus* with Gen. is found twice in the phrase *aula onusta auri* in Aul. 611, 617; on the other hand *compos*, which usually takes Gen., appears with Abl. in Capt. 217 ea (*scil.* copia) facitis nos compotes; also Naevius trag. 5 eam nunc esse inventam probris compotem scis, Accius 37 magnis compotem et multis malis (cf. Abl. with *compotire*, 68). From the other Dramatists may be cited Pacuvius 291 postquam ést oneratus frugum et floris Liberi, Pomponius 101 domus haec fervit flagiti. *Vitae* seems to be Gen. in Stich. 18 haec res vitae me, soror, saturant.

15. A similar concurrence of Gen. and Abl. is seen with another Adj., *dignus*, for we find once in Trin. 1153 non ego sum salutis dignus?; possibly too with the Adj. *cupidus*, for the Abl. (Dat.?) is attested in Pseud. 183 vino modo cupidae estis.

16. Along with the Gen. of Price, e.g. *pluris (minoris) aestimare* (cf. *pluris preti* Bacch. 630), huius non faciam Ter. Adelph. 163, we find *plure (minore)* in Republican Latin (cf. Charisius p. 109, 10 K. plure aut minore emptum antiqui dicebant; see Wölfflin in Archiv lat. Lexikographie 9, 107), an Abl., like *magno (parvo)*, although it may also be a Loc.; for -*i* (later -*e*) was the Loc. suffix

with Cons.-stems, as *-ei* (later *-ī*) with O-stems (see 29). The Gen. (or Loc.) *nihili* of *nihili facere*, etc., becomes an Adj. in the phrase *homo nihili*; cf. *non homo trioboli* Poen. 463. This Gen. (or Loc.) of Price is found with *refert*, e.g. Rud. 966 nihilo pol pluris tua hoc quam quanti illud refert mea. The phrase in Pseud. 809 is curious: me nemo potest minoris quisquam nummo, ut surgam, subigere (i.e. 'hire my services,' said by a cook).

17. The 'Objective Gen.' has been already mentioned (4). In Asin. 77 sq. the Verb takes the Dat., the Verbal Noun the Gen., *obsequi gnato meo . . obsequium illius*. Interesting Plautine examples of this Gen. are Truc. 145 (cf. 223) rei male gerentes, and the obscure *iuris coctiores (doct.?)* Poen. 586.

18. Of the 'Possessive Gen.' these examples are noteworthy: Curc. 230 estne hic Palinurus Phaedromi? (*scil.* servus); Rud. 481 heus, Agasi Ptolemocratia, cape hanc urnam tibi (? *scil.* uxor; cf. Virgil's Hectoris Andromache), Ter. Adelph. 582 ubi ad Dianae (*scil.* aedem) veneris. With a Gen. like Capt. 583 est miserorum ut malevolentes sint, may be compared the use of the Possessive Pronoun, e.g. *non meum est* 'that is not my habit' (cf. **IV**, 2). We also find *officium* in this type of expression, e.g. Truc. 436 non amantis mulieris, sed sociai unanimantis, fidentis fuit officium facere quod modo haec fecit mihi.

On the Gen. with *par* (as with *similis*), see below, 26.

19. **Dative.** (H. Peine: de dativi apud priscos scriptores usu. Strasburg (diss.) 1878.)

The Dative in Early Latin plays much the same parts as in the classical period. That peculiarly Latin usage, the Predicative Dative, is much affected by Plautus. Noteworthy examples are: Trin. 356 habemus . . aliis quī *cōmitati* simus; Curc. 72 (with a play on words that reminds us of Shakespeare).

> A. me inferre Veneri vovi iaientaculum. ('that I would offer.')
>
> B. quid? te ante pones Veneri *iaientaculo*? ('will you put yourself on the table?')

Most. 922 at enim ne quid *captioni* mihi sit, si dederim tibi; Pseud. 418 ita nunc per urbem solus *sermoni* omnibust (-ni *A*, -ne *P*); Most. 154 parsimoniā et duritiā *discipulinae* aliis eram; Truc. 704 quom hoc iam volupest, tum illuc *nimio magnae mellinae* mihi; Mil. 671 quibus nunc me esse experior *summae sollicitudini*; Poen.

1217 A. gaudio ero vobis—B. at edepol nos voluptati tibi. A. *libertatique* (cf. Trin. 629, where the 'Dative of Purpose' is suggested: si in rem tuam, Lesbonice, esse videatur, *gloriae* aut *famae*, sinam); of Verbal Nouns of the Fourth Decl. may be noticed: Mil. 771 quam ad rem *usui* est?; Mil. 740 quanto *sumptui* fuerim tibi; Poen. 626 ut *quaestui* habeant male loqui melioribus; Poen. 1281 tum profecto me sibi habento scurrae *ludificatui ;* Cist. 366 remque nostram habes *perditui et praedatui.* The Nom. often competes with the Predicative Dat., e.g. Poen. 145 si tibi lubido est aut voluptati, sino; Truc. 466 id illi morbo, id illi seniost, ea illi miserae miseriast, Ter. Heaut. 920, Eun. 940. Only *miseria est* (e.g. Mil. 68), *flagitium est* (e.g. Mil. 694) seem to be used; but both *lucro est* (e.g. Mil. 675) and *lucrum est* (e.g. Merc. 553), *exitio est* (e.g. Bacch. 953) and *exitium est* (e.g. Bacch. 945 exitium, excidium, exlecebra fiet hic equus hodie auro senis; cf. 947, 1054; Ennius trag. 46 V. eum esse exitium Troiae, pestem Pergamo). *Cordi* is not Dat. but Abl.; cf. Cist. 109 in cordi est tamen.

20. As examples of the Dat. of Purpose may be noticed *quoi rei* 'why?' 'for what purpose?' (passim) and (with the Verb *auspico*) Rud. 717 non hodie isti rei auspicavi, Pers. 689 lucro faciundo ego auspicavi in hunc diem; Ter. Heaut. 837 hasce ornamentis consequentur alterae (*scil.* minae). Other examples of the Gerundive (cf. decemviri legibus scribundis, etc.) are, e.g. Mil. 745 serviendae servituti ego servos instruxi mihi, hospes, non qui mi imperarent; Most. 288 purpura aetati occultandae est. The *aetati agundae* of Trin. 229 is equivalent to the *ad aetatem agundam* of v. 232:

229 utram aetati agundae arbitrer firmiorem.
232 utra in parte plus sit voluptatis vitae ad aetatem agundam

(for a similar use of the Gen. of the Gerund. see 5, above). From phrases like Pers. 792 ferte aquam pedibus, Most. 308 cedo aquam manibus, we cannot dissociate Curc. 578 linteumque extersui. This use of the Dative of Verbal Nouns of the Fourth Declension was much in favour in the homely Latin of the camp (e.g. *receptui canere* 'to sound a retreat') and of the farm (e.g. in Cato's and Varro's books on husbandry we find phrases like: oleas esui optime condi Varro R. R. i. 60).

21. Not far removed are phrases like *arraboni dare* 'to give as earnest-money,' e.g. Most. 645; *pignori ponere*, e.g. Capt. 433

(cf. 655 reliqui pigneri putamina; cf. Most. 978 quadraginta etiam dedit huic quae essent pignori); *quaestioni dare (accipere) servos*, e.g. Most. 1088.

22. The equivalence of the Dat. to the combination of a Prep. (*ad, in*) with the Acc. (see VII, 2), which led to the 'Auxiliary' formation of the Dat. in the Romance languages, is prominent even in Plautus' time. Thus we find *dare ad*, e.g. Capt. 1019 hunc .. ad carnificem dabo (cf. Amph. 809 haec me modo ad mortem dedit; but Merc. 472 ibi me toxico morti dabo), Pseud. 1100 ut det nomen ad Molas coloniam; similarly Cist. 786 nunc quod ad vos, spectatores, relicuum relinquitur; while *mitto* is used with the Dat. in Capt. 692 te morti misero. But in Ter. Andr. 70 ex Andro commigravit huic viciniae, we should probably read *huc viciniae*, like *hic viciniae* Phorm. 95. A truer anticipation of Virgil's *it clamor caelo* is Ennius Ann. 94 V. praepetibus sese pulchrisque locis dant (of the vultures seen by Romulus; cf. Ann. 401).

23. The Dativus Commodi too is as common in Plautus' time as later, and provides a quibble in Capt. 866 A. esurire mihi videre. B. mi quidem esurio, non tibi. Our Grammars describe as a 'Dat. of Reference[†]' that similar use of this Case in lines like Trin. 971 neque edepol tu is es neque hodie is umquam eris, auro huic quidem 'so far as this gold is concerned.' It comes very near the function of the Abl. (with *ab*) after a Passive Verb in one or two places, e.g. Epid. 154 ubi tibi istam emptam esse scibit (cf. the old legal formula *emptus mihi esto pretio*, and see G. Landgraf: Beitraege zur historischen Syntax der lat Sprache. Munich (progr.), 1899).

This Dat. is associated with Adjectives, e.g. Pseud. 783 eheu! quam illae rei ego etiam nunc sum parvulus!, Most. 532 scelestiorem ego annum argento faenori numquam ullum vidi. Sometimes the Dat. exercises the function of a Gen., e.g. Amph. 66 eant per totam caveam spectatoribus, Rud. 935 monumentum meae famae et factis, Trin. 204 qui illorum verbis falsis acceptor fui. With *esse* the Dat. is always used with *cognatus, patronus*, etc., but without *esse*, the Gen. We find both *pater est alicuius* (e.g. Capt. 4, 974) and *pater est alicui* (e.g. Capt. 633, 1011),

---

[†] Akin is the 'Dat. of the Person Judging,' e.g. Ennius Ann. 280 V. hostem qui feriet, mihi erit Carthaginiensis.

etc. (For details see Landgraf in Archiv lat. Lexikographie, 8, 66.)

24. The Dat. of Possession is equally common. The Verb *sit* is suppressed in the phrase *vae victis* Pseud. 1317 and in the formula for toasts, e.g. Pers. 773 bene mihi, bene vobis, bene meae amicae! (On the use of the Acc. in toasts, see below, 46.)

25. Much the same Verbs govern the Dat. in Plautus as in Cicero, e.g. *credo, ignosco, impero*. We have the full construction, Dat. of Person and Acc. of Thing, in lines like Bacch. 1185 ut eis delicta ignoscas (but Merc. 997 ora ut ignoscat delictis tuis atque adulescentiae), Poen. 490 an mi haec non credis?, Mil. 1159 nunc hanc tibi ego impero provinciam. But we find both Acc. and Dat. with *curo*, e.g. Stich. 679 meis curavi amicis, . . amicos meos curabo; *decet* (see Seyffert in Berliner Philologische Wochenschrift 24, 141), e.g. Amph. 820 nostro generi non decet (contrast 838 ut pudicam decet), Ter. Adelph. 491 ut vobis decet (contrast Heaut. 1054, etc., ut te decet); *vito* has Dat. in Plautus (Cas. 211 huic verbo vitato, Poen. 25 vitent ancipiti infortunio, Stich. 121 qui potis est mulier vitare vitiis?), but the Acc. is found, e.g. Rud. 168 fluctus devitaverint. *Ausculto* with Acc. means 'I hear,' with Dat. 'I obey'[5]; so editors change *me* of the MSS. into *mi* in Trin. 662 nisi mi auscultas atque hoc ut dico facis.

The distinction between the function of the Dat. (Indirect Object) and the Acc. (Direct Obj.) is seen with *timeo* in Ter. Andr. 210 si illum relinquo, eius vitae timeo; sin opitulor, huius minas; and with the two uses of *ludos facio* (1) with Acc. 'to make game of,' even in Passive, e.g. Bacch. 1090 hocine me aetatis ludos bis factum esse indigne! (2) with Dat. 'to honour, divert one with a comedy,' often approaching the other sense, e.g. Most. 427 ludos ego hodie vivo praesenti huic seni faciam, quod credo mortuo numquam fore.

26. A like freedom of construction with Gen. or Dat. appears in some Adjectives, e.g. *par*, usually with Dat., e.g. Poen. 376, but with Gen. in Rud. 49 ei erat hospes par sui Siculus senex (parvi *MSS*.), Accius 465 quodsi ex Graecia omni illius par nemo reperiri potest. But editors are perhaps right in rejecting all cases

[5] Cf. *audiens sum* with Dat., e.g. Amph. 991 eius dicto, imperio sum audiens. The phrase *dicto audiens esse* became stereotyped as a synonym of *oboedire* and took Dat. of Person, e.g. Amph. 989 ego sum Jovi dicto audiens, Cato Agric. 142 dominoque dicto audiens sit. Cf. Pers. 378 futura's dicto oboediens an non patri?

of Dat. with *similis*; for the evidence for this construction is weak (see my note on Capt. 582). *Studiosus* takes Dat. in Mil. 802 qui, nisi adulterio, studiosus rei nulli aliaest improbus. (On Pseud. 183 vino modo cupidae estis, see above, **15**.)

Conscius (with *esse*) seems to take the Dat. (Abl. ?) in Rud. 1247 ne conscii sint ipsi maleficiis suis (-ci *Pylades*). This Dat. is of the same type as Ter. Adelph. 671 auctor his rebus quis est?, and the examples, *cognatus esse*, etc., quoted above, **23**.

27. The 'Dative of Capacity' (cf. oneri ferendo esse, etc.) appears in Stich. 720 nulli rei erimus postea; 'we shall be fit for nothing afterwards,' Cato inc. 3 J. qui tantisper nulli rei sies, dum nihil agas (which can hardly be Gen., as Priscian 1. p. 227, p. 266 H. prefers to make it, or Loc., like *nihili*); cf. Ter. Adelph. 357 qui aliquoi reist, etiam eum ad nequitiem adducere. To it should be referred the common phrase (*bonae*) *frugi esse*. In Early Latin *frux* in the Singular had the metaphorical sense of 'good conduct' in various phrases, e.g. Poen. 892 erus si tuus volt facere frugem, Trin. 270 certa est res ad frugem applicare animum, Pseud. 468 tamen ero frugi bonae. The phrase with the Dat. obtained a firm footing (cf. **III. 3**).

28. The curious appositional use of the Dative of a Personal Name in a phrase like 'nomen est mihi Gaïo' is also Plautine, e.g. Rud. 5 nomen Arcturo est mihi, Men. 1068 mihi est Menaechmo nomen, Stich. 174 Gelasimo nomen mi indidit parvo pater. But it seems to be a rule with Plautus that, when the Dat. of the Person is put between the word *nomen* and the Name, the Name shall not stand in the Dat. Case, e.g. Truc. 12 hic habitat mulier, nomen quoi est Phronesium. (For additional examples see Asmus: de Appositionis apud Plautum et Terentium collocatione, Halle, 1891, p. 49; Seyffert in Bursian's Jahresbericht 1894, p. 331; Becker in Studemund's Studien 1, pp. 170-1.)

On *suus sibi* 'his own' see **IV, 2**.

29. Locative (see J. Heckmann in Indogermanische Forschungen, 18, pp. 296 sqq.).

Comparative Philology has corrected the old notion that -*ī* was in all Declensions the Loc. suffix (e.g. Romai, Corinthi, Carthagini), and has shewn that in Ā-stems (1 Decl.) the suffix was -āi, a diphthong (while the Gen. suffix was disyllabic -āī), in O-stems (2 Decl.) -ōi (cf. Gk. οἴκοι) which became -ēi, and later (after Plautus' time) -ī, in Cons.-stems (part of 3 Decl.) -ĭ, which became -ĕ.

This Cons.-stem Loc. was used in Latin as Abl., e.g. *Carthaginĕ*, *patrĕ*, in Greek as Dat., e.g. πατρί. Instead of this Abl.-Loc. *-ĕ* in Cons.-stems we find occasionally *-ī* in Plautus, e.g. *militi*, which seems to be the I-stem Abl. (originally -id), e.g. *navī, classī*. Just as the Cons.-stem suffix *-ĕ* was often used in I-stems, e.g. *navĕ, classĕ*, and (in Plaut.) *marĕ*, so the I-stem suffix *-ī(d)* found its way into Cons.-stems. If this be the true explanation, *Carthagini*, *mani*, etc., and in Plautus *Accherunti* 'in the lower world,' e.g. Capt. 998, are Ablatives, not Locatives.

30. In the classical Latin period the Loc. had lost its identity. In the first Decl. both Loc. āī and Gen. -āī had become *-ae*, so that *Romae habitare* was indistinguishable from *Romae conditor;* and similarly in the second *agri* (older *-ei*) *habitare* and *agri cultor*. Thus in these two Declensions the Loc. became merged in the Gen., as in the third (and probably the fourth and fifth) it was identified with the Abl. In Plural Nouns of all Declensions Dat., Loc., and Abl. had apparently been fused into one Case from a remote period.

31. How far a Roman of Plautus' time recognised the Loc. as a special case is difficult to say. It certainly plays a greater part in Plautine Latin than in Ciceronian; witness expressions of place like *proxumae viciniae* 'next door' (passim), *meae viciniae* Rud. 613; of time like *die septimi* Men. 1156; of value like *trioboli, flocci, nauci, aequi facere* Mil. 784.

32. But the notion of Price (Loc. *tanti, plure;* see above, 29) could be expressed equally by an Abl., e.g. *minimo* (cf. Epid. 295 quanti emi potest minimo?), and by a Gen., e.g. *pluris* (cf. Asin 858 sq. minimi mortalem preti . . . nihili). And beside *animi anxius* (cf. Epid. 326 angas te animi) we have *desipere mentis*[h] (see above, 4) as well as *animo ferox*, Mil 1323 et quia tecum eram, propterea animo eram ferocior. So that the way was paved for the identification of the Loc. with the Gen. in the First and Second Decl. and with the Abl. in the Third.

33. The Loc. seems to be loosely used for the Acc. after a Verb of Motion in Pers. 731 transcidi loris omnes adveniens domi, Epid. 361, adveniens domi extemplo ut maritus fias, just as the Acc. is sometimes loosely used after a Verb of Rest (see 39); although this use of *domi* is open to question.

[h] This is strong evidence in favour of *animi* being really Gen. and not Loc.

34. And the laws of Classical Latin for the expression of 'at' (also 'to' and 'from') without a Preposition in the case of towns and small islands and with a Preposition in the case of countries were not strictly enforced in Early Latin. Even Terence uses *in Lemno* nearly as freely as *Lemni* and allows *in Lemnum* (iter esset) beside *in Ciliciam* in Phorm. 66, while he actually seems to prefer *ex Andro, e Corintho*, etc. (see below, **39, 54**).

On *boni consulere* see above, 11.

35. Accusative (Biese 'de objecto interno apud Plaut. et Ter.' Kiel, 1878).

This Case plays so many parts in Plautus and so often usurps the function of other Cases that we are occasionally reminded of the Late Latin Declension (reflected in the Romance languages), in which all the Oblique Cases are merged in the Accusative.

The Cognate Acc. is much in evidence. Early Lat. did not recognize the restriction that the Acc. should always contain some additional notion besides that contained in the Verb; for the early legal phrase, 'to be a slave,' was *servitutem servire* (cf. Quintilian 7, 3, 26), a phrase of frequent occurrence in the Comedies and also used by the historian Livy. Other Plautine examples are: Most. 42 olere unguenta exotica, 39 oboluisti ālium, Aul. 152 lapides loqueris, Capt. 467 ita venter gutturque resident esuriales ferias. The Acc. Neut. of a Pronoun is used with all kinds of Verbs, e.g. Amph. 346 quid veneris 'for what purpose,' Most. 786 quod me miseras, adfero omne impetratum, Pers. 177 amas pol, misera; id tuus scatet animus, Most. 306 haec qui gaudent, gau- deant perpetuo suo semper bono, Mil. 392 id me insimulatam ... neque me quidem patiar probri falso impune insimulatam. It gives occasion to a pun in Cas. 460 illuc est, illuc quod ('that is why') hic hunc fecit vilicum; et idem me pridem ... facere atriensem voluerat sub ianua.

36. From this Cognate Acc. it is an easy transition to the Adverbial Acc., e.g. Rud. 69 increpui hibernum; *meam vicem*, e.g. Most. 355; Poen. 413 maiorem partem in ore habitas meo, Cist. 22 decet pol, mea Selenium, hunc esse ordinem benivolentes inter se. In Amph. 301 editors change *modum maiorem* to *multo maiorem*, igitur magis modum maiorem in sese concipiet metum. *Quod genus* and *id genus* are not found in Plaut. or Ter., but are familiar to Lucilius (see Arch. Lat. Lex. 5, 387). On *cetera, ceterum* see below, **VIII, 2**; on *circum*, **VII, 2**.

37. For the Acc. of Time (see T. Kane: Case Forms with and without Prepositions used by Plautus and Terence to express time. Baltimore, 1895) may be cited the quasi-Adverb *aetatem* 'for one's lifetime[i]' (e.g. Amph. 1023 ut profecto vivas aetatem miser, Asin. 21 ut tibi superstes uxor aetatem siet, Asin. 274 aetatem velim servire, Libanum ut conveniam modo), Asin. 848 cum hac annum ut esses, Pers. 21 plusculum annum (with ellipse of *quam*), Pers 628 si hanc emeris, numquam hercle hunc annum vortentem, credo, servibit tibi. We find already in Plautus that curious misuse of the Acc. for the Abl. in expressions like Mil. 618 tibi istuc aetatis homini, Merc. 290 quid tibi aetatis videor?, just as we find *omni in aetate* for *omnem aetatem* in Poen. 228 quae noctes diesque omni in aetate semper ornantur. *Abhinc* takes an Acc. of Time, as in classical Latin, e.g. Bacch. 388 hoc factumst ferme abhinc biennium, Ter. Andr. 69 abhinc triennium, Turpilius 134; but the MSS. shew the Abl. (cf. *anno* 'a year ago' Amph. prol. 91 etiam histriones anno quom in proscaenio hic Jovem invocarunt, venit, auxilio is fuit; see below, 63) in Most. 493 qui abhinc sexaginta annis (-os *edd*.) occisus foret.

38. As examples of Acc. of Space these may serve: Poen. 837 (cf. Rud. 1294) cubitum longis litteris, Aul. 56 si hercle tu ex istoc loco digitum transvorsum aut unguem latum excesseris, Bacch. 424 digitum longe a paedagogo pedem ut efferres aedibus.

39. The Acc. of Motion (see J. Heckmann in Indogermanische Forschungen, 18, pp. 296 sqq.), which is in class. Lat. confined to names of towns, *domus*, *rus*, etc., had a wider range in Plautus' time, e.g. Curc. 206 parasitum misi nudiusquartus Cariam (cf. Livius Andronicus Odyss. 14 partim ('in groups') errant, nequinont Graeciam redire; although we also find *in Cariam*[k], etc., e.g. Curc. 67 nunc hinc parasitum in Cariam misi meum), Cas. 448 hunc Accheruntem praemittam prius, Poen. 814 domos abeamus nostras, sultis,

---

[i] The corresponding Adj. is *aeternus*, e.g. Capt. 897 aeternum tibi dapinabo victum.

[k] It is sometimes said that Plautus regarded Caria and Elis as towns and not countries. Such an explanation is obviously unsuitable to Egypt (cf. Most. 440). The truth is that Plautus does not follow the strict laws of class. Lat. with regard to geographical names. He uses *in Ephesum ire* as well as *Ephesum ire*, and the like (cf. Ter. Phorm. 66). Egypt, it should be noticed, receives the same treatment from writers of Cicero's time and later as from Plautus, e.g. Cic. Nat. Deor. 3, 56 Aegyptum profugisse (but *in Aegyptum* Pis. 49, as in Plaut. Most. 994). Varro has *Aegypto* 'in E.' Ling. Lat. 5, 57.

nunciam; cf. Men. 1020 edepol, ere, nae tibi suppetias temperi adveni modo, Pseud. 1086 quique infitias non eat. (*Exsequias ire* Ter. Phorm. 1026 is Acc. of Object, like Poen. 698 is, leno, viam.) Both *malam crucem ire* and *in malam crucem ire* are used, e.g. Poen. 496 A. nisi aut auscultas aut is in malam crucem. B. malam crucem ibo potius; usually *in malam rem*, but Truc. 937 malam rem is et magnam, Ter. Eun. 536 malam rem hinc ibis? (See below, **V, 42**, on ı Supine.)

It is sometimes loosely used with Verbs of Rest, e.g. Men. 51 siquis quid vostrum Epidamnum (-ni *alii*) curari sibi velit, just as *huc* is used for *hic* in Aul. 640 ostende huc, or as *in* governs the Acc. in Epid. 191 in amorem (-re *alii*) haerere. (On O. Lat. *in manum esse, in potestatem esse*, see 51.)

And it is most in evidence after a Compound Verb, being, in a manner, governed by the Prep. with which the Verb is compounded (see below, **43**).

40. The main function of the Acc., the expression of the Object of the Verb of the sentence, is pushed to the widest possible extent. The use of the Neut. Acc. of Pronouns with all manner of Verbs has been already noticed in connexion with the Cognate Acc. (above, **35**). 'Constructio ad Sensum' is the usual explanation in Grammars for lines like Capt. 969 quid dignus siem (= merear), Poen. 860 aliquem id dignus qui siet, Ter. Phorm. 519 quod es dignus; in Pseud. 643 hoc inicere ungulas, *hoc* may be the O. Lat. form of *huc* (see below, **IV, 20**). On *manum inicere* (= comprehendere) with Acc. and on other examples of Acc. in 'Constructio ad Sensum,' see **I, 4**. *Perditus esse* with the sense of *deamare* takes its construction, Mil. 1253 ut, quaeso, amore perditast te misera! (cf. Cist. 132).

The passage of Intransitives into Transitives had already begun in Plautus' time, and the Acc. with them admits of the same explanation as the Acc. with *perditus esse*. Examples are: *pereo*, e.g. Poen. 1095 earum hic alteram efflictim perit; *depereo*, e.g. Bacch. 470 meretricem indigne deperit; *demorior*, e.g. Mil. 970 ea demoritur te; *calleo*, e.g. Most. 279 ut perdocte cuncta callet!; *convenio* 'I meet,' e.g. Men. 401; *conloquor*, e.g. Pseud. 252 non licet conloqui te?; (on *consuesco*, see below, **70**); *studeo*, e.g. Mil. 1437 minus has res studeant (see above, **8**); *pecco*, Bacch. 433 si unam peccavisses syllabam; *queror*, Amph. 176 satiust me queri illo modo servitutem; *exeo*, Ter. Hec. 378 iam ut limen exirem (cf. Mil. 1432); *aversor*, Ennius Ann. 464 V. aversabuntur semper vos vostraque vulta.

41. In Most. 100 simul gnarūres vos volo esse hanc rem mecum, we may say that *gnarures esse* has the sense and takes the construction of *novisse*, as in Amph. 879 quod gravida est (= concepit). We may also say that the Verbal Adj. governs the same Case as the Verb itself (cf. Turpilius 65 at enim scies ea quae fuisti inscius); although this treatment of Verbal Adj. and Verbal Noun, so common in Greek, is at the time of Plautus in process of disappearing. It is almost wholly confined to Verbal Nouns in *-tio* (see Landgraf in Archiv lat. Lexikographie 10,401), when used in interrogative sentences which begin with *quid*, e.g. Truc. 622 quid tibi hanc aditio est?, Curc. 626 quid tibi istum tactio est?, Amph. 519 quid tibi hanc curatio est rem, verbero, aut muttitio? This use of the Acc. is peculiarly Plautine; for Terence, though he allows this type of phrase, uses the Gen. in Eun. 671 quid huc tibi reditiost? vestis quid mutatiost?

We may add Capt. 519 neque exitium exitio est, and Pseud. 385 ad eam rem usust hominem astutum (see below, 56). (In Ter. Andr. 202 nihil circumitione usor es (usus es *MSS.*) may be the true reading; but in Amph. 34 *iusta* is a doubtful emendation, for the *iuste* of the MSS. may stand for *iustae* Dat., nam iustae (*sc.* rei) ab iustis iustus sum orator datus). In Poen. 410 quid nunc mi es auctor?, the phrase *es auctor* takes the construction of its equivalent, *suades*.

That *facio* can be used like *me facio* 'play the part of' is not absolutely proved by Mil. 1034 facito fastidi plenum (*al.* face te), Most. 890 ferocem facis quia te erus amat (te ἀπὸ κοινοῦ?). Cf. Ter. Phorm. 476 tum Phormio itidem in hac re ut [in] aliis strenuom hominem praebuit; and see below, **V, 4.**

42. This claim of the Acc. to denote the Object of the sentence is seen in the anticipatory use (cf. Gk. οἶδά σε ὅστις εἶ), for which Plautus shews an extraordinary predilection, e g. Merc. 483 quo leto censes me ut peream?, Rud. 390 eam veretur ne perierit, Pseud. 1061 nunc ego Simonem mi obviam veniat velim. (For a full list of instances see Lindskog: Quaestiones de Parataxi et Hypotaxi apud priscos Latinos. Lund, 1896, pp. 76 sqq.) It is the normal construction with *facio*, e.g. Pers. 414 possum te facere ut argentum accipias?, Most. 389 satin habes, si ego advenientem ita patrem faciam tuum ... ut fugiat longe ab aedibus? (but e.g. Pseud. 819

quae illis qui terunt, prius quam triverunt, oculi ut exstillent facit). Not unlike is Pseud. 1319 hoc ego nunquam ratus sum fore me ut tibi fierem supplex.

43. With some Compound Verbs the use of the Acc. may be referred to the Prepositional part of the compound, e.g. *circumduco*, Most. 843 eho, istum, puere, circumduce hasce aedes et conclavia; also various Compounds with *ad*, such as *adhinnio*, Cist. 308 adhinnire equolam possum ego hanc; *accido*, e.g. Stich. 88 sonitus aures accidit; *accumbo*, 'sit next, at table,' e.g. Bacch. 1189 scortum accumbas; *accedo*, e.g. Most. 689 igitur tum accedam hunc, Lucilius 112 Ma. ut Setinum accessimus finem; with *in*, such as *inhio*, e.g. Mil. 715 bona mea inhiant; *incumbo*, Cas. 308 gladium faciam culcitam eumque incumbam; *insisto*, e.g. Mil. 793 erro quam insistas viam; *insto*, e.g. Poen. 918 tantum eum instet exiti, Pers. 514 nescis quid te instet boni; *impendeo*, e.g. Ter. Phorm. 180 tanta te impendent mala; *inmitto*, e.g. Capt. 548 ne tu quod istic fabuletur aures inmittas tuas; *inlucesco*, Amph. 547 ut mortales inlucescas luce clara et candida, Bacch. 256 Volcanus, Luna, Sol, Dies, di quattuor, scelestiorem nullum inluxere alterum; *invado*, e.g. Trin. 28 (see above, 1); with *ob*, such as *obrepo*, e.g. Trin. 61 me inprudentem obrepseris; *occento*, Pers. 569 occentabunt ostium (cf. *accento* Stich. 572); *occurso*, Mil. 1047 ita me occursant multae (*mi* Bothe) (cf. Afranius 183); *obstino*, Aul. 267 ea affinitatem hanc obstinavit gratia; although many Compounds with *ob* take the Dat., *occubo*, e.g. Mil. 212 quoi bini custodes semper totis horis occubant; *obsŏno*, Pseud. 208 quom sermone huic obsonas 'you drown his words with your talk.'

44. The competition of Acc. with Dat. has been already mentioned (25) in connexion with *ausculto*, etc. To the Compound Verbs which take Acc. as well as Dat. (e.g. Epid. 135 nunc iam alia cura impendet pectori), we may add *inservio*, Most. 190 matronae, non meretricium est unum inservire amantem, Most. 216 si illum inservibis solum; *indulgeo*, e.g. Ter. Heaut. 988 te indulgebant (cf. Eun. 222), Lucilius 900 Ma, tu qui iram indulges nimis, Afranius 391 qui nos tanto opere indulgent in pueritia. Also the Simple Verbs *servio*, Turpilius 39 modice atque parce eius serviat cupidines; *studeo*, e.g. Mil. 1437 minus has res studeant, Truc. 337 illum student iam, Titinius 85 Ferentinatis populus res Graecas studet; *medeor*, e.g. Ter. Phorm. 822 cupiditates, quas, quom res advorsae sient, paulo mederi possis (cf. *medicari* with Acc. Most. 387 ego istum lepide medicabo metum; with Dat. Amph. frag. viii. advenienti morbo medicari iube). *Anteeo* (*antideo*) takes Acc. with an Abl. of Respect, e.g. Bacch. 1089 solus ego omnes longe antideo stultitia et moribus indoctis, but otherwise Dat., e.g. Pers. 778 solus ego omnibus antideo facile, Amph. 649 virtus omnibus rebus anteit. *Parco* has Acc. and Dat. indiscriminately, e.g. Mil. 1220 ne parce vocem, ut audiat (cf. Most. 104, and the old formula, like Gk. εὐφήμει, used at sacrifices *parcito linguam*), Pers. 682 tace, parce voci (cf. Poen. 1145).

45. The Acc. competes with the Abl. in the construction of the Deponents *potior* (see above, 7), *fungor, fruor, utor*, etc. Apparently the Acc. is the older usage. It appears normally with *fungor*, e.g. Trin. 1 sequere hac me, gnata, ut munus fungaris tuum; also with *abutor*, e.g. Trin. 682 qui abusus sum tantam rem patriam, and *fruniscor*, e.g. Rud. 1012. But with *fruor* and *utor* it has been almost wholly supplanted by the Abl. (for full statistics see Langen in Archiv lat. Lexikographie 3, pp. 329 sqq.). *Careo* too may take Acc. in O. Lat., e.g. Ter. Eun. 223 tandem non ego illam caream, si sit opus, vel totum triduom?, Turpilius 32 meos parentes careo.

46. The use of the Acc. after the Interjection *em* is natural; for *em* was originally the 2 Sing. Imperat. of *emo*, 'I take' (see chap. IX). Natural too is Most. 845 apage istum a me perductorem! Either to Analogy of *apage* (ἄπαγε) or to the ellipse of some Verb the Acc. with *ultro* (which is related to *ultra* as *citro* to *citra*; cf. **VII, 2**, s.v. intra) is usually ascribed, e.g. Capt. 551 ultro istum a me!, Amph. 320 ultro istunc qui exossat homines!, Most. 607 ultro te! Ellipse of obsecro is the usual explaflation of *tuam fidem* in lines like Aul. 692 Iuno Lucina, tuam fidem! (see **V, 7, IX**). In toasts, etc., we have seen (**24**) that the Dat. was used, e.g. *bene mihi, bene vobis* (sc. *sit*). We find also the Acc., e.g. Stich. 709 bene vos, bene nos, bene te, bene me, bene nostrum etiam Stephanium, Asin. 905 (at a throw of dice) te, Philaenium, mihi atque uxoris mortem.

Similarly instead of the usual *vae tibi!* we have in Asin. 481 *vae te!*

47. In all kinds of Exclamations the Acc. is as common as the Gen. (cf. **6**, above; e.g. Most. 912 di immortales, mercimoni lepidi!) is rare. Examples are: Most. 1071 o mortalem malum! Bacch. 759 o imperatorem probum!, Poen. 324 A. Milphio.

B. edepol Milphionem miserum!, Rud. 686 edepol diem hunc acerbum!, Mil. 977 hercle occasionem lepidam!, Mil. 1056 eu hercle odiosas res!, Bacch. 991 eugae litteras minutas!, Cist. 685 ilicet me infelicem et scelestam!; often without any Interjection, e.g. Trin. 1035 A. more fit. B. morem improbum!, Mil. 1385 facetum puerum!, Asin. 931 bellum filium!, Bacch. 1177 lepidum te!, Mil. 248 nimis doctum dolum! Often we find a construction of this kind: Amph. 882 durare nequeo in aedibus. ita me probri, stupri, dedecoris a viro argutam meo!, Mil. 837 bono subpromo et promo cellam creditam! Beside the common exclamation *gerrae!* (e.g. Trin. 760) we find the Acc. *nugas!* (e.g. Most. 1087, Pers. 718, etc.). The ellipse of *dicis* or *fabularis* is suggested by Rud. 1322 sq. :

    A. quid dare velis qui istaec tibi investiget indicetque?
       eloquere propere celeriter. B. nummos trecentos. A. tricas!
    B. quadrigentos. A. tramas putidas! B. quingentos. A. cassam glandem!
    B. sescentos. A. curculiunculos minutos fabulare.

48. The suppression of a Verb is certainly the explanation of the Acc. in lines like Cas. 319 quam tu mi uxorem?, Poen. 972 quid tu mihi testes?, Most. 908 A. quoiusmodi gynaeceum? quid porticum? B. insanum bonam (see below, **V**, 7).

49. The Acc. is found with the Participle *indutus*, e.g. Epid. 223 quid erat induta? an regillam induculam an mendiculam?, 225 utin impluvium induta fuerit?, Men. 511 non ego te indutum foras exire vidi pallam? Either *indutus* is Middle, not Passive, or *indutus* takes Acc. on the analogy of *gestare*. But Cist. 641, utrum hac me (hacine *Brix*) feriam an ab laeva latus?, Men. 858 hunc senem osse fini dedolabo assulatim viscera, are doubtful instances of the 'Acc. of Limitation.' They rather shew Apposition, like Cas. 337 quis mihi subveniet tergo aut capiti aut cruribus?, for the Greek Acc. is alien to Plautus. Ennius in his 'Annals' ventured on this Acc. in v. 311 V. perculsi pectora Poeni, and found imitators in subsequent Dactylic poets (e.g. Lucr. 1, 12 perculsae corda tua vi). It is probably a Graecism, although the Acc. in another line of the Annals (v. 400 V.) succincti corda machaeris, might be classed with the Syntax of *indutus*. (On the gradual extension of this use of the Acc. in Latin, see Landgraf in the Archiv lat. Lexikographie, 10, 209 sqq.)

50. The same variation of construction that appears in class. Lat. with verbs like *circumdo*, (1) c. murum urbi, (2) c. urbem muro, is seen with *instruo* in Plautus, e.g. Mil. 981 aurum atque ornamenta quae illi instruxti mulieri. *Impertio* 'aliquem aliqua re' is the usual construction, e.g. Epid. 127 Stratippoclem impertit salute servus Epidicus, Ter. Eun. 270, etc., but 'aliquam rem alicui' (usual with Cicero) appears occasionally, Pseud. 41 Phoenicium Calidoro amatori suo .. salutem impertit (cf. Vidul. 39, Novius 11).

51. The Double Acc., of person and thing, is found even with, e.g. *consulo*, Men. 700 consulere hanc rem amicos; *insimulo*, e.g. Amph. 859 sic me insimulare falso facinus tam malum!; *circumduco* (cf. 43, above); *eludo*, Curc. 630 illum anulum, quem parasitus hic te elusit; *cogo* (when Acc. of Thing is Neut. Pron.), e.g. Amph. 164 haec eri immodestia coegit me, Ter. Adelph. 490, and other verbs, besides the usual *doceo*, *celo*, *posco*, etc., e.g. *incuso*, Ter. Phorm. 914 quae .. me incusaveras; *condono*, e.g. Phorm. 947 argentum .. condonamus te (cf. Eun. 17); Afranius 173 id aurum me condonat litteris; *privo*, Novius 69 quot res vis hunc privari pulchras?

Lastly may be mentioned the O. Lat. use of *in* with Acc. instead of Abl., e.g. *in mentem est* (like *in mentem venit*) (see VII, 2).

(On the use of the Acc. with the Infinitive, see V, 34.)

52. **Vocative.** (W. Ferger: de Vocativi usu Plautino Terentianoque. Strasburg, 1889.)

In Latin the Voc. is distinguished in form from the Nom. only in the Sing. of the Second Decl.; and that not always in Plautus, in the colloquial language of endearment, e.g. Stich. 763 meus oculus, da mihi savium, Asin. 664 da, meus ocellus, mea rosa, mi anime, mea voluptas, Cas. 137 meus festus dies, meus pullus passer, mea columba, mi lepus.

But Plautus and Terence recognize a distinction between *puere* Voc. and *puer* Nom. (sometimes Voc.) which has disappeared by the classical period. *O* is added to a Vocative in emotional utterance, e.g. Trin. 1072 certe is est, is est profecto. O mi ere exoptatissume!, in the invocation of absent persons, etc., e.g. Trin. 617 O ere Charmides, quom absenti hic tua res distrahitur tibi, utinam te rediisse salvom videam!; but is usually omitted, e.g. Capt. 1009 salve, Tyndare, Pers. 725 heus, Saturio, exi, Most. 373 Callidamates, Callidamates, vigila. *O Iuppiter!* is common in Terence, but

Plautus uses *Iuppiter!* without *O*. (*Pro Iuppiter!* is also used by both.)

53. Ablative. (On Abl. of Place and Motion see J. Heckmann in Indogermanische Forschungen, 18, pp. 296 sqq.; on Abl. of Time, Kane: Case forms .. to express Time. Baltimore, 1895.)

The Latin Abl. combines in itself the Indo-European (1) Abl., (2) Instrumental, a Case denoting instrument, accompaniment, description, etc. There is a play on these two senses of instrument and description in Amph. 368 A. immo equidem tunicis consutis huc advenio, non dolis. B. at mentiris etiam : certo pedibus, non tunicis venis. In Plautine Latin we find the Abl. with all the functions which it has in classical literature, viz. Motion from, Instrument, Description, Cause, Time, Place, Price, Abl. Absolute, etc. A few of the more notable examples under each head will suffice.

54. The Abl. of Motion, confined in class. Lat. to names of towns, with *domus* and *rus*, has (like the Acc. of Motion, above, 39) a wider range in Plautus, e.g. Most. 440 triennio post Aegypto advenio domum (cf. 39 note, and Lucilius 1276, quoted below), Curc. 225 paves parasitus quia non rediit Caria (though we also find the Prep. used, e.g. Capt. 1005 erus alter eccum ex Alide rediit). Corresponding to the Loc. *militiae, viciniae* (cf. above, 31), we have Truc. 230 eum mittat militia domum. (On *viciniā* Most. 1062, see the next paragraph). But also *ab domo* Aul. 105 quia ab domo abeundum est mihi, Epid. 681 (see p. 11). We find it not merely with such Verbs as *abscedo*, e.g. Epid. 285 et repperi haec te qui abscedat suspicio, where we may ascribe it to the Prep. in Tmesis (like *inmittere verba aures*, 43), but with *salio* Trin. 266 peius perit quasi (= quam si) saxo saliat, although the Prep. is usually supplied with Simple Verbs (cf. above, 1).

55. Provenience is indicated by Abl., not merely of town-names, etc., e.g. Mil. 648 non sum Animula 'I do not hail from A.', Asin. 499 Periphanes Rhodo mercator dives, Merc. 940 video ibi hospitem Zacyntho (cf. Ter. Andr. 892 civem hinc), but with the same freedom as the Abl. of Motion in O. Lat. Corresponding to Loc. *viciniae*, we have Most. 1062 foris concrepuit proxuma vicinia (cf. *hinc* Mil. 1377, hinc sonitum fecerunt fores). Lucilius admits *Aegypto sargus* (1276 Ma.) along with *Syracusis sola* 'bootsoles from S.' (446 Ma.). Compare also phrases like Pers. 251 Ope gnatus (but Mil. 1081 ex Ope natust); also the Abl. in the phrase *stare sententia*, e.g. Curc. 250 ea omnes stant sententia (cf. Rud. 808 age alter istinc, alter hinc adsistite; Men. 799 hinc stas, illim causam dicis).

56. The Abl. with *opus est* is usually explained as a relic of the Instrumental Case, e.g. opus est gladio 'there is a work (to be done) with a sword'[1]. In Plautus we find also the Nom., e.g. Capt. 164 opus Turdetanis, opust Ficedulensibus, iam maritumi omnes milites opus sunt tibi; but whether the Grammarian Nonius Marcellus (482 Me.) is right in saying that the Acc. was also used is doubtful. Cf. Truc. 88 (of uncertain text), 902 puero opust cibum (-bo *edd.*), Ter. Phorm. 666 opus est sumptu (-tum *A*) ad nuptias. It might be defended on the analogy of *usus est* with Acc., of which we have a probable example in Pseud. 385 ad eam rem usust hominem astutum, doctum, cautum et callidum. In this line the Verbal Noun *usus* seems to take the earlier construction (see above, 45) of the Verb *utor* (whence a use of the Gerundive like *haec utenda sunt*). Some however prefer to ascribe the Abl. with *opus est* to the analogy of the Abl. with *usus est* (the usual construction, just as *utor* in Plautus normally takes Abl.). Both *usus est* and *opus est* are found with Abl. of Perf. Part. Pass., e.g. Amph. 505 citius quod non factost usus fit quam quod factost opus. Cf. Pers. 584 A. opusne est hac tibi empta? B. si tibi venisse est opus, mihi quoque empta est.

57. With *facio* 'I sacrifice,' 'make an offering,' we find the Abl., e.g. Stich. 251 quot agnis fecerat? Also in the sense of 'disposing of,' e.g. Most. 636 quid eost argento factum?, Capt. 952 meo minore quid sit factum filio, Epid. 152 quid illa fiet fidicina igitur? Similarly with *esse*, etc., e.g. Trin. 157 siquid eo fuerit, Mil. 299 quid fuat me nescio, Caecilius 180 quid hoc futurum obsonio est? (but the Dat. is also used, e.g. Truc. 633 quid mihi futurum est?). Also, e.g. Men. 266 quid eo vis? 'what do you want with it?'

The Abl. with *vescor*, lit. 'feed myself,' appears to be Abl. of Instrument; similarly with *victito*, e.g. Mil. 321 mirumst lolio victitare te, tam vili tritico. On the construction of *utor*, *fungor*, *fruor*, etc., see 45; of *potior*, 7.

---

[1] In Sanscrit the Instr. Case is used with the corresponding phrase, arthō bhavati 'opus est.'

To the Agent the Gen. would be as appropriate as the Abl. to the Instrument, e.g. Most. 412 id viri doctist opus. We find the Gen. of the thing in Lucilius 334 Ma. nummi opus (see Marx's note).

58. The Adverbial Abl. is much in evidence, e.g. Mil. 450 nisi voluntate ibis, Aul. 477 sapienter factum et consilio bono, Trin. 362 id nunc facis haud consuetudine (cf. *more*, e.g. Aul. 246 more hominum facit), Rud. 729 *ioculo*[m], like *ioco* (the opposite of the Adv. *serio*), for which we also find *per iocum*, e.g. Amph. 964 A. me dixisse per iocum. B. an id ioco dixisti? equidem serio ac vero ratus. Cf. Bacch. 268 rebus ceteris 'in other respects' (see **4**, above). Like Capt. 689 clueas gloriā (= gloriose), is Poen. 1192 si quod agit cluet victoriā, Asin. 142 sordido vitam oblectabas pane in pannis inopiā.

59. The Abl. Absolute (see E. Bombe 'de abl. abs. apud antiquiss. Romanorum scriptores usu.' Greifswald, 1877) is sometimes loosely used of the Subject of the sentence, e.g. Amph. 542 ut quom absim me ames, me tuam te absente tamen, Ter. Heaut. 913 qui se vidente amicam patiatur suam; cf. Rud. 712 meas mihi ancillas invito me eripis, Most. 230 quam te me vivo unquam sinam egere aut mendicare, Stich. 132. Similar is an Abl. (without a Noun) like *auspicato*, Pers. 608 vide ut ingrediare auspicato (cf. praefinito Ter. Hec. 94), and (without a Verb) e.g. Poen. 728 quid si recenti re aedes pultem?, Most. 916 me suasore atque impulsore. Other examples of this Abl. (sometimes called in Grammars the 'Abl. of Accompaniment' or of 'Attendant Circumstances') are Trin. 446 bonis tuis rebus meas res irrides malas (tuis in rebus *A*), Trin. 376 tua re salva, Truc. 75 re placida atque otiosa, victis hostibus (but Poen. 524 praesertim in re populi placida atque interfectis hostibus; cf. Pseud. 1021), Bacch. 599 tuo ego istaec igitur dicam illi periculo, Mil. 513 quam magno vento plenumst undarum mare ('when the wind is high'), and the curious phrase in Cas. 525 nunc enim tu demum nullo scito scitus es (cf. Leo's note on Pseud. 1047). This may be the true explanation of the O. Lat. use of *fini* 'as far as' with Abl., Men. 859 osse fini dedolabo assulatim viscera, Cato R.R. 31, 2 operito terra radicibus fini, lit. 'the bone being the limit,' 'with the roots as limit.'

60. The Abl. of Price has been already mentioned (16, 32). Here may be added these instances: Asin. 87 argentum accepi,

[m] The Diminutive scarcely survives except in this Adverbial use. Stereotyped Adverbial Ablatives of obsolete Nouns, e.g. *astu*, are numerous in Latin, as in our own language obsolete Nouns survive in Adverbial use, e.g. *stead*.

dote imperium vendidi; Pers. 668 non edepol minis trecentis carast.

It is often accompanied by the Adv. *contra* (cf. below, VII, 2), e.g. Truc. 538 iam mi auro contra constat filius.

61. For the Abl. of Cause we may quote Pseud. 799 A. cur conducebas? B. inopia: alius non erat, Most. 196 te ille deseret aetate et satietate, 840 aetate non quis obtuerier, Poen. 509 scibam aetate tardiores, Capt. 808 quarum odore praeterire nemo pistrinum potest, Amph. 1066 qui terrore meo occidistis prae metu, Ter. Adelph. 409 lacrimo gaudio (*prae* is used in Stich. 466, etc.), Phorm. 998 delirat miser timore; also *ea re* (cf. *quare*), e.g. Aul. 799 ea re repudium remisit aunculus causa mea, *hoc*, etc., e.g. Pseud. 807 hoc ego fui hodie solus obsessor fori, Rud. 1234 isto tu pauper es, quom nimis sancte piu's; hence *eo . . . quia*, etc.

62. The Abl. of Description, often the equivalent of an Adj., competes with the Gen. (see above, 9), e.g. Mil. 1369 dicant te mendacem nec verum esse, fide nulla esse te, Pseud. 1218 rufus quidam, ventriosus, crassis suris. The Abl. seems to predominate in Plautus, the Gen. in the Silver Age. (For details, see Edwards and Woelfflin in Archiv lat. Lexikographie 11, pp. 197 sqq., 469 sqq.) *Cum* is used in sentences like Aul. 554 quingentos coquos cum senis manibus, just as it is an alternative expression of other functions of the Abl. (see VII, 2), e.g. Merc. 811 rediit .. cum quidem salute familiai maxuma (contrast Men. 134 avorti praedam ab hostibus nostrum salute sociûm).

63. Abl. of Time ('at' or 'within'): e.g. Most. 505 quae hic monstra fiunt anno vix possum eloqui. *Anno* can also mean 'within the past year,' 'a year ago,' Amph. prol. 91, Men. 205 quattuor minis ego emi istanc anno uxori meae (cf. above, 37). The Pron. *hic* often accompanies the Abl., e.g. Pers. 504 neque istuc redire his octo possum mensibus, Poen. 872 iam his duobus mensibus volucres tibi erunt tuae hirquinae (*scil.* alae), Most. 238 nam neque edes quicquam neque bibes apud me his decem diebus. Like *ludis* 'at the games,' e.g. Pers. 436, is Aul. 540 si nitidior sis filiai nuptiis.

64. Abl. of Place ('at' or 'within'): e.g. Merc. 51 conclamitare tota urbe, Cas. 763 omnes festinant intus totis aedibus; Amph. 568 homo idem duobus locis ut simul sit. With a Compound Verb (see above, 1), e.g. Rud. 907 qui salsis locis incolit pisculentis. The phrase *capite sistere* 'to be tumbled on one's head' is common,

e.g. Curc. 287 quin cadat, quin capite sistat in via de semita. The Locative Abl., e.g. *Carthagine, Athenis*, has been already mentioned (29—34), and the greater freedom of its use in Plautine than in class. Lat., e.g. Capt. 330 filius meus illic apud vos servit captus Alide (usually *in Alide;* see my note on v. 94).

The Abl. expresses also 'along,' 'by a route' (cf. *recta via*), e.g. Poen. 631 si bene dicetis, vostra ripa vos sequar : si male dicetis, vostro gradiar limite.

65. Of the Abl. of Difference we may take as example the joke in Rud. 1305 A. immo edepol una littera plus sum quam medicus. B. tum tu mendicus es (which shews that Plautus spelt *mendicus* with *i*, not *ei*); Stich. 498 uno Gelasimo minus est quam dudum fuit ' there's one G. less,' Cas. 359 te uno adest plus quam ego volo, Pers. 684 duobus nummis minus est, Truc. 304 (of a wall) quae in noctes singulas latere fit minor 'loses a brick each night.' If *quī* be really Instr., not Abl., of *quis*, there is evidence of the Instrumental origin of this function, for *ecquī, numquī, siquī* are the forms used with Comparatives, e.g. numquī minus? (but *quo minus*, e.g. Ter. Andr. 655).

66. The Abl. of Comparison is used not merely with Comparatives, but with *aeque*, e.g. Curc. 141 qui (= quis) me in terra aeque fortunatus erit? (On the use of *aeque* with the Comp. of an Adj., e.g. *aeque miserior*, see III, 2). Some appeal to a line like Amph. 704, ex insana insaniorem facies, in support of the theory that the Abl. of Comparison is a developement of the Abl. of Motion or Provenience.

67. The Abl. with *dignus* is associated in some Grammars with the Abl. of Comparison, in others with the Abl. of Price. In Plautus we find not only *dignus aliqua re*, but *dignus ad*, e.g. Mil. 968 ad tuam formam illa una dignast. (On *id dignus esse*, see above, 40). He gives *decorus* the same Abl. as *dignus* in Mil. 619 neque te decora neque tuis virtutibus.

68. The Abl. of Plenty and Want has been discussed above (14), in connexion with the similar use of the Gen., e.g. Mil. 1033 quia tis (Gen.) egeat, quia te (Abl.) careat, a line which exemplifies Plautus' invariable construction of these two Verbs ; Turpilius 157 expers malitiis ; also the Abl. with *compos*, which follows the construction of the Verb *compotire* (*-ri*), e.g. Rud. 911 piscatu novo me uberi compotivit, Rud. 205 ita hic sola solis locis compotita sum.

69. The Abl. of Respect, indicating the sphere in which the Verb operates: e.g. Most. 708 atque pol nescio ut moribus sient vostrae, 'in respect of character'; Pers. 238 malitia certare tecum; with *deficio*, e.g. Asin. 609 quem si intellegam deficere vita.

This Abl. plays the part of a Cognate Acc. in lines like Most. 1158 scis solere illanc aetatem tali ludo ludere, Pseud. 24 ludis iam ludo tuo.

70. Of other Verbs with Abl. may be noticed: *desisto*, e.g. Mil. 737 istis rebus desisti decet; *supersedeo*, e.g. Epid. 39 supersede istis rebus iam; *emungo* 'swindle,' e.g. Bacch. 1101 me auro esse emunctum; *tango* 'swindle,' e.g. Poen. 1286 aere militari tetigero lenunculum; *circumduco* 'swindle,' e.g. Poen. 1287 nanctus est hominem mina quem argenti circumduceret; *tondeo* 'swindle,' Bacch. 242 itaque tondebo auro usque ad vivam cutem; *eluo*, Asin. 135 nam in mari repperi, hic elavi bonis; *interficio*, e.g. Truc. 518 salve qui me interfecisti paene vita et lumine (hence *interficere*, sc. vitā, 'to kill'); *prohibeo*, e.g. Asin. 515 illo quem amo prohibeor, Pseud. 13 id te (Abl.) Juppiter prohibessit!, Ter. Phorm. 425 aut quidem cum uxore hac ipsum prohibebo domo; *abstineo*, e.g. Rud. 1108 abstine maledictis, Aul. 601 qui ea curabit abstinebit censione bubula, Rud. 424 potin ut me abstineas manum?; *caveo*[a], e.g. Bacch. 147 cave malo; *excido*, Ter. Andr. 423 erus, quantum audio, uxore excidit; *consuesco*, Ter. Adelph. 666 qui illa consuevit prior (*v.l.* illam).

On *refert meā*, see above, I, 4.

III. THE ADJECTIVE.

1. Just as an Adj. may play the part of a Noun, e.g. *boni* 'good men,' *bonum* 'a good thing' (cf. *proxumum* 'next door,' e.g. Asin. 54; Rud. 767 quin *inhumanum* exuras tibi 'cauterize your inhumanity'), so a Noun occasionally plays the part of an Adj. Instances from Plautine Latin are *turbo ventus* 'whirlwind,' *lapis silex* 'flintstone,' *Philippus nummus* (but *Philippeus* Poen. 714;

---

[a] Sometimes with *ab* and Abl., e.g. Men. 151 abs te caveo, Pers. 317 cave sis a cornu. The Acc. is also found, not merely of Neut. Pron., e.g. Men. 265 ego istuc cavebo, but of Nouns, e.g. Asin. 43 cave sis malam rem. In the legal sense 'to take surety' the Verb takes *cum* with Abl., e.g. Pseud. 909 malus cum malo stulte cavi.

cf. Poen. 781), Most. 1049 ut senatum congerronem (-num B^2) convocem, Poen. 543 obsecro hercle, operam celocem hanc mihi, ne corbitam date 'express-boat service, not lugger service.' Of the equivalence of an Adj. to the Gen. Case of a Noun the common phrase *erilis filius* 'our young master' may serve as example.

An Adj. plays the part of an Adv. in lines like Men. 154 dies quidem iam ad umbilicum est dimidiatus mortuus. Besides *invitus* (e.g. Mil. 449 vi atque invitam ingratiis .. rapiam te domum, Aul. 106 invitus abeo), we often find *totus, miser, divorsus, citus* used Adverbially, e.g. Aul. 410 totus doleo atque oppido perii, Bacch. 208 misera amans desiderat, Poen. 368 discrucior miser (*misere* is Terentian but hardly Plautine in such phrases; Sjögren 'de part. cop'., p. 60 cites Aul. 14, 315), Rud. 1252 sed quom inde suam quisque ibant divorsi domum, Truc. 787 divorsae state 'stand apart,' Amph. 1115 citus e cunis exilit, etc. Adj. and Adv. are often found side by side, e.g. Capt. 960 recte et vera loquere (cf. Ter. Adelph. 609), Trin. 268 sunt tamen quos miseros maleque habeas, Bacch. 474 tu Pistoclerum falso atque insontem arguis. (For other examples see Sjögren 'de part. copulat.', p. 58.)

On the use of the Pron. Adj. for a Conjunction, *nullus* for *non*, e.g. Asin. 408 is nullus venit, 'he did not turn up,' see IV, 28. The Adj. *varius* plays the part of a Perf. Part. Pass. *variatus* in Mil. 216 nisi quidem hic agitare mavis varius virgis vigilias.

2. In regard to the Comparison of the Adj. (see W. Fraesdorff: de Comparativi Gradus usu Plautino. Halle, 1881), two Plautine peculiarities call for notice, the pleonastic use of *magis* with a Comparative (see Seyffert in Bursian's Jahresbericht, 1895, p. 296), e.g. Capt. 644 quin nihil, inquam, invenies magis hoc certo certius (cf. Trin. 1029), and the association of *aeque* (*adaeque*) with the same Degree, e.g. Merc. 335 homo me miserior nullust aeque, opinor.

The genesis of the phrase, common both in Plautine and class. Lat., *certiorem facere* 'to inform,' may be seen in lines like these: Pseud. 18 face me certum quid tibist 'inform me' (cf. scientem facere, e.g. Asin. 48, Ter. Heaut. 872 nam te scientem faciam quidquid egero), Pseud. 1097 epistula atque imago me certum facit 'makes me certain,' Pseud. 965 sed eccum qui ex incerto faciet mihi quod quaero certius, Amph. 347 numquid nunc es certior? Similarly we find *potior fieri*, Cas. 112 hercle me suspendio, quam tu eius potior fias, satiust mortuum. On the Positive, use of the Comparative *ocius*, see **VI, 4**.

Some Participles receive Comparison like Adjs., often with comical intention, e.g. Cas. 694 occisissimus sum omnium qui vivunt, Trin. 397 factius nihilo facit, Poen. 581 quin edepol condoctior sum quam tragoedi aut comici, Stich. 118 utra siet condicio pensior, virginemne an viduam habere?, Most. 441

> A. credo, exspectatus veniam familiaribus.
>
> B. nimio edepol ille potuit exspectatior
>   venire qui te nuntiaret mortuum,

Ter. Heaut. 645 ignoscentior. Other examples of comic Comparison are Poen. 991 nullus me est hodie Poenus Poenior, and the often quoted *ipsissumus* (cf. αὐτότατος), Trin. 989 A. is ipsusne es? B. aio. A. ipsus es? B. ipsus, inquam, Charmides sum. A. ergo ipsusne es? B. ipsissumus. Notice that the construction 'verior quam gratior,' etc., is unknown to Plautus and Terence. There is an example in a speech of Cato (10, 2) quantoque suam vitam superiorem atque ampliorem atque antiquiorem animum inducent esse quam innoxiorem. On *quam* and *atque* after Comparatives, see **VIII, 2**.

The **Predicative use** of the Adj. may be illustrated by these lines: Mil. 953 immo omnes res posteriores pono atque operam do tibi, Cist. 193 nihil est perpetuum datum.

3. **Indeclinables.** *Nequam*, lit. 'nohow,' is an Adj. in the colloquial Latin of Plautus' time, e.g. Pers. 453 si malus aut nequamst, male res vortunt quas agit; sin autem frugist, eveniunt frugaliter; Truc. 157 postremo illi sunt improbi, vos nequam et gloriosae. Like other Adjectives, it may act as a Noun, e.g. Poen. 159 A. vin tu illi nequam (= malum) dare nunc? B. cupio. A. em, me dato. *Frugi bonae* Dat. (II, 27) was shortened to *frugi*°, and associated with *frugalis*, as may be seen from these lines: Truc. 34 temptat benignusne an bonae frugi sies (cf. 41), Cas. 268 ut enim frugi servo detur potius quam servo improbo, Pers. 454 (just quoted) sin autem frugist, eveniunt frugaliter. *Nihili* (II, 32) too became an Adj., e.g. Cas. 257 armigero nihili atque improbo, Asin. 472

° Ennius coined the word *frux* for 'homo frugi' in Ann. 314 V. dictum factumque facit frux.

impure, nihili 'you good for nothing,' Mil. 180 propter nihili bestiam.

4. **Numerals.** *Unus.* (M. Paul: Quaestionum Grammaticarum part. I. De 'unus' nominis numeralis apud priscos scriptores usu. Jena (diss.) 1884.) The colloquial use with the Superl. is frequent in Plautus (cf. Seyffert in Bursian's Jahresbericht, 1895, p. 293). Other notable uses are: Epid. 453 pol ego magis unum (= quendam) quaero meas (*scil.* pugnas) cui praedicem; Trin. 166 unos (= tantummodo) sex dies; Most. 677 iterum iam ad unum (= idem) saxum me fluctus ferunt; *unus populus* 'a whole people,' Mil. 584 nam uni satis populo improbo merui mali; Poen. 226 sed vero duae, sat scio, maxumo uni populo quoilubet plus satis dare potis sunt. Some find an anticipation of the Indefinite Article of the Romance languages in a line like Capt. 482 dico unum ridiculum dictum de dictis melioribus.

Mille is a Neut. Noun, and takes the Gen., e.g. Trin. 959 si hunc possum illo mille nummûm Philippûm circumducere, Mil. 1079 quin mille annorum perpetuo vivunt, Ter. Heaut. 601 huic drachumarum haec argenti mille dederat mutuum (cf. Aul. Gell. 1, 16. In Truc. 485 editors change *mille memorari potest* to *pote*).

IV. THE PRONOUN.

1. **Personal.** (W. Kaempf: de pronominum personalium usu et collocatione apud poetas scaenicos Romanorum. Berlin, 1886.)

The pleonastic strengthening of Pronouns (see below, 3) is a feature of language, especially of colloquial language, as in English 'this here man' 'my very own self.' We see it in the emphatic forms of the Pers. Pron. *egomet, tute*, where *-mĕt* and *-tĕ* are mere repetitions of the 1 Pron. stem and the 2 Pron. stem, e.g. Most. 369 A. tutin vidisti? B. egomet, inquam. These forms are especially used in the phrases *egomet mihi* (or *me*) and *tute tibi* (or *te*), for which we find also *ego mihi* and *tu tibi*. The reduplicated *sese* is the emphatic form of the Reflexive *se*. In the normal *ipsus* (not *-se*) *sibi* (or *se*) we have a parallel to *egomet mihi, tute tibi*, e.g. Trin. 321 qui ipsus sibi satis placet . . qui ipsus se contemnit (cf. Rud. 730 tu ipsus te ut non noveris).

On the colloquial use of *hic* (homo, etc.) for *ego*, see below, 13; and on the occasional careless use of *is* for the Reflexive (and vice versa), 15. *Vos* seems (but, I think, only seems) to be used for *tu* in Mil. 862 (Lurcio to Palaestrio) ne dixeritis obsecro huic vostram fidem, Most. 62 (Grumio to Tranio) ervum daturin estis, bubus quod feram?, Pers. 501 salutem dicit Toxilo Timarchides et familiae omni; si valetis, gaudeo. In his note on Ter. Adelph. 774 in peccato maxumo quod vix sedatum satis est potastis, scelus, Donatus remarks: oratorie 'potastis' dicit, cum unum ebrium cernat. (Cf. Truc. 401, 953, Ter. Hec. 263; in Stich. 255, Truc. 358, Poen. 1372, Pseud. 1217, etc., the two families of MSS. offer 2 Sing. and 2 Plur. respectively.)

2. **Possessive.** To *meus, tuus, suus, noster, vester* we must add *quoius* (of Rel. and Interrog.), *alienus* (of *alius*), e.g. Trin. 82 ego meo sum promus pectori: suspicio est in pectore alieno sita. We know from the parody: dic mihi, Damoeta, 'cuium pecus' anne Latinum?, that the Possessive of *qui* and *quis* was discarded by purists. Perhaps the reason was that it was regarded as an incorrect use of the Gen. Sing. In a line like Rud. 1021 si veniat nunc dominus quoiust (*scil.* vidulus), we might parse *quoius* either as Possessive or as Gen. Sing. of *qui*.

The pleonastic strengthening of *suus* by the addition of *sibi* is a feature of colloquial Latin (see G. Landgraf in Archiv lat. Lexikographie 8, 43), which, especially in the proverb *suo sibi gladio hunc iugulo* 'hoist with his own petard,' survived to late times. It looks as though it were fashioned on the pattern of phrases like Bacch. 994 tuus tibi servus tuo arbitratu serviat, Rud. 712 meas mihi ancillas invito me eripis (the juxta-position of Possessive and Personal Pron. is normal) with *sibi* instead of *ei* (cf. 15); cf. Trin. 156 reddam suum sibi, Poen. 1083 suam sibi rem salvam sistam, si illo advenerit. But the Dat. *sibi* has usually no place in the construction of the sentence, e.g. Capt. 5 sed is quo pacto serviat suo sibi patri, 81 suo sibi suco vivunt. Like *sua sibi pecunia* of Pers. 81 is Truc. 698 ubi male accipiar mea mihi pecunia.

Other notable uses of the various Possessives are: *mea*[p] for *era mea*, etc., e.g. Mil. 1263, Ter. Adelph. 289, etc., mea tu; *noster* in the expression of welcome and approval *noster esto* 'be one of our set' (like Horace's scribe tui gregis hunc), e.g. Bacch. 443,

---

[p] The vagueness of this use of the Possessive is utilized for keeping Euclio at cross-purposes between his 'ducats and daughter,' Aul. 744 quid tibi ergo meam me invito tactiost?, where *meam* is meant by Euclio for 'meam ollam,' but is understood by Lyconides as 'meam filiam.'

Mil. 899; *nostri* similarly for 'ex nostra familia' or possibly for 'nosmet ipsi' in Mil. 431 persectari hic volo, Sceledre, nos nostri an alieni simus (cf. Amph. 399 certo edepol tu me alienabis numquam quin noster siem). In Rud. 1245 Daemones says to his slave: minime istuc faciet noster Daemones, using *noster* in the slave's sense of the word.

In Plautus, as in class. Lat., a Possessive may play the part of a Pers. Pron. with a Prep. like *ob, propter*, e.g. *tuus* for *ob te* in Capt. 133 ego qui tuo maerore maceror, Amph. 1066 qui terrore meo occidistis prae metu; it may express the sense of 'characteristic' or 'appropriate,' e.g. *non est meum* Mil. 1363, etc.; cf. Trin. 445 haud nosco tuum, Ter. Eun. 1066 non cognosco vestrum tam superbum, Most. 789 antiquum obtines hoc tuum, tardus ut sis; also Pers. 579 si quidem hanc vendidero pretio suo.

The Possessive is sometimes omitted with *erus* 'master' (for 'my master,' 'your master'), e.g. Rud. 347. The arrangement of phrases like Capt. 875 tuum Stalagmum servum, Amph. 1077 tua Bromia ancilla, is normal (I, 4). (For statistics, see M. Nilsson: quomodo Pronomina, quae cum substantivis coniunguntur, apud Plautum et Terentium collocantur, Lund, 1901, p. 23.)

3. **Relative, Interrogative, Indefinite.** (A. Prehn: Quaestiones Plautinae de Pronominibus Indefinitis. Strasburg (progr.), 1887; with it read Seyffert's remarks in Bursian's Jahresbericht, 1890, pp. 15 sqq.)

Pleonastic strengthening (see I, 11) of the Interrogative and Indefinite Pronouns appears in lines like Most. 256 *quid . . quicquam?*, Aul. 810 *quis . . quisquam?*, Asin. 785 *nequid . . quicquam*, Rud. 896 *nequid* significem *quippiam* mulierculis, Mil. 431 nedum *quispiam* nos vicinorum imprudentes *aliquis* immutaverit, Pers. 648, etc., *nemo . . quisquam*, Asin. 146, etc., *nihil quicquam*. The Relative is occasionally strengthened by the addition of *is, ille*, e.g. Trin. 1023 *quorum eorum* unus surrupuit currenti cursori solum, Epid. 329 quid illum ferre vis, *qui*, tibi quoi divitiae domi maxumae sunt, *is* nummum nullum habes nec sodali tuo in te copiast (cf. Pseud. 225); and this suits the theory that *cuius* (older *quoius*) represents 'quo-eius,' *cui* (older *quoiei*) represents 'quo-eiei,' with addition of the cases of *is* to the Relative-stem. We find also *qui . . ego*, e.g. Epid. 388 vel ego, *qui* dudum fili causa coeperam *ego* med excruciare animi (cf. Epid. 329, just quoted).

4. **Doubling of the Pronouns, to express indefiniteness, appears**

not merely in *quisquis* (never in Plur.), etc., but also in, e.g., *quantumquantum* Poen. 738 (cf. *ubiubi* Rud. 1210). The same sense is given by the addition of *vis*, *lubet*[q], *cumque* (*quomque*), e.g. Pers. 210 quoi pol quomque occasio est (cf. Bacch. 252 *ubi* fit *quaque* mentio); also of *-que*, e.g. *quandoque*, *quisque* (= *quisquis*), e.g. Mil. 156 quemque in tegulis videritis alienum. (On *quisque* 'each,' and on *quisquis* with the function of *quisque*, see below, 25.)

5. Although a phrase like 'quae tua est prudentia (qua es prudentia, cuius es prudentiae), nihil te fugiet' is unknown to Plautus, the beginnings of this use of the Relative may be seen in lines like Mil. 951 quin tu tuam rem cura potius . ., quae tibi condicio nova et luculenta fertur. (In Mil. 801 Parataxis is preferred: ille, eiusmodi est, cupiet miser. On Terence's *utist audacia* and *ut est dementia*, see VIII, 2 s.v. ' ut.')

6. The old Instrumental Case (cf. II, 65) of *qui* and *quis* retains its instrumental function in lines like Curc. 705 A. quodne promisti? B. quî promisi? A. linguā. B. eādem nunc nego; but its transition to a mere Conjunction is patent in its frequent association with a Plural Antecedent, e.g. Aul. 502 vehicla quî vehar. And it has already in Plautus' time sunk to this last stage, e.g. *quî fit ut* . . *?* (see below, VIII, 2). With the Particle (Interrogative, and perhaps also Negative) *-nĕ*, it becomes the Conjunction *quin* (see below, VIII, 2). But *quin* may be also Nom. Masc., like *quaen* or *quaene*, Nom. Fem., in Cist. 654 quae (Neut. Plur.) dudum fassast mihi quaene infitias eat?, Mil. 66 A. itane aibant tandem? B. quaen me ambae obsecraverint? 'why! they both implored me,' *quoin* Dat. Masc. in Mil. 588 quoin id (*scil.* quod vidit) adimatur, ne id quod vidit viderit? (For more examples see Rauterberg: Quaestiones Plautinae. Wilhelmshaven (progr.), 1883.)

7. By a grammatical laxity *is* appears instead of a repeated *qui* in a line like Trin. 1141 quem ego nec qui esset noram, neque eum ante usquam conspexi prius (cf. Poen. 624 fortunati omnes sitis,

---

[q] We see the origin of these forms in lines like Trin. 570 quid tibi lubet tute agito cum nato meo, Stich. 698 vide utram tibi lubet etiamnunc capere, cape provinciam, Bacch. 866 pacisce ergo, obsecro, quid tibi lubet . . pacisce quidvis, Rud. 854 A. utrum vis opta, dum licet. B. neutrum volo, Mil. 1031 impera, siquid vis, Merc. 182, etc., siquid vis, roga. But the form *quidvis* is already crystallized in Mil. 500 an, quia latrocinamini, arbitramini quidvis licere facere vobis, verbero? *Quovis* is not equivalent to *quo* (*tu*) *vis* in Most. 888 cibo perduci poteris quovis.

quod certo scio nec fore nec Fortunam id situram fieri). On the common Attraction of the Antecedent to the Relative and the very rare Attraction of the Relative to the Antecedent, see above, **I, 8, 9.**

8. The Indefinite Pronoun appears in the form *quis* in classical Latin after certain Conjunctions only, *ne, si, num*, etc., but is less restricted in the Dramatists' time (cf. *an quis* Asin. 717, etc., Pacuvius 25). We may take as examples: Most 749 iam de istis rebus voster quid sensit senex?, Bacch. 274 etiamnest quid porro?, Stich. 201 i quando quem auctionem facturum sciunt, Men. 664 opera reddetur, quando quid tibi erit surruptum domo, Stich. 178 nam illa artes omnes perdocet, ubi quem attigit, Ter. Eun. 511 roget quis. And *quis* plays the part of *quisquis* in lines like Merc. 991 supplici sibi sumat quid volt, Pers. 398 vel tu me vende vel face quid tibi lubet (cf. *quidvis, quidlubet*).

9. *Quisquam* (normally Subst., as *ullus* is normally Adj.) is not confined to Negative[r] and Interrogative Sentences, for we find also, e.g., Cas. 677 tibi infesta solist plus quam cuiquam (cf. Cas. 128). *Quispiam*, only found in Sing. in the Comedians, is not used by Plaut. (but by Ter. Eun. 873) in direct statements, but only in questions or after *si, ubi, nisi, ne*, etc. The same is true of the Adv. *uspiam*.

10. The Interrogative Pronouns are strengthened by the addition of Particles like *tandem, nam*, e.g. Poen. 619 ecquidnam adferunt? et ille chlamydatus quisnam est qui sequitur procul? (On *quianam?* 'why?' of Epic Poetry, see **VIII, 2**). *Ecquid* is sometimes a mere Particle, e.g. Mil. 1106 ecquid fortis visast? 'did she seem good-looking?' (cf. **VIII, 7**). On *quid* 'why?,' *quidni* 'why not?' see **VIII, 2.**

11. The phrase *quot calendis* 'on the first day of each month,' Stich. 60 vos meministis quot calendis petere demensum cibum, affords an interesting contrast to *quoti-die* (*cottidie*).

Plautus' use of *qui, quod* for class. Lat. *quis, quid* (and vice versa) belongs rather to Accidence than to Syntax (Statistics will be found in Seyffert's article in the Berliner Philologische Wochenschrift 1893, p. 278). The use of Subj. and Ind. Mood with Relative Pronouns is treated in **V, 30.**

12. Demonstrative and others. (J. Bach: de usu pronominum

---

[r] On *numquam quisquam*, see below, 28.

demonstrativorum apud priscos scriptores Latinos, in vol. II. of Studemund's 'Studien auf dem Gebiet des archäischen Lateins.' Berlin, 1891.)

To the Demonstratives *hic, iste* (or *istic*), *ille* (or *illic*), *is*, must be added *homo*, which, in the colloquial Latin of Plautus and Terence, often has the function of *is* or *ille*, e.g. Most. 1124 Philolaches venisse dixit mihi suum peregre huc patrem, quoque modo hominem advenientem servus ludificatus sit, Trin. 952 si forte eumpse Charmidem conspexeris, . . . noverisne hominem?, Trin. 45, etc., adgrediar hominem 'I'll go up to him,' Ter. Phorm. prol. 2, Hec. 828. It is often appended to another Pron., e.g. Mil. 684 tu homo et alteri sapienter potis es consulere et tibi, Mil. 624 novo modo tu homo amas 'you're a new type of lover.'

13. The distinction between *hic* 'the person beside me or us,' *iste* (often *iste tuus*) 'the person beside you,' *ille* 'the person at a distance from me or us' is carefully observed in the Comedies and often reveals to us the position occupied at the moment by the several actors on the stage. *Hic* (usually *hic homo*, etc.) for *ego* is a well-known usage of colloquial Latin, e.g. Ter. Andr. 310 tu, si hic sis, aliter sentias. In Epid. 291 it has this sense, even though in a neighbouring line (v. 286) it has the sense of 'he.' Common too is *hoc habet* 'a hit!,' e.g. Most. 715; *hoc age* 'exert yourself' (cf. Mil. 458 vin tu facere hoc strenue?). *Hoc* means 'the sky' 'the day' in e.g. Amph. 543 lucescit hoc iam (cf. Mil. 218, Ter. Heaut. 410), acting in fact as Subject of the Impersonal Verb; 'the door' in e.g. Amph. 1020 aperite hoc. heus! ecquis hic est? ecquis hoc aperit ostium? (cf. Trin. 870). On *hoc est quod* 'this is the reason of,' see VIII, 2, s.v. quod. Terence's *quidquid huius* (Neut.) may also be mentioned, e.g. Heaut. 961 quidquid ego huius feci, tibi prospexi et stultitiae tuae, Eun. 202 et quidquid huius feci, causa virginis feci, 980.

The contemptuous use of *iste*, even of an absent person, is apparently found in Plautus, see Seyffert in Bursian's Jahresbericht, 1895, p. 300), e.g. Cas. 275 Hercules dique istam perdant, where the speaker is alone on the stage. Other phrases with this Pronoun are: *Quid istuc?* 'what is the meaning of your conduct?' e.g. Capt. 541 quid istuc est quod meos te dicam fugitare oculos? It is to be distinguished from *quid istic* (Adv.) ?, the formula of unwilling assents, e.g. Rud. 1331 A. proin tu vel aias vel neges. B. quid istic? necessumst, video. The full form of the last appears in Epid. 141 quid istic ('in that matter urged by you') verba facimus?

Ille became the Definite Article of certain Romance languages. In a few lines of Plautus it seems to play something like this part, e.g. Trin. 493 aeque mendicus atque ille opulentissimus censetur censu ad Accheruntem mortuus, Stich. 133 placet ille meus mihi mendicus (cf. Ital. il mio). Of phrases with *ille* may be mentioned: *hic ille est*, e.g. Most. 162 haec illa est tempestas mea 'this is the storm I mentioned (in v. 108)'; *nunc illud est quom*, e.g. Capt. 516 nunc illud est quom me fuisse quam esse nimio mavelim (cf. Ter. Adelph. 299; the abnormal *nunc id est quom* of Rud. 664, a Cretic line, seems due to metrical convenience); *ille Juppiter* 'J. in heaven above,' e g. Curc. 26 nec me ille sirit Juppiter, Most. 398 (Pseud. 922) ita ille faxit Juppiter (*ille* is explained in Pers. 818 ille qui supra nos habitat); *ille alter* and *illi ceteri* (cf. French ces autres), Mil. 168 nihili facio quid illis faciat ceteris; *illud—volui dicere*, in correcting a slip of the tongue, e.g. Mil. 819 A. sorbet dormiens. B. quid, sorbet? A. illud 'stertit' volui dicere.

The rhetorical use of *hic—ille* as 'the latter—the former,' e.g. Accius 6 haec fortes sequitur, illam indocti possident, is naturally rare in the Comedians, e.g. Bacch. 397 illum laudabunt boni, hunc (hoc MSS.) etiam ipsi culpabunt mali (see Seyffert in Bursian's Jahresbericht, 1895, p. 307). But *hic—hic* and *ille—ille* 'the one' —'the other' are characteristic of the colloquial Latin of Plautus' time and later, e.g. Most. 778 vehit hic clitellas, vehit hic autem alter senex, Ter. Phorm. 332 quia enim in illis fructus est, in illis opera luditur; also *huc illuc, hinc illinc*, etc. In this connexion may be mentioned that phrase of Most. 605 with its curiously modern ring: A. cedo faenus, redde faenus, faenus reddite!.. B. faenus illic, faenus hic! ('interest here, interest there!') nescit quidem nisi faenus fabularier.

14. *Is* in O. Lat., as in class. Lat., is the Demonstrative which (1) refers to some thing or person previously mentioned, (2) accompanies a Relative Pronoun, e.g. *is . . qui*. (On its use instead of a repeated Relative, see above, 7.) This function is shared by the Conjunctions and Adverbs formed from the same Pronominal Stem: *ita* (see **VIII**, 2), *ibi*[a], *inde, eo*, etc.

---

[a] In Livius Andronicus Odyss. 9 *ibi* seems to be used differently. Homer's line (Od. 2, 317) ἢὲ Πύλονδ' ἐλθὼν ἢ αὐτοῦ τῷδ' ἐνὶ δήμῳ is thus rendered: ⟨aut⟩ n Pylum deveniens aut ibi ommentans. But we do not know the context.

15. By a grammatical laxity *is* (*ille*) and the Reflexive Pron. seem occasionally to be confused, e.g. Rud. 1378 si vidulum hunc redegissem (Orat. Obl.) in potestatem eius (= suam), iuratust dare mihi talentum magnum argenti (cf. Bacch. 1098), Merc. 238 dicit capram, quam dederam (Orat. Rect.) servandam sibi (= ei), suai uxoris dotem ambedisse oppido.

16. We find *ille* put for *is* sometimes, e.g. Mil. 21 peiuriorem hoc hominem siquis noverit, aut gloriarum pleniorem quam illic (= is) est. Editors are chary of allowing *hic* to stand for *is* in Plautus (for examples in Terence, see Bach, p. 364) and alter Capt. prol. 19, 335, Men. 650. Certainly the notorious confusion of these Pronouns by scribes (especially *i* and *hi*, *is* and *his*) and in late Latin makes it difficult to be sure that the error is to be ascribed to Plautus and not to a copyist (cf. Seyffert: Studia Plautina. Berlin (progr.), 1874, p. 17; and especially H. Ziegel: de 'is' et 'hic' pronominibus quatenus confusa sint apud antiquos. Marburg, 1897). And undoubtedly lines like Rud. 751 nam huic alterae quae patria sit profecto nescio, nisi scio probiorem hanc (= eam) esse quam te, impuratissume, Mil. 275, (see above, I, 8) are no evidence. But it is impossible to ignore the use of *hoc* for *eo* 'on that account,' e.g. Pseud. 808, 822, Mil. 850. (For other examples see Meader: Latin Pronouns. New York, 1901, pp. 36 sqq.). In Truc. 533 his te dono (contrast 531), the Demonstrative Pron. marks the actual presentation. (On a like confusion of *sic* and *ita* see below, VIII, 2.)

17. *Is* may be referred to *ego*, *tu*, e.g. Amph. 177 hodie qui fuerim liber, eum nunc potivit pater servitutis, Merc. 632 egomet credidi homini docto rem mandare, is lapidi mando maxumo, Bacch. 123 quem ego sapere nimio censui plus quam Thalem, is stultior es barbaro Poticio.

18. *Is* is pleonastically used (as with the Rel. *qui*; cf. 3, above) with the Subject (or Object) of the Sentence (cf. Homeric ὅ), e.g. Poen. 1069 pater tuus, is erat frater patruelis meus, Poen. 302 aurum, id fortuna invenitur, natura ingenium bonum, Bacch. 387 homini amico . . ei, Men. 678 immo edepol pallam illam, amabo te, quam tibi dudum dedi, mihi eam redde, Ter. Adelph. 452 (see Seyffert in Bursian's Jahresbericht, 1895, p. 301). Similarly the Neut. Sing. of various Pronouns may stand in anticipatory apposition to a whole sentence (see Redslob in Literarisches Centralblatt, 1895, p. 1761), e.g. Men. 107 id quoque iam, cari qui instruuntur

deserunt, Men. 536 istuc, ubi illae armillae sunt quas una dedi?, Pseud. 391 ergo utrumque, tibi nunc dilectum para ex multis [atque] exquire ex illis unum qui certus siet. It is not far removed from a mere Particle in lines like Poen. 840 nam id quidem, illi, ut meditatur, verba facit emortuo, Capt. 267 ne id quidem, involucre inicere voluit, Asin. 149 at scelesta viden ut ne id quidem, me dignum esse existumat quem adeat. From a similar use of the Neuter of *uter* has arisen the Disjunctive Interrogative *utrum* (see below, VIII, 2). *Illud quidem* 'I mean to say' is common, e.g. Stich. 589 A. hunc hercle ad cenam ut vocem, te non vocem. B. advorsum te fabulare. A. illud quidem, ambos ut vocem. The fuller phrase *illud volui dicere* has been already mentioned (13).

The loose colloquial use of the Neut. Acc. as Object of the Verb has been discussed in II, 35, e.g. Mil. 1158 id ('on that account') nos ad te, siquid velles, vēnimus, Trin. 35 quam id quod ('wherein') prosint pluribus.

19. As we have seen *tuus*, etc., used for *ob te*, etc. (2, above), so *is, hic*, etc., may play the part of *ob id*, etc., e.g. Pers. 756 eas vobis grates habeo atque ago (cf. Poen. 1255), Rud. 631 si speras tibi hoc anno multum futurum sirpe et laserpicium, eamque (= eorumque) eventuram exagogam Capuam salvam et sospitem, Amph. 924 da mihi hanc (= de hac re) veniam, ignosce, irata ne sies.

20. The Pronominal Adverbs often play the function of Cases (whence Fr. en = *inde*, dont = *de-unde*), e.g. Rud. 1409 dimidium tibi sume, dimidium huc (= *huic*) cedo, Rud. 1387 dandum huc (= *huic*, i.e. mihi) argentum est probum; id ego continuo huic ('to Daemones') dabo, Mil. 712 sacruficant, dant inde (= ex eo sacrificio) partem, Mil. 676 est te unde hospitio accipiam ('the means of'), Stich. 142 quo dedisti nuptum, abire nolumus, Stich. 80 si manere hic sese malint, potius quam alio nubere, Men. 703 immersit aliquo sese, credo, in ganeum, Amph. 111 utrimque est gravida, et ex viro et ex summo Iove; also the common phrases *eo addere, eo accedere*, e.g. Curc. 344 (cf. VI, 3).

21. These Adverbs shew the same Pleonastic strengthening as the Pronouns themselves (cf. 1, 3, above), e.g. Mil. 666 *hinc indidem* expromam tibi, Most. 482 *hic* . . . *ibidem*. In this connexion may be mentioned the common combination of *nemo* (originally *nĕ-hemo*, i.e. non homo) and *homo*, e.g. Most. 901 homo nemo hinc quidem foras exit, Pers. 211 nemo homo umquam ita arbitratust, Ter. Eun. 549 nemo homost, Lucilius 836 Ma. quis tu

homo es? nemo sum homo. Also *hic tantus, hic talis*, e.g. Stich. 769 qui Ionicus aut cinaedicust qui hoc tale facere possiet? Plautus revels in conglomerations like *haec hinc huc*, etc. (the Pronoun normally preceding the Adverb), e.g. Mil. 377 quo modo haec hinc huc transire potuit, Men. 845 qui hunc hinc tollant. (For examples, see Seyffert in Bursian's Jahresbericht, 1890, p. 15 *n*.)

22. The Deictic use of Demonstr. Pronouns may be illustrated by Trin. 483 non hercle hoc longe 'not an inch,' Most. 393 non hoc longe, Delphium; nam intus potate hau tantillo ('not a scrap') hac quidem causa minus. On the combination of the Interjection *ecce* with the Demonstratives *hic, ille, iste* in the forms *eccum, (-am,* etc.), *eccistum (-am,* etc.), *eccillum (-am,* etc.) and of *em* with *ille* in the form *ellum*, see IX. *Eccistum* and *eccillum* have apparently furnished the Demonstratives of some Romance languages, e.g. Ital. questo 'this,' quello 'that.'

23. *Ipse* (W. Niemoeller: de pronominibus 'ipse' et 'idem' apud Plautum et Terentium. Halle, 1887) appears also in the form *ipsus*, a form appropriate to use with the Reflexive Pron., (see above, 1).

This Pron. often bears the colloquial meaning of 'master,' e.g. Aul. 356 si a foro ipsus redierit, Cas. 790 ego eo quo me ipsa misit. *Issula* 'mistress' in Cist. 450 meae issula sua aedes egent is Diminutive of that form which is so well known to us from Martial's pretty poem on the lapdog *Issa* 'My Lady.' On the comical Superlative *ipsissumus*, see above, III, 2.

24. *Idem* (Niemoeller l.c.), older *isdem* (Amph. 945), is formed like *ibi-dem, itidem,* etc., by addition of a Particle (cf. *demum*) with the sense of 'very' 'precise,' so that *is-dem* means 'that very'[t]. It is usually followed by *qui*, but sometimes by *atque* (see below, VIII, 2). With suppression of *operā* Abl. (cf. *eādem operā* Capt. 450, etc., *unā operā* Ter. Hec. 798; also Pseud. 319 qua opera credam tibi, una opera alligem fugitivam canem agninis lactibus) we find the Adverb *eādem*, used (in Asyndeton normally) with Fut. or Fut. Perf., e.g. Capt. 293 sequere hac me igitur: eadem ego ex hoc quae volo exquisivero (in Pers. 445 with Fut. Imperat.).

---

[t] *Is* without the addition of this Particle sometimes has this function, e.g. Bacch. 265 infit dicere adulterinum et non eum esse symbolum, Men. 468 non faxo eum esse dices: ita ignorabitur.

25. *Quisque* 'each' has also, as we have seen (**4**), the function of *quisquis* 'whoever,' e.g. Asin. 404 quisque obviam huic occesserit irato, vapulabit (cf. Pennigsdorf: de 'quisque' et 'quisquis' pronominum apud comicos latinos usu. Halle, 1878). Similarly *quisquis* occupies the place of *quisque* in lines like Trin. 881 si unum quidquid singillatim et placide percontabere, Most. 831 ut quidquid magis contemplo, tanto magis placet, Aul. 198 ubi quidquid tetigerunt, tenent (but Asin. 945 ubi quicque occasionis sit), and in the Plautine phrase *cum eo cum quiqui*, Poen. 536, etc., 'in any case.' The MSS. seem often to confuse the two words, e.g. Truc. 225 adridere ut quisquis (*P*: quisque *A*) veniat blandeque adloqui, and in Trin. 218 many editors substitute through metrical reasons *quidque* for *quidquid* of the MSS. (*AP*):

> quod si exquiratur usque ab stirpe auctoritas,
> unde quidquid auditum dicant.

The two Pronouns are rightly distinguished in Poen. 483 sqq.:

> quemquem visco offenderant,
> tam crebri ad terram decidebant quam pira :
> ut quisque acciderat, eum necabam ilico.

By a similar laxity of usage, the Abl. (Instr.) of *quisque* is, if this be the right reading, used in the phrase *suo quique loco*, Poen. 1177 in suo quique loco sita munde (*v.l.* quicque), Most. 254 suo quique (*v.l.* quicque, strongly supported by Nonius' remarks) loco viden capillum satis compositumst commode? (cf. Stich. 62, Titinius 130). So in Cato (R.R. 23, 4 suo cuique dolio) and Varro (L.L. 10, 48 sui cuiusque generis). The classical use of *quisque* with Ordinal Numerals is also a usage of Plautus, e.g. Trin. 524 in quinto quoque sulco moriuntur boves. With a Superlative he uses it only once, and in the Plural, Most. 155 optumi quique expetebant a me doctrinam sibi. (For examples of *ubi quisque*, see Seyffert in Berliner Philologische Wochenschrift, 16, p. 14.)

The use of *quisque* and *uterque* with a Plural Verb is discussed in **I, 6**.

26. *Alter* seems to be construed (like a Comparative) with the Abl. in Asin. 492 neque me alter est Athenis hodie quisquam cui credi recte aeque putent, although the Abl. may be really dependent on *aeque* (cf. **II, 66**).

27. *Ambo* is sometimes accompanied by *duo* in a way that reminds us of expressions in the Romance languages like Ital. ambe due 'both,' e.g. Amph. 974 iam hisce (Nom. Plur.) ambo, et servus et era, frustra sunt duo (see Seyffert in Berliner Philologische Wochenschrift, 1896, p. 845).

28. Just as the Conjunction *non* (older *noenum*) originated from the Adverbial use of the Neut. Sing. of *nĕ-unus* (older *oenus*), so *nullum* is used for *non* in the colloquial Latin of Plautus, e.g. Cas. 795 qui amat, tamen hercle, si esurit, nullum esurit; also *nihil* for *non*, e.g. Mil. 625 nihil amas, umbra es amantis, Mil. 469 etc. nihil opust, and for *ne*, e.g. Mil. 1007 hercle hanc quidem nil tu amassis. *Nullus* (*nulla*, etc.) is found in the same senses, e.g. Rud. 143 ille qui vocavit nullus vēnit, Trin. 606 at tu edepol nullus creduas. Cf. Rud. 340 A. quasi non sit intus! B. neque pol est neque huc quidem ullus vēnit; Pers. 226 huc nullam attuli, Rud. 1135 tu mihi nullum ostenderis (*sc.* vidulum), Mil. 48 at nullos habeo scriptos, sic memini tamen. And this suggests an explanation of the Lucretian *noenŭ* as *noenus* (like *nullus* beside *nullum*), and to be printed *noenu'* like *nullu' sequetur* (for 'non s.') Lucil. 507 (but Lucil. 987 si noenŭ molestumst). *Nullus* (Adj.) is often used for *nemo* (Pron.) e.g. Bacch. 190 A. qui scire possum? B. nullus plus; *nullum* appears for *nihil* in Livius Andronicus 22 B. namque nullum peius macerat homonem quamde mare saevom (cf. Pomponius 3), and *nullius* and *nullo* came to supersede *neminis* and *nemine*, although Plautus does not refuse the Gen. and Abl. of *nemo*, e.g. Capt. 764, Mil. 1062.

Nullus is the equivalent of *nihili* in Cas. 305 si id factum est, ecce me nullum senem!, and *nullus esse* of *perire* in Bacch. 193 si abest, nullus est. Instead of *nemo* (for *nĕ-homo*) we often find the redundant phrase. *nemo homo* (see above, 21), e.g. Truc. 300 nemo homo hic solet perire apud nos.

Nemo umquam is not unknown (e.g. Amph. 566); but the favourite expression is *numquam quisquam*, e.g. Stich. 77 (for full statistics see J. Lange in Neue Jahrbücher f. Philologie, 1894, pp. 275 sqq.; Seyffert in Bursian's Jahresbericht, 1895, p. 312).

29. *Tantus* in the Deictic sense of 'ever so much,' e.g. Curc. 286 nec demarchus nec comarchus nec cum tanta gloria, has already been mentioned (22). Another of its usages may be seen in lines like Bacch. 1034 sescenta tanta reddam, si vivo, tibi, Bacch. 1184 quem quidem ego ut non excruciem, alterum tantum auri non meream, Trin. 530 tribus tantis illi minus redit quam obseveris.

Tantumst 'enough!,' e.g. Trin. 22, the Dramatists' equivalent of Cicero's *sed haec hactenus*, reveals its origin in lines like Merc. 282 A. numquid amplius? B. tantumst, Ter. Eun. 996 A. numquid est aliud mali damnive quod non dixeris relicuom? B. tantum est. With *tanto melior* 'so much the better,' e.g. Bacch. 211, and similar phrases the Substantive Verb is normally omitted (see V, 8). *Tanta* (instead of *tanto*) figures in a curious usage of O. Lat., which has not yet been satisfactorily explained (see Havet and Leo in Archiv lat. Lexikographie 11, 579 and 12, 100): Rud. 521 multo tanta miserior, Stich. 339 multo tanta plus, Men. 800 multo tanta amplius, Men. 680 bis tanta pluris (cf. Cic. Verr. 3, 225 quinquies tanta amplius). Whether the later use of *tanti* for *tot* is anticipated in Amph. 1057 is doubtful:

> ita tanta mira in aedibus sunt facta.   vae miserae mihi!

On *hic tantus*, see above, 21.

V. The Verb.

(Vol. III. of the new Historische Grammatik der lateinischen Sprache (Leipzig, 1903), edited by a group of German Scholars, contains an account of the Latin Verb, its Classes, its Tenses and its Moods, with full details of Plautine usages.)

1. The history of the Italic Verb is full of difficulty. The Passive in *-r* it shares with some other Indo-European languages; and from a consideration of these, as well as of the Italic Dialects, it would seem that this Passive was originally an Impersonal governing an Accusative Case. The Latin Passive, as far back as we can trace it, has Person-endings, and therefore must have followed that tendency which appears in the occasional change of an Impersonal to a Personal Verb in Early Latin (cf. Priscian 1, pp. 432, 561 H.), e.g. Aul. 491 quo lubeant, nubant, Trin. 211 dum illud quod lubeant, sciant, Stich. 51 (post Plautine?) et me quidem haec condicio nunc non paenitet, Ter. Andr. 481 quae adsolent quaeque oportent, Adelph. 754 non te haec pudent?, Pacuvius 31 paenitebunt, and also in the curious phrase, Rud. 1241 mihi istaec videtur praeda praedatum irier (see below, 41). Like *me veretur* for class. Lat. *vereor* (see above, II, 8) is *mihi dolet*, for *doleo* (see my note on Capt. 928) e.g. Men. 439 mihi dolebit, non tibi, siquid ego stulte fecero, Ter. Phorm. 162. But we see in Plautus a marked predilec-

tion for the 3 Sing. Pass. used impersonally, e.g. *caletur* (always in speaking of hot weather, while *calet* means 'this or that thing is hot'); Pseud. 273 A. quid agitur, Calidore? B. amatur atque egetur acriter, Pseud. 457 A. quid agitur? B. statur hic ad hunc modum (cf. Ter. Eun. 270), Pers. 17 A. quid agitur? B. vivitur, Pers. 386 non tu nunc hominum mores vides, quoiusmodi hic cum mala fama facile nubitur?, Pers. 448 dum stas, reditum oportuit, Ter. Hec. 457 creditur 'I believe you,' and the common phrase *facere certumst* 'I have decided to do it;' and this may be, in a way, a survival of the old Impersonal stage. [Whether we find also survival of the primitive construction, the government of an Acc. Case by this 3 Sing. Pass. is not certain.] I think that we do in lines like Cas. 185 pessumis me modis despicatur domi (*des.* is Pass. of *despico*; cf. v. 189), Mil. 24 epityra estur insanum bene, 254? inducamus vera ut esse credat quae mentibitur, Pseud. 817 teritur sinapis scelera, 1261 ubi mammia mammiculā opprimitur, Ennius trag. 100 R. incerte errat animus, praeterpropter vitam (*alii* -ta) vivitur 'life is lived casually.' (On *vitam vivere*, see II, 35.)

The intermixture of Act. and Pass. Inf. in a passage like Most. 959 is thoroughly Plautine:

> triduom unum est haud intermissum hic esse et bibi,
> scorta duci, pergraecari, fidicinas, tibicinas
> ducere.

2. Another feature of the Italic Verb is its formation of Tenses by means of Auxiliaries. This tendency asserts itself in Plautine Latin in the use of *dare, reddere, habere* (see P. Thielmann in Archiv Lat. Lexikographie, 2, pp. 272—423) with Perf. Part. Pass., e.g. Pers. 457 nunc ego lenonem ita hodie intricatum dabo, Mil. 1174 si tibi meum opus ita dabo expolitum ut improbare non queas, Mil. 1214 A. si impetras. B. reddam impetratum, Mil. 886 nam ego multos saepe vidi regionem fugere consili prius quam repertam haberent; also in the periphrastic Tense-formations mentioned below, 15, 44.

3. The lines of distinction between Active, Passive, and Deponent are not so strictly marked in Plautine as in Classical Latin. Thus Plautus uses Active *opino*, but also *opinor*, with Perf. *opinatus sum; ludifico* (sometimes *-or*), *-atus sum; vago* and *vagor; mereo* and *mereor; apiscor* is Passive in Trin. 367, etc. (For other examples see Langen: Beiträge zur Kritik und Erklärung des

Plautus. Leipzig, 1880, pp. 59 sqq.; cf. Naev. com. 67 populus patitur, tun (*v.l.* tu non) patias?). How far this Variation is connected, on the one hand, with the use of the Verbal Adj. in *-tus* along with the Subst. Verb as a Perfect Tense Passive (see **45**) and, on the other, with the old Intransitive or Subjective use of the Deponent (or Middle, e.g. Greek ἀκούσομαι, ὄψομαι, etc.), has not yet been investigated. Certainly a type of Conjugation like *soleo* (Act.), *solitus sum* (Dep.) was widely extended in Early Latin (cf. Turpilius 33 A. iurasti? B. non sum iurata).

4. Latin does not possess a Middle Voice like Greek. The Latin Deponent often corresponds to the Greek Middle, e.g. *sequor* to ἕπομαι, and Verbs like *accingor* (e.g. Ter. Phorm. 318; cf. Amph. 308 cingitur, certe expedit se), *vescor, amicior* (e.g. Pers. 307 subnixis alis me inferam atque amicibor gloriose) really have the Reflexive function, that as a rule belongs to the Act. with the Refl. Pron., e.g. *se accingere*. *Indutus* takes an Act. Epid. 223 quid erat induta? an regillam induculam an mendiculam?, 225 utin impluvium induta fuerit? (**II, 49**). In Amph. 238 we seem to have a mixture of *converti* and *se convertere*: sed fugam in se tamen nemo convortitur 'but still no one turns to flee;' cf. Stich. 306 meditabor me ad ludos Olympios; but the colloquial Latin of Plautus' time (and later) loves to use in this sense the Act. Verb without any Refl. Pron., e.g. *recipere* for *se recipere* Pers. 51, Merc. 498, Bacch. 294, Rud. 880 (also *se recipere*, e.g. Pers. 46, Merc. 881); *capessere* (cf. *facessere* 'to be off') Rud. 178 for the usual *se capessere* (e.g. Rud. 172); *quo* (unde) *agis?* for *quo te agis?* Pers. 216, Poen. 333, Bacch. 1106 (also *quo te agis?*, e.g. Trin. 1078); *capite sistere*, e.g. Curc. 287, Mil. 850 (**II, 64**); *male res vortunt* Pers. 453; *foris aperit* 'the door opens' Pers. 300 (cf. Aul. 411). Apparently *habere* for *se habere* is to be similarly explained, e.g. Ter. Phorm. 429 bene habent tibi principia (cf. εὖ ἔχει); also *praebeo* for *se praebeo* in Ter. Phorm. 476, and the like. Cf. Pomponius 66 age, anus, *accinge* ad molas; perhaps Ter. Eun. 912 *move* vero ocius (but cf. Andr. 731). In a passage of the Cistellaria we have *insinuavit se* (v. 89) followed by *insinuavit* (v. 92 inde in amicitiam insinuavit cum matre). While *lavĕre* is the Transitive Verb, *lavare* is the Reflexive 'to bathe,' 'take a bath,' e.g. Mil. 251 dormit, ornatur, lavat, which however appears as Deponent-Middle in Poen. 229 ornantur, lavantur, tergentur.

5. Another feature of colloquial Latin, much in evidence in the Comedies, is the use of Frequentative Verbs, e.g. *fores pultare* 'to

knock at the door;' cf. Amph. prol. 7 quasque incepistis res quasque inceptabilis, 821 tu si me impudicitiai captas, capere non potes, Most. 116 usque mantant neque id faciunt. But *habeo* is equally used with *habito* (e.g. Trin. 12) in the sense of 'dwelling,' e.g. Trin. 193 ubi nunc adulescens habet? Cf. *verti* for *versari* in Most. 639 iam homo in mercatura vortitur.

Intransitive Verbs have already in Plautus' time begun to govern an Acc. on the analogy of their Transitive equivalents, e.g. *depereo* (on the Analogy of *deamo*), *calleo* (of *scio*) (see II, 40).

6. The curious Assimilation of *coepi* and *desino* to the Mood of a Pass. Inf. in class. Lat., *urbs coepta est (desita est) oppugnari* (cf. Men. 718 itaque adeo iure coepta appellari est canes), instead of 'coepit' ('desiit'), has a slightly wider range in Early Latin, e.g. frag. 109 retrahi *nequitur*, Rud. 1064 ut *nequitur* comprimi!, Ter. Hec. 572 forma in tenebris nosci non *quita est*, Eun. 22 magistratus quom ibi adesset, *occeptast* agi, Caecilius 279 si non sarciri *quitur*, Pacuvius 390 sed quom contendi *nequitum* vi, Accius 664 neque vi impelli neque prece *quitus sum*, Pacuvius 100 siqua *potestur* investigari via (contrast Plautus' use of *potest* with Inf. Pass, e.g. Curc. 451 ita non potuere uno anno circumirier).

7. The omission of the Verb is common in Terence, who cleverly in this respect reproduces the unconventional utterance of every-day, e.g. Phorm. 440 A. siquid opus fuerit, heus domo me (*sc.* arcessito). B. intellego, Andr. 300 A. verbum unum cave de nuptiis (*sc.* dicas), ne ad morbum hoc etiam (*sc.* accedat). B. teneo.

It is not so marked a feature of Plautus' style, although it is by no means absent, e.g. Rud. 1086 quid istuc tuā? (*scil.* refert).

8. Most frequent is the omission of the Substantive Verb (see W. Olsen: quaestionum Plautinarum de Verbo Substantivo specimen. Greifswald, 1884; with it read Seyffert's corrections in Bursian's Jahresbericht 1886, p. 52), e.g. Amph. 56 sed ego stultior, and the common phrases *tanto melior* (e.g. Truc. 953), *quae res?* (e.g. Mil. 1344, Cas. 844) and the like. (On *nimirum* and *mirum ni, mirum quin*, see VIII, 2.) *Potis* (*pote*) often appears instead of *potest*, e.g. Ter. Phorm. 337 non pote satis.

This is often found in Tenses where *sum* is an Auxiliary, e.g. *quae facta* (passim); *factum* 'true,' 'quite right,' (e g. Trin. 429, Ter. Adelph. 561, etc.) for *factum est;* Amph. 964 an id ioco dixisti? equidem serio ac vero ratus, with *ratus* for *ratus sum;* Trin. 1049 illis quoque abrogant etiam fidem, qui nil meriti; Men.

119 nunc adeo, ut facturus, dicam, with *facturus* for *facturus sum*, Stich. 54 faciendum id nobis. *Esse* is often omitted in the Passive (Gerundive and Perfect) and Active (Fut. [u]) Infinitive, evidently with the view of shortening the cumbrous phrases *faciendum esse, factum esse, facturum esse*. (For examples see Reinkens : über den accusativus cum infinitivo bei Plautus und Terentius. Düsseldorf (progr.) 1886, pp. 14, 15, 23). With *oportet* [x] the omission of *esse* from the Perf. Inf. Pass. is usual in Plautus and invariable in Terence, e.g. Adelph. 213 morem gestum oportuit.

9. The use of an Abstract Noun with *est* in periphrasis for a Verb is characteristically Plautine, e.g. Mil. 229 confidentiast (= confido) nos inimicos profligare posse, Trin. 626 est lubido (= lubet) orationem audire duorum adfinium.

TENSES.

10. **Sequence of Tenses.** (Wirtzfeld : de consecutione temporum Plautina et Terentiana. Siegburg, 1888.) That the strict laws of Sequence should often be defied by the colloquial Latin of Plautus is only natural. The following examples will give an idea of the extent to which this was done:

Men. 784 sqq.   A. quotiens tandem edixi tibi ut caveres (Imperf.) neuter ad me iretis cum querimonia ?
B. qui ego istuc, mi pater, cavere possum ? A. men interrogas ?
B. nisi non vis. A. quotiens monstravi tibi viro ut morem geras ? (Pres.)

Bacch. 689 sqq. A. ego patrem exoravi. B. nempe ergo hoc ut faceret (Imperf.) quod loquor ?
A. immo tibi ne noceat (Pres.) neu quid ob eam rem suscenseat. (Pres.)

Amph. 745 sq.   quippe qui ex te audivi, ut urbem maxumam expugnavisses (Plup.) regemque Pterelam tute occideris. (Perf.)

---

[u] Another theory regards *facturum* as the original form of the Fut. Inf. Act., from which *facturum esse* was afterwards developed. See Postgate in Class. Rev. 18,450.

[x] *Factum oportet* is thus adapted to the pattern of *facto opus est* (see II, 56).

Bacch. 352 sq.	ita feci ut auri quantum vellet sumeret, quantum autem lubeat reddere ut reddat patri.
Most. 715.	hoc habet! repperi ('I have found') qui senem ducerem. (Contrast Epid. 285 repperi haec te qui abscedat suspicio.)
Capt. 1002 sqq.	nam ubi illo adveni . . . haec mihi advenienti upupa qui me delectem datast.
Cist. 567 sqq.	iam perducebam illam ad me suadela mea : anus ei amplexa est genua plorans, obsecrans ne deserat se.
Mil. 131 sq.	dedi mercatori quoidam qui ad illum deferat (*sc.* litteras) . . ., ut is huc veniret.
Pseud. 795 sq.	quin ob eam rem Orcus recipere ad se hunc noluit, ut esset hic qui mortuis cenam coquat.
Poen. 602 sqq.	(adsimulabimus) quasi tu nobiscum adveniens hodie oraveris liberum ut commonstraremus tibi locum et voluptarium, ubi ames, potes, pergraecere.
Pers. 537 sq.	tua ego hoc facio ('am doing') gratia, ut tibi recte conciliandi primo facerem copiam.

After the Historical Pres. we find Pres. in lines like :

Amph. 205   Telebois iubet sententiam ut dicant suam,

but Past in lines like :

Amph. 214 sq.   respondent bello se et suos tutari posse, proinde uti

propere suis de finibus exercitus deducerent,

or both Pres. and Past in lines like :

Amph. 225   convĕnit, victi utri sint eo proelio,

urbem, agrum, aras, focos seque uti dederent.

(On Conditional Sentences, see **VIII**, 5.)

11. **Present.** We find in Plautus the same types of this Tense as in all periods of Latin, such as the Pres. of unachieved action, e.g. Mil. 36 A. quid illuc quod dico (= volo dicere)? B. ehem! scio iam quid. vis dicere; *longum est* 'it would be tedious,' etc., e.g. Mil. 694 flagitiumst, si nihil mittetur (but also Past, e.g. Mil.

725 aequom fuit deos paravisse uno exemplo ne omnes vitam viverent, Mil. 755 hominibus sat erat decem, Ter. Hec. 284 quanto fuerat praestabilius); the Historical Pres., e.g. Mil. 287 sq. forte fortuna per impluvium huc despexi in proxumum : atque ego illi aspicio osculantem Philocomasium (often with *quom, quoniam* and other temporal Conjunctions, VIII, 10).

In all languages the Pres. may play the part of a Fut., especially with the Verb 'to go,' e.g. 'I go to-morrow,' and in Attic Greek this usage has been carried so far that εἶμι is the recognised Fut. Tense. In O. Lat. this use of the Pres. is less in evidence than in modern languages and is mostly confined to some Verbs of motion, especially *eo* and its Compounds. In Plautus with *redeo* the Pres. is normal in a phrase like *iam ad te redeo* (Mil. 1020, etc.), (but the Fut. of *revertor*, e.g. Pseud. 1159, and the Fut. Perf. of *revenio*, e.g. Bacch. 1066); with *eo, exeo, transeo*, etc., also with *viso*[y], *inviso*, the Pres. is more frequent than the Fut., while with *sum* (e.g. iam ego hic ero), *adsum*, and other Verbs the Fut. is used. (For details see Sjögren : Gebrauch des Futurums im Altlateinischen. Upsala, 1906, chap. i.) The Pres. is also normal with *non*, after a Command. e.g. Stich. 93 A. adside hic, pater. B. non sedeo istic, vos sedete: ego sedero in subsellio; also with *quam mox* and *iam* in questions, e.g. Truc. 208 quam mox te huc recipis?, Mil. 1400 iamne ego in hominem involo? Also in various types of Conditional Sentences. (see VIII, 5), e.g. *si sapis* (or *sapies*), *tacebis ; si vivo, te ulciscar; hoc faciam, si possum exorare* 'in hope to'; especially after *nisi* in threats, e.g. Cas. 730 dabo tibi μέγα κακόν . . . nisi resistis. In questions, when asking the advice of another, *quid ago?*, not 'quid agam?,' is Plautus' phrase, but *quid faciam?* is used both in dialogue and soliloquy ; also however *quid fit?*

The use of the Pres. for the Fut. in Temporal Sentences with *dum, priusquam*, etc., is discussed in VIII, 10. On the use of the Pres. Subj. in a Future sense, e.g. Trin. 1136 sed 'maneam etiam, opinor, and the Dubitative Pres. Subj., see below, 26.

12. The Pres. Inf. is quite legitimate after *dico, promitto*, etc., in Plautine Latin, where the Fut. Inf. is normal in class. Lat., e.g. Capt. 194 ad fratrem, quo ire dixeram, mox ivero, lit. ' I had spoken of going,' the Inf. being treated as a Verbal Noun, the Object of *dixeram*, Trin. 5 si quidem operam dare promittitis. The two

[y] *Viso* seems to be of the same formation as the old Futures (or S-Aor. Subj.) *dixo, amasso*, etc.

constructions are found side by side in Most. 633 A. dic te daturum, ut abeat. B. egon dicam dare?

13. Imperfect. (A. L. Wheeler : ' The Syntax of the Imperfect Indicative in Early Latin' in Classical Philology, I. 357—390.) Instead of the usual Imperfect sense, an Aoristic meaning seems often to be attached to a Verb like *aibam*, and (as in class. Latin) *eram*, e.g. Pseud. 1083 A. malum et scelestum et periurum aibat esse me. B. pol hau mentitust (see below, **22n**). In a line like Mil. 755, nam idem hoc hominibus sat erat decem, we seem to have the same use of the Imperfect *erat* as in Horace's tempus erat dapibus, sodales (cf. above, **11**). Cf. *tune hic eras ?* 'are you here?' Ter. Hec. 340 (cf. Phorm. 858, 945).

14. The Imperatival use of the Imperfect Subj. (never Pluperf. in O. Lat.), e.g. Merc. 633 quid tu faceres, men rogas? *requireres, cogitares,* is mentioned below, **25.** It is the Past of the Imperatival Pres. Subj., e.g. *requiras, cogites,* just as the Imperfect *quid facerem ?* ' what was I to do?' is the Past of the Dubitative Pres. Subj. *quid faciam?* 'what am I to do?' On the distinction of the Imperf. from the Pluperf. Subj. in Conditional Sentences, see VIII, 5. The ' Potential' use of 2 Sing. Imperf. Subj. (e.g. *crederes, putares,* is not unknown), e.g. Curc. 331 scires velle gratiam tuam (see below, **31**). *Vellem, mallem,* etc., are common, e.g. Poen. 1066 patrem atque matrem viverent vellem tibi, Curc. 512 tacuisse mavellem. In Wishes, the Imperf. Subj. is, as in class. Lat., appropriate to unrealizable wishes for the present, e.g. Rud. 533 utinam fortuna nunc anetina uterer, as the Pluperf. Subj. to the same wishes for the past, e.g. Truc. 375 utinam item a principio rei repersisses meae, ut nunc repercis saviis. But the Imperf. is not unknown where classical Latin would require the Pluperf., e.g. Capt. 537 utinam te di prius perderent quam periisti e patria tua.

15. Future. (Sjögren : Gebrauch des Futurums in Altlateinischen. Upsala, 1906.) The substitution of the Pres. for the Fut. of *eo* and its Compounds has just been treated (**11**). The competition of the Pres. Subj. (especially in 1 Sing.) with the Fut. Ind. in O. Lat. is discussed below, **26**, e.g. Bacch. 1058 taceam nunciam. It has left its mark on the language in the 3rd Conj. 1 Sing., e.g. *dicam,* the only form in use in Plautus' time, as later, and in the 4th Conj. 1 Sing., e.g. *audiam,* which competed with *audibo* in Plautus' time. There is apparently no rule which determines Plautus' use of *audibo* and *audiam, scibo* and *sciam.* The love of

Latin for Auxiliary Verbs is seen in the three periphrastic forms of the Future in Plautine Latin, (1) *-urus sum*, e.g. Cist. 47, 507, Pers. 778, Curc. 75, (2) *volo* with Inf., (3) *eo* with 1 Supine, e.g. Truc. 559 ipsus perditum se it (for other examples, see below, 42; and on the use of (1) and (3) to form Fut. Inf. Act. and Fut. Inf. Pass., see 40, 41).

In Colloquial Latin, early and later, the Fut. often has the peculiar sense shewn in these examples from Plautus: Asin. 734 hic inerunt viginti minae 'you will find 20 minae to be inside here,' Pseud. 677 hoc sic erit 'you will find this to be the case' (cf. Ter. Heaut. 1014). It looks like the use of the Fut. in general statements such as Most. 289 pulcra mulier nuda erit quam purpurata pulcrior, and may be compared with the Fut. in this type of Conditional sentences, Most. 1041 qui homo timidus erit, . . nauci non erit. Or it may be explained like the Epistolary Imperfect, which is due to the writer's putting himself in the place of the man to whom he is writing, and so regarding the time from another's point of view.

16. *Amabo* 'prithee,' in O. Lat. chiefly used by women, and always accompanying a question or a command[1], is to be referred to a suppressed Protasis '(do this); if you do, I will love you.' Poen. 250 sqq. throws light on its origin:

A. soror, parce, amabo. . . . B. quiesco. A. ergo amo te.

In the Inf. we find *amare* (not 'amaturum esse'), e.g. Men. 524 amare ait te multum Erotium, etc. (For details, see Lindskog: Quaestiones de Parataxi et Hypotaxi apud priscos Latinos, pp. 19 sqq.) On Fut. Imperat. see below, 32.

17. **Future Perfect.** (Sjögren: Gebrauch des Futurums im Altlateinischen. Upsala, 1906.) The Fut. Perf. has the appearance of a Subj., the Perf. Subj. of an Opt., so that *fuero* and *fuerim* may be said to differ as *edam* and *edim* (see 24). However that may be, it is certain that the two Tenses are often hardly distinguishable, e.g. *fuerint* is 3 Plur. of both. (On the close relation of Fut. and Pres. Subj. see 15, 26). Why Plautine (and Terentian) Latin should use only the Fut., never the Fut. Perf., of *oportet, possum, volo*, is not clear. As regards other Verbs, the Tense sometimes has its true function, e.g. Bacch. 708 hoc ubi egero, tum istuc agam, but often has practically the same function as the Fut. It

---

[1] Sometimes expressed by *ut* and Subj., e.g. Truc. 872 immo amabo ut hos dies aliquos sinas eum esse apud me.

is normal after *si* in threats, e.g. si attigeris, vapulabis, where an Aoristic sense is perhaps conveyed; while after *nisi* the Pres. is normal, e.g. nisi abis, vapulabis. Cicero's use of *videro*, in postponing the consideration of a difficulty, is clearly seen in Terence, e.g. Hec. 701, Adelph. 538; not so clearly in Plautus (Merc. 448, 450).

The Fut. Perf. Deponent and Passive can take as Auxiliary *fuero* in the sense of *ero*, e.g. Men. 471 non hercle ⟨ego⟩ is sum qui sum, ni hanc iniuriam meque ultus pulchre fuero.

18. With the Fut. Perf. may be included O. Lat. S-Futures (or rather Aorist Subjunctives) like *faxo*. The difference in Plautus' use of *faxo* and *fecero* seems to be that *fecero* is only used absolutely, in answer to a request, e.g. Stich. 351: A. cape illas scopas. B. capiam. A. . . . convorre. B. ego fecero. *Faciam* may be used in the same way, e.g. Stich. 354 A. pinge, humum consperge ante aedes. B. faciam; *faxo*, on the other hand, governs a Verb syntactically, e.g. faxo scias, faxo ut scias, or paratactically faxo scies. This paratactic use is not found with *faciam*, but only the syntactic, e.g. Capt. 65 si erit, ego faciam ut pugnam inspectet non bonam.

19. **Perfect.** The various class. Latin types of Perfect are all found in Plautus: the Perf. of what is past and gone, e.g. Capt. 516 nunc illud est quom me fuisse quam esse nimio mavelim, Bacch. 151 vixisse nimio satiust iam quam vivere, Pers. 637 omne ego pro nihilo esse duco quod fuit quando fuit (cf. Rud. 1321, Ter. Haut. 93); the Perfect with Present function, such as *novi*, e.g. Bacch. 789 A. nosce signum. B. novi (cf. 986). *Scivi* would appear to follow the analogy of *novi* in lines like Poen. 724 A. scitis? B. scivimus, Poen. 629 ego male loquendi vobis nescivi viam, Capt. 265 siquid nescivi, id nescium tradam tibi.

Also the Perf. Ind. for Pluperf. Subj., e.g. Mil. 1112 ad equas fuisti ('you would have been') scitus admissarius; a Perfect like *perii* used of Future time in Conditional sentences, e.g. Amph. 320 perii, si me aspexerit, Asin. 243 interii, si non invenio; the Perf. Inf. for Pres. Inf., e.g. Aul. 828 non potes probasse nugas; especially after *volo* or *nolo* in prohibitions, e.g. Poen. 872 nolito edepol devellisse, Ter. Hec. 563 interdico ne extulisse extra aedes puerum usquam velis. This Perf. Inf. is a characteristic of the early legal style, e.g. (Sen. Cons. de Bacchanalibus) ita exdeicendum censuere, neiquis eorum Bacanal habuise velet . . Bacas vir nequis adiese velet (*i.e.* adiisse vellet), with which we may compare Livy's version

(39, 14, 8): nequis, qui Bacchis initiatus esset, coiisse aut convenisse causa sacrorum velit. Horace imitates it (Sat. 2, 3, 187) nequis humasse velit Aiacem, Atrida, vetas cur?

20. The Perf. Deponent and Passive can take as Auxiliary *fui* in the sense of *sum*, e.g. Most. 694 non mihi forte visum ilico fuit. The substitution of *fui* gives precision to the Preterite sense, which is often obscured in Perfects like *solitus est* = *solet*, *lubitum est* = *lubet*. Similarly with *fuerim* for *sim* in Perf. Subj., e.g. Epid. 225, Pers. 379.

21. On the use of the Perf. Subj. in Prohibitions, see below, **VIII, 9**. Its Potential use, e.g. *crediderim* 'I could believe,' *dixerim* 'I would say' (all Verb-forms in *-im* were originally Optatives; see below, 24) is not unknown to Plautus and Terence, e.g. Asin. 491 praefiscini hoc nunc dixerim, Ter. Andr. 203 ubivis facilius passus sim quam in hac re me deludier. But the Concessive use, e.g. *fuerit verum* 'allowing it to be true,' is not earlier than Cicero.

22. **Pluperfect.** (H. Blase: Geschichte des Plusquamperfekts im Lateinischen. Giessen, 1893.)

Plautus often seems to use the Pluperfect as the equivalent of the Perfect, e.g. Merc. 760 A. uxor ... quam dudum dixeras te odisse. B. egon istuc dixi tibi?, Curc. 426, 560; Mil. 132 meum erum qui Athenis fuerat, has the same sense as Mil. 127 meum erum Athenis qui fuit. (In Asin. 356 ego me dixeram adducturum, editors change *dixeram* to *dixi erum*.) The ambiguity of *fueram* with Perf. Part. Pass. is turned to account by the cunning slave in Most. 821 A. eo pretio emptae fuerant olim. B. audin 'fuerant' dicere?

Two explanations are possible. One is that Tense-signification[a] is not so definite and precise in the early stage of a language as in the later, so that *amaveram* and *amavi* may have been as interchangeable in Plautine Latin as *amavero* and *amabo* (see above, 17). Another theory restricts the interchange to the Verb *sum*, and tries to prove that, while Plautus uses *fueram* (conceivably a mixture of

---

[a] The latest theories regarding the Indo-European Verb make out the character of an action (instantaneous, protracted, completed), rather than the time of its occurrence, to have differentiated the Indo-European Verbal formations. Thus the Present Tense would have originally no sense of Present Time, but would merely characterize an action as a process; traces of this tense-less use survive in Latin in sentences conveying general maxims, e.g. Plaut. Capt. 232 quod sibi volunt (homines), dum id impetrant, boni sunt.

fui and *eram*) for *fui*, he never uses, e.g., *amaveram* for *amavi*; this extension of the license from *sum* to other Verbs was, according to this theory, a gradual process in Latin, and culminated in that Late Latin substitution of Pluperf. for Perf. which is reflected in the Romance Conjugation, e.g. O. Fr. vidra (= Lat. viderat) 'he saw.' (See my note on Câpt. 17.)

In the Pluperf. Deponent and Passive we find the same use of *fueram* beside *eram* as of *fui* beside *sum* in the Perf. (20) and of *fuero* beside *ero* in the Fut. Perf. (18).

23. The Pluperf. Subj. is used, as in class. Latin, for unrealizable wishes for the past, e.g. Amph. 386 utinam istuc pugni fecissent tui, Ter. Phorm. 157 quod utinam me Phormioni id suadere in mentem incidisset. But the Imperf. Subj. (see above, 14) occasionally takes its place in O. Lat. (not in class. Lat.), e.g. Rud. 495 utinam te, prius quam oculis vidissem meis, malo cruciatu in Sicilia perbiteres.

In 'Jussive' Sentences, e.g. ne poposcisses 'you should not have asked,' the Imperf. Subj. (see above, 14) is invariably found in O. Lat., e.g. Men. 611 at tu ne clam me comesses prandium, never the Pluperf. Subj. On the distinction of the two Tenses in Conditional Sentences and on the occasional use of Plup. Ind. for Plup. Subj., see below, **VIII, 5**.

SUBJUNCTIVE.

24. The Latin Subjunctive combines the functions of the Greek Subjunctive and Optative. Comparative Philology tells us that forms in *-im* were originally Optative-forms; thus *sim*, older *siēm*, is the Latin equivalent of Gk. $\dot{\epsilon}(\sigma)i\eta\nu$, while the Latin Fut. *ero* (from *eso*) is the equivalent of the Gk. Subj. $\ddot{\omega}$, older $\ddot{\epsilon}(\sigma)\omega$. O. Lat. forms like *amassim, prohibessim, faxim* were apparently originally S-Aorist Optatives, and in the language of Plautus' time they still retain traces of their origin; for in 3 Pers. they are in independent sentences mainly used in prayers and curses, e.g. di melius faxint (passim), Iuppiter prohibessit Pseud. 14; in 1 Pers. they are appropriate to Conditional statements, e.g. haud (non) ausim Aul. 474, etc.; in 2 Pers. to Prohibitions, e.g. ne dixis Asin. 839, etc., cave respexis Most. 523. (For a full account of these *-sim* forms in independent sentences in Plautus, see Morris in Amer. Journ. Phil. 18, 165 sqq.)

25. The Subj. can play the part of an Imperative at all periods of Latin. Madvig shewed that in Cicero *ne* with 2 Sing. Pres. Subj. was restricted to general[b] prohibitions, whereas Plaut. and Ter. use, e.g. *ne me mone* and *ne me moneas* as equivalents (cf. 32, below). This Imperatival or, as it is usually called, Jussive Subj. is found in the Imperf. (not Pluperf.), when past time is referred to, e.g. Pseud. 437 vel tu ne faceres tale in adulescentia (cf. above, 14).

26. In early Greek the Subj. sometimes plays the part of a Fut., e.g. Homer Il. 1, 262 οὐ γάρ πω τοίους ἴδον ἀνέρας οὐδὲ ἴδωμαι. So in early Latin, e g. Amph. 1060 nec me miserior femina est neque ulla videatur magis, Trin. 1136 quid ego cesso hos colloqui? sed maneam ('I will wait') etiam opinor, Bacch. 1058 taceam nunciam, Ter. Phorm. 140 ad precatorem adeam, credo, qui mihi sic oret. This usage is mainly confined to 1 Sing. and must have something to do with the employment (from very early times) of 1 Sing. Subj. as Fut. in the Third Conjugation, e.g. *dicam, faciam* (while *dixo, faxo* are like *amasso, prohibesso,* the S-Aor. Subj.), and (at a later stage apparently) in the Fourth, e.g. *sciam* beside *scibo, audiam* beside *audibo* in Plaut. In a sentence like Rud. 1356, etc., *sed conticiscam*, it is impossible to say whether the verb is Subj. (like *taceam*) or Fut. (like *tacebo*). From this use of 1 Sing. *taceam* 'I will be silent,' 'I had better be silent,' it is but a step to the ordinary uses (in all periods of Latin) of 1 Plur., e.g. *taceamus* 'let us be silent,' 'we had better be silent,' and of all Persons in Conditional Sentences, e.g. *taceam, si sapiam; taceamus, si sapiamus; taceas, si sapias.* Similarly it is but a step from Pseud. 240, modo ego abeam, to the use of *ut (uti)* in Pers. 575 modo uti sciam, quanti indicet, 'only I wish to know what price he offers.' To disentangle the various threads of which the Latin Subj. is composed is not easy. For example, Plautus uses *velim* and *volo* almost indiscriminately, but it baffles us to detect the precise original sense of *velim* (Optative? Future? Potential?). In Amph. 928 valeas, tibi habeas res tuas, reddas meas, the three Subjunctives would, if they occurred in separate sentences, be classified as Optative, Permissive and Imperative respectively. But the crudeness of such a distinction is evident when we find them together in the same line. In Greek the Optative Mood has retained a separate existence; but Latin

---

[b] On the general or indefinite use of 2 Sing. Pres. Subj. in Latin see below, 31. Madvig's law has been questioned (Elmer, Amer. Journ. Phil. 1894, pp. 132 sqq.).

Optatives, *sim, velim, edim, duim, creduim,* etc., were all merged in the Subjunctive mood before the time of Plautus, whose language retains only doubtful traces of the distinction between *edam* (Subj.) and *edim* (Opt.), *creduam* (Subj.) and *creduim* (Opt.) (see my Latin Language, p. 514; and on the occasional Potential use of the Perf. Subj., above, 21). Even in the Indo-European language the provinces of Fut. and Subj. were not definitely discriminated, nor even of Fut. and Opt. In Pers. 16 Fut. and Subj. (= Opt.) seem to play the same part:

> A. O Sagaristio, di ament te. B. O Toxile, dabunt di quae exoptes,

but *dabunt* (cf. ita me di amabunt Ter. Heaut. 463; cf. Poen. 869) may conceivably be an affirmation like the Fut. in Ter. Heaut. 161 A. utinam ita di faxint! B. facient.

(On the Tenses of the Subjunctive used in Prohibitions, see **VIII, 9.**)

27. In Dependent Clauses the use of the Subj. in Plautus' colloquial language was not at all so strictly regulated as in the literary language of the Augustan Age. It is extremely difficult to say with certainty: 'in this or that Dependent Clause Plautus could not use the Ind.' or 'could not use the Subj.' In most types of clause we find both Moods used, but never quite at random. There is always a particular nuance of thought expressed by the one and the other. The use of the Ind. makes the statement more a definite statement of actual fact, the use of the Subj. makes it more indefinite, more dependent on external agency. The distinction is most clearly seen in Oratio Obliqua, where the Plautine and the classical usage scarcely differ, e.g. Bacch. 735:

> Chrysalus mihi usque quaque loquitur nec recte, pater,
> quia tibi aurum *reddidi* et quia non te *defraudaverim.*

Here *quia non defraudaverim* is Chrysalus' remark, while *quia aurum reddidi* is the remark of the speaker himself. Cf. Mil. 981 and 974, Mil. 300 and Epid. 19. Also in sentences not far removed from Oratio Obliqua, e.g.:

> Cist. 179 et eam cognoscit esse quam *compresserat* (the remark of the speaker).
> Aul. 29 is scit adulescens quae sit quam *compresserit* (= scio quae sit quam compressi Or. Rect.).

Similarly after an Impersonal Verb, the use of the Subj. makes a dependent clause less definite, more a possibility than a fact, e.g.:

Pseud. 460 decet innocentem qui *sit* atque innoxium
    servom superbum esse apud erum potissumum.
Amph. 836 quae non *deliquit* decet audacem esse.

28. Parataxis (see Lindskog: Quaestiones de Parataxi et Hypotaxi apud priscos Latinos. Lund, 1896) is characteristic (1) of the early stage of a language, (2) of colloquial, as opposed to literary language. Naturally it is strongly in evidence in the colloquial Latin of Plautus' time, e.g. Trin. 161 alium fecisti me, alius ad te veneram. Most of all in Indirect Questions, which in Plautus are as often Direct (with Ind.) as Indirect (with Subj.), e.g. Bacch. 557 dic quis est, Bacch. 555 dic modo hominem qui sit, the two Moods often appearing side by side, e.g. Amph. 17 nunc quoius iussu venio et quam ob rem venerim dicam, Pers. 515 nescis quid te instet boni neque quam tibi Fortuna faculam lucriferam adlucere volt, Most. 969, Ter. And. 650, Hec. 874; cf. *nescioquis* with Ind. in Early, as in Class. Lat., and the similar phrase *scin quid* in lines like Pseud. 276 sed scin quid nos volumus? (For full statistics see E. Becker: de Syntaxi Interrogationum Obliquarum, in vol. I, Part i, of Studemund's Studien auf dem Gebiet des archäischen Lateins. Berlin, 1873.) Even where the Subj. appears, there may often be Parataxis, e.g. Stich. 333 A. quid agis? B. quid agam rogitas?, for a similar Subj. is found in independent sentences, e.g. Capt. 139 A. ne fle. B. egone illum non fleam?, Ter. Andr. 915 A. bonus est hic vir. B. hic vir sit bonus? Similarly with other dependent Subjunctives; e.g. Men. 683 may be printed as two separate sentences or as one main sentence with a dependent clause: mihi tu ut dederis pallam et spinter? numquam factum reperies. Compare lines like Trin. 485 semper tu hoc facito Lesbonice, cogites, Trin. 59 vin commutemus?, Poen. 909 ita di faxint, ne apud lenonem hunc serviam. Of recent years a great deal has been done in the way of tracing back the use of a Subj. in Dependent Clauses to a similar use in Early Latin in Independent Sentences.

29. In phrases like Asin. 44 *di tibi dent quaecumque optes*, Asin. 780 *quom iaciat, 'te' ne dicat*, the Subj. (*optes, iaciat*) is conventionally ascribed to 'Attraction.' But similar Subjunctives are found in other circumstances too; and, if 'Attraction' has played any part, it may rather be that the presence of a Subj. in a neighbouring clause has ensured the retention of the old construction, has in fact aided the old Mood to resist the encroachments of the Indicative. This so-called 'Subj. by Attraction' is a feature of the other Italic dialects and evidently belongs to the earliest Italic period, e.g. Oscan *pun far kahad, nip putiiad edum*, which would be in Latin ' quom far incipiat, ne possit esse,' 'when he takes food, may he not be able to eat.' These dialects shew a similar Subj. where the neighbouring clause contains an Imper., e.g. Umbrian *pone esonom e ferar . . ere fertu* (in Latin ' quom in sacrificium feratur . . is ferto'), just as we find in Plautus sentences like Amph. 439 ubi ego Sosia *nolim* esse, tu esto sane Sosia, Asin. 29 dic, obsecro hercle, serio quod te *rogem* (cf. Men. 1105 uterque id, quod *rogabo*, dicite). Plautus uses the Ind. as well as the Subj., e.g. Bacch. 224 veniat quando *volt*, Truc. 233 aequo animo, ipse si nil habeat, aliis, qui *habent*, det locum. It is perhaps true that the two moods give a different nuance to the clause, the Ind. implying that the thing is a fact, e.g. Epid. 19 (with Ind.) quid tibi vis dicam nisi quod *est?*, compared with Mil. 300 (with Subj.) quid tibi vis dicam nisi quod *viderim?*; Trin. 351 quod *habes*, ne habeas, Aul. 482 invidia nos minore utamur quam *utimur*. (Contrast Pers. 293 and Asin. 44.) But it is often hard to perceive the distinction. Compare Rud. 1137 (with Ind.), sed, si *erunt* vera, tum obsecro te ut mea mihi reddantur, with Rud. 1128 (with Subj.) ac, si istorum nil *sit*, ut mihi reddas; Merc. 425 (with Ind.), dum ne minoris vendas quam *emi*, with Rud. 1242 (with Subj.) ut cum maiore dote abeat quam *advenerit;* Trin. 1042 (with Ind.), et metuo, si *compellabo*, ne aliam rem occipiat loqui, with Trin. 1171 (with Subj.), metuo, si tibi *denegem* quod me oras, ne te leviorem erga me putes. The truth is that the Ind. had begun before Plautus' time to encroach on the sphere of the Subj., just as in our own time 'if I am' has almost usurped the sphere of 'if I be.' It is seldom that we find the Subj., where the Ind. would seem more natural, e.g. Capt. 237 quod tibi *suadeam*, suadeam meo patri (cf. Curc. 484; on Most. 1100 quod *agas*, id agas, see 31, below); and in this example the term 'Attraction' seems not inappropriate; although it is not absolutely certain that Plautus did not write *suadeo*[o]. Almost the only rule that can be suggested for the use of

[o] Lorenz's argument for altering the reading is however unsound, viz. that 'Attraction' is impossible in a clause that precedes the ruling clause. It is less usual, but not impossible. Cf. Cist. 497 A. di me perdant. B. quodcumque *optes*, tibi velim contingere, etc., etc.

the Ind. and Subj. in these by-clauses, is that the Ind. must be used where the time indicated in the two clauses is different, e.g. Men. 1104 utinam efficere quod pollicitu's (Perf.) possies (Pres.), Trin. 6 nunc .. quae illaec siet (Pres.), huc quae abiit (Perf.) intro, dicam; especially when a Temporal Adverb (e.g. *nunc*) is used, e.g. Ter. Andr. 339 ubi inveniam Pamphilum ut metum in quo nunc est adimam? But the rule is not without exceptions, e.g. Aul. 29 (quoted above) scit .. quae sit quam *compresserit*. The Ind. is also preferred in a clause that stands first in the sentence, e.g. Rud. 379, si *amabat*, rogas, quid faceret?; but we have sometimes the Subj., e.g. Merc. 344 neque is quom *roget* quid loquar cogitatumst.

This so-called Subj. by 'Attraction' is so marked a feature of Plautine Syntax that more examples, taken from different types of sentence, will be useful:

Bacch. 656 furetur quod *queat;* Aul. 491 quo *lubeant* nubant; Capt. 548 ne tu quod istic *fabuletur* auris immittas tuas; Epid. 588 non patrem te nominem, ubi tu tuam me *appelles* filiam?; Bacch. 1190 egone, ubi filius *corrumpatur* meus, ibi potem?; Asin. 838 putem ego, quem *videam* aeque esse maestum ut quasi dies si dicta sit?; Mil. 426 quin ego hoc rogem quod *nesciam ?*, Amph. 434 quid ego ni negem qui egomet *siem ?;* Amph. 871

> nam mea sit culpa, quod egomet *contraxerim,*
> si id Alcumenai innocentiae expetat;

Poen. 681 videre equidem vos vellem, quom huic aurum *darem;* Merc. 152 me rupi causa currendo tua, ut quae *scirem* scire actutum tibi liceret; Bacch. 550 ille .. accuratum habuit quod *posset* mali faceret in me.

It will be well to add examples taken from Indirect Questions and Reported Speech, in order to shew how similar is the Plautine treatment in all cases of dependent sentence:

> Aul. 17 coepi observare ecqui maiorem filius
> mihi honorem haberet quam eius *habuisset* pater;

Asin. 442 aibat reddere ('said he would pay'), quom extemplo *redditum esset;* Curc. 425 quod istic scriptumst (Ind.), id te orare iusserat profecto ut faceres, suam si *velles* gratiam.

30. Various uses of the Subj. in Dependent Clauses, such as the Causal use, e.g. Aul. 769 sanus tu non es, qui furem me voces, Capt. 546 (cf. 565) si te odit, qui istum appelles Tyndarum pro Philocrate; the Concessive, e.g. Men. 362 te hic stare foris, fores quoi pateant;

the Subj. of Limitation, e.g. *quod sciam* 'so far as I know,' Epid. 638 A. non me novisti? B. quod quidem [d] nunc veniat in mentem mihi, Merc. 520 de lanificio neminem metuo, una aetate quae sit, are common to Plautine and classical Latin and need not detain us. But attention must be called to the freedom of the Subj. in Plautus' time in contrast to certain restrictions which attached to it later. The rule that Causal (and Concessive) *quom* requires the Subj., is, as will be shewn in Chap. VIII, unknown to Plautus. He usually employs the Ind., e.g. Mil. 1211 saltem id volup est, quom ex virtute formai evēnit tibi; although he can say, e.g. Mil. 1342 nequeo quin fleam, quom abs te abeam, Most. 896 tibi obtemperem, quom tu mihi nequeas? (cf. Capt. 146 quom .. feras), just as he uses Ind. as well as Subj. after Causal *qui* in Poen. 1030:

A. servum hercle te esse oportet et nequam et malum,
   hominem peregrinum atque adverſam qui *irrideas*.
B. at hercle te hominem et sycophantam et subdolum,
   qui huc *advenisti* nos captatum.

In class Lat. *quamvis* postulates the Subj., *quamquam* the Ind. But to Plautus *quamvis* means 'as you wish,' 'as much as you wish,' and scarcely has acquired the sense of 'although' (see VIII, 4). With *est qui, sunt qui, est ubi*, etc., it is not always easy to see what determines the use of the Subj. (e.g. Poen. 884 quid est quod metuas?) and the Ind. (e.g. Ter. Andr. 448 est quod suscenset tibi; cf. the frequent *sunt quae volo*, etc., e.g. Capt. 263 sunt quae ex te solo scitari volo). (For fuller statistics see Dittmar: Studien zur lateinischen Moduslehre. Leipzig, 1897, pp. 10 sqq.) Here are some examples of the Subj. and Ind. in Dependent Clauses:

Aul. 810	quis me Athenis nunc magis quisquam est homo cui di sint propitii?
Bacch. 807	quis homost qui dicat me dixisse istuc?
Accius 458	quis erit qui non me spernens .. turpi fama differet?
Mil. 994	numquis [nam] hic prope adest qui rem alienam potius curet quam suam?

[d] *Qui quidem* with Subj. has not only this limitative function (with Ind., e.g. Ter. Adelph. 692 perdidisti .., quod quidem in te fuit; cf. p. 71), but others too. Thus it is the equivalent of class. Lat. *quippe qui* in a line like Bacch. 1132 merito hoc nobis fit, qui quidem huc venerimus. Other examples are Poen. 1213, Trin. 552, 953.

Pomponius 158	numquis hic restitit qui nondum labeas lirarit mihi?
Capt. 997	vidi ego multa saepe picta, quae Accherunti fierent cruciamenta.
Men. 143	enumquam tu vidisti tabulam pictam in pariete, ubi aquila Catamitum (= Ganymedem) raperet?
Trin. 543	nemo exstat qui ibi sex menses vixerit.
Merc. 335	homo me miserior nullust aeque, opinor, neque advorsa cui plura sint sempiterna.
Curc. 248	vah! solus hic homost qui sciat divinitus.
Trin. 89	haben tu amicum aut familiarem quempiam quoi pectus sapiat?
Mil. 784	eam des quae sit quaestuosa, quae alat corpus corpore, quoique sapiat pectus.
Mil. 1376	stulte feci, qui hunc amisi.
Men. 309 sqq.	insanit hic quidem, qui ipse male dicit sibi. . . nam tu quidem hercle certe non sanu's satis, Menaechme, qui nunc ipsus male dicas tibi.
Most. 362	sed ego sumne infelix, qui non curro curriculo domum?
Trin. 1057	sed ego sum insipientior, qui rebus curem publicis, potius quam, etc.
Trin. 905	A. novistin hominem? B. ridicule rogitas, quocum una cibum capere soleo.
Mil. 984	vah! delicatu's: quae te tamquam oculos amet.
Truc. 769	de nihilo nihil est irasci, quae te non flocci facit.
Amph. 1021	tibi Juppiter dique omnes irati certo sunt, qui sic frangas fores.
Mil. 59	amant ted omnes mulieres, neque iniuria, qui sis tam pulcher.
Mil. 180	vae mihi misero, quoi pereundumst propter nihili bestiam!
Stich. 395	Hercules, qui deus sis, sane discessisti non bene.
Amph. 506	nimis hic scitust sycophanta, qui quidem meus sit pater.
Men. 203	A. hoc animo decet animatos esse amatores probos. B. qui quidem ad mendicitatem se properent detrudere.

Syntax of Plautus.

Truc. 832	non vinum viris moderari, sed viri vino solent, qui quidem probi sunt.
Epid. 180.	A. pulchra edepol dos pecuniast. B. quae quidem pol non maritast.
Pers. 634	tactus lenost: qui rogaret ubi nata esset diceret, lepide lusit.
Poen. 233	miror equidem, soror, te istaec sic fabulari, quae tam callida et docta sis et faceta.
Mil. 764	haud centensumam partem dixi atque, otium rei si sit, possum exponere.
Mil. 20	nihil hercle hoc quidemst praeut alia dicam, quae tu numquam feceris.
Asin. 816	suspendam potius me quam tacita haec tu auferas.
Cist. 533	perdam operam potius quam carebo filia.

For examples with *quod, quippe qui, utpote qui,* etc., see **VIII, 2.**

In Conditional Sentences we see the utmost freedom in Plautus. The difficulty of framing rules for his use of Ind. and Subj. is often very difficult (see **VIII, 5**).

31. Lastly may be mentioned that the curious Latin use of 2 Pers. Sing. of this Mood in general statements, not referring to a definite person, is as early as Plautus, e.g. Bacch. 63 ubi periclum facias ('when one makes trial'), aculeata sunt, Truc. 569 quod des, devorat, Trin. 914 fieri istuc solet : quod in manu teneas atque oculis videas, id desideres.

Like it is the 'Potential' *credas* 'one would think,' etc , e.g. Most. 243 videas eam medullitus me amare, Ter. Hec. 58 per pol quam paucos reperias meretricibus fideles evenire amatores, Syra. To the Pres. *credas* of Accius 395, interruptum credas nimbum volvier, the Imperf. *crederes* of Accius 321, Mavortes armis duo congressos crederes, stands in the same relation as the Imperf. to the Pres. of the Jussive Subj. (see above, 14.)

32. **Imperative.** (Loch : 'zum Gebrauch des Imperativus bei Plautus.' Memel (Schulprogr.), 1871.) The competition of the Subj. with the Imperative has already been mentioned. That there is a different signification in Imperatives like *vale* and Subjunctives like *valeas* (e.g. Truc. 433 A. valeas. B. vale) is hard to prove. Similarly in Prohibitions, e.g. Asin. 826 ne mone, Mil. 1378 ne me moneatis (see below, **VIII, 9**).

The Fut. Imperat. is usually reserved for its proper sense, the expression of commands relating to future time, e.g. Pseud. 859—864 quoquo hic spectabit, eo tu spectato simul; si . . gradietur . . . progredimino, etc.; Rud. 813 si appellabit quempiam, vos respondetote; and a command in Pres. Imperat. is often followed by a further command in Fut. Imperat., e.g. Asin. 740 Leonida, curre, obsecro, patrem huc orato ut veniat. But *bene ambulato* is used beside *bene ambula, salveto* beside *salve* (cf. Havet in Archiv lat. Lexikographie, 9, 287), etc. And the Pres. Imperat. is occasionally found where the Fut. Imperat. would be normal, e.g. Ter. Andr. 848 ubi voles, accerse.

33. **Infinitive.** (Walder: der Infinitiv bei Plautus. Berlin, 1874; and, especially for Terence, P. Barth: de Infinitivi apud scaenicos poetas Latinos usu. Berlin, 1882.)

The Inf. has its original function of a Verbal Noun in lines like these, where it is Object of a Finite Verb: Curc. 28 ita tuum conferto amare ('so arrange your loving') semper, si sapis; Bacch. 158 hic vereri perdidit 'he has lost all sense of shame'; Poen. 313 A. at ego amo hanc. B. at ego esse et bibere 'eating and drinking'; Capt. 88 nisi qui colaphos perpeti potis parasitus frangique aulas in caput 'having dishes broken across his head.' Or in these, where it is Subject: Mil. 354 A. praecepta facito ut memineris. B. totiens monere mirumst, Most. 705 ire dormitum odiost, Capt. 750 vis haec quidem hercle est, et trahi et trudi simul. From this origin comes the association of various Verbs and Verbal Phrases with the Inf., e.g. *volo* (cf. Aul. 201 nunc hic eam rem volt, scio, mecum adire ad pactionem, Merc. 868 A. quid me voltis? 'what do you want of me?' B. ire tecum), *pudet* (cf. Most. 1165 si hoc pudet, fecisse sumptum, supplici habeo satis). *Occipio* prefers an Inf. to any other object, but *incipio* in Plautus' time is not yet so freely used with an Inf. as with the Acc. of a Noun or Pronoun. The Inf. plays the part of a Gerund in lines like Epid. 197 per omnem urbem quem sum defessus quaerere, Ter. Phorm. 589 neque defetiscar umquam adeo experirier (contrast, e.g., Amph. 1014 sum defessus quaeritando), Trin. 76 ut te videre audireque aegroti sient, Poen. 1212 facere occasio est (contrast, e.g., Epid. 271 nunc occasiost faciundi), Pseud. 1141 operam fac compendi quaerere, Men. 233 nam quid modi futurum est illum quaerere? ('our seeking him'), Rud. 223 omnia iam circumcursavi atque omnibus latebris perreptavi quaerere conservam ('seeking'),

Ter. Phorm. 885 summa eludendi occasiost mihi nunc senes et Phaedriae curam adimere argentariam. Also in its use with *est* (like Virgil's *cernere erat*), which is better attested for Terence (Heaut. 192 miserum? quem minus credere est? (crederes *alii*), Adelph. 828 scire est (scires *alii*) liberum ingenium atque animum) than for Plautus (Truc. 501 ?).

34. The Subject of the Inf. itself is put in the Acc.[*], even when it is also the Subject of the Finite Verb, in class. Lat. with *dico*, etc., in Plautine Lat. also with *volo*, etc., e.g. Pseud. 167 magnufice volo me viros summos accipere, ut mihi rem esse reantur, 853 an tu coquinatum te ire quoquam postulas (contrast 851 an tu invenire postulas quemquam coquum?, and see Abraham 'Studia Plautina' p. 189); although we also find the Nom. in Plautus, not merely with *volo*, etc., but (as in Greek) with *dico* in Asin. 634 quas hodie adulescens Diabolus ipsi daturus dixit (unless we should read *daturum*). But it is often, especially with Pres. Inf., left unexpressed, e.g. Merc. 410 uxori meae mihique obiectent lenocinium facere, Epid. 238 dissimulabam earum operam sermoni dare, Men. 461 quoi tam credo datum voluisse (*scil.* eum), quam me video vivere. Accordingly in Curc. 72 vovi me inferre 'I made a vow that I would offer' is by a quibble misapprehended as 'I vowed that I would offer myself' (the passage is quoted in II, 19).

On *promitto dare*, lit. 'I promise giving,' 'I promise the gift,' see 12, above.

(For a list of the Verbs with which we find Acc. and Inf. in Plautus and Terence, see J. Reinkens: über den Acc. c. Inf. bei Plautus u. Terentius, Düsseldorf (Schulprogr.), 1886.)

35. Of the Verbs with which Plautus uses the Inf. may be mentioned: *obtineo*, e.g. Mil. 186 earumque artem et disciplinam obtineat colere; *abstineo*, e.g. Curc. 180 dum mi abstineant invidere; *teneo*, e.g. Merc. 52 omnes (Nom.) tenerent mutuitanti credere; *occupo*, e.g. Most. 566 sed occupabo adire, Titinius 145 ergo occupa foras exire; *intendo*, e.g. Mil. 380 pergin, sceleste, intendere hanc arguere?; *maturo*, e.g. Mil. 1093 iube maturare illam exire huc; *quiesco*, Most. 1173 A. Tranio, quiesce, ⟨si⟩ sapis. B. tu quiesce hanc rem modo petere; *exsequor*, e.g. Merc. 913 ut, si haec non sint vera, inceptum hoc itiner perficere exsequar; *perpetro*, e.g. Truc. 465 male quod mulier facere incepit, nisi ⟨id⟩ efficere per-

---

[*] See I, 10, on lines like Poen. 523 servoli esse duco festinantem currere.

petrat; *omitto*, e.g. Pers. 431; *parco, comperco*, e.g. Bacch. 910 cave parsis in eum dicere, Poen. 350; *compesco*, e.g. Bacch. 463 compesce in illum dicere iniuste; *tempero*, e.g. Poen. 22 vel dormire temperent, Ennius trag. 45 temperaret tollere; *neglego*, e.g. Amph. 586 erus quod imperavit neglexisti persequi; *praetereo*, Merc. 402 quod praeterii dicere; *ploro*, e.g. Aul. 308 aquam hercle plorat, quom lavat, profundere; *duro*, e.g. Truc. 326 non quis parumper durare opperirier?; *offirmo*, e.g. Pers. 222 offirmastin occultare quo te immittas, pessume?

36. Of the Verbal Phrases: *nil moror, nihili facio*, etc., e.g. Pers. 224 nihili facio scire; *immemor esse*, e.g. Pseud. 1104 nihilist autem suom qui officium facere immemor est, nisi est admonitus; *occupatus esse*, e.g. Merc. 288 non sum occupatus umquam amico operam dare; *neglegens esse*, e.g. Most. 141 postilla obtegere eam neglegens fui; *animum inducere*, e.g. Bacch. 1191 facere inducam animum; *ferox* ('proud') *esse*, e.g. Asin. 468 ferox est viginti minas meas tractare sese; *maestus esse*, e.g. Most. 796 sed ut maestust sese hasce vendidisse (cf. Rud. 397 id misera maesta est, sibi eorum evenisse inopiam); *aegritudo est*, e.g. Capt. 783 tanto mi aegritudo auctior est in animo, ad illum modum sublitum os esse mi hodie (or Inf. of Exclamation); *opus est*, e.g. Pers. 584 A. opusne est hac tibi empta? B. si tibi venissest opus, mihi quoque emptast; *occasio est*, e.g. Pers. 726 nunc est illa occasio inimicum ulcisci; *operam perdere, sumere*, e.g. Aul. 341 ne operam perdas poscere, Men. 244 operam praeterea numquam sumam quaerere. The Inf. in Lucilius 414 Ma., solvere nulli lentus, looks like a Graecism.

37. The O. Lat. Inf. *bibere* in the phrase *dare bibere (biber)*, e.g. Pers. 821 bibere da usque plenis cantharis, Titinius 78 date illi biber, Lucilius 222 Ma. da bibere ab summo (but Cist. 18 raro nimium dabat quod biberem, Stich. 757 date bibat tibicini), is in some Grammars explained like *aquam dare*, in others as an Inf. of Purpose. The Inf. of Purpose is a common usage, e.g. Asin. 910 ecquis currit pollinctorem arcessere?, Pseud. 642 reddere hoc non perdere erus me misit, Bacch. 631 militis parasitus modo venerat aurum petere hinc, Truc. 167 nunc ad amicam venis querimoniam referre, Ter. Eun. 528 misit porro orare ut venirem serio, Hec. 345 tum filius tuus intro iit videre, ut venit, quid agat, Turpilius 154 progredior foras visere quid hic tumulti ante fores. In this function the First Supine competes with the Inf., e.g. Most. 594 venisti huc te extentatum? (see below, 42), also *ut* (or Relative Pron.) and

Subj. These two are combined in Ter. Andr. 514 missast ancilla ilico obstetricem arcessitum ad eam et puerum ut adferret simul.

38. From phrases like Bacch. 237 nam meus formidat animus nostrum tam diu ibi desidere neque redire filium, Capt. 600 crucior lapidem non habere me, ut illi mastigiae cerebrum excutiam, Asin. 407 quid hoc sit negoti, neminem meum dictum magni facere?, Asin. 127 sicine hoc fit, foras aedibus me eici?, it is but a step to the Inf. of Exclamation, e.g. Pers. 42 sicine hoc te mihi facere?, Amph. 882 durare nequeo in aedibus: ita me probri, stupri, dedecoris a viro argutam meo!, Asin. 580 edepol senem Demaenetum lepidum fuisse nobis!, Ter. Andr. 870 tantum laborem capere ob talem filium!, Eun. 755 militem secum ad te quantas copias adducere! It is usually in the form of a question, e.g. Bacch. 152 magistron quemquam discipulum minitarier?, Pseud. 202 huncine hic hominem pati colere iuventutem Atticam?, Ter. Heaut. 749:

> ita me di amabunt, ut nunc Menedemi vicem
> miseret me: tantum devenisse ad eum mali.
> illancin mulierem alere cum illa familia?

The same function may be taken by a Subjunctive clause, e.g. Bacch. 375 egone ut haec conclusa gestem clanculum?, Curc. 193 quod quidem mihi polluctus virgis servus sermonem serat! (see below, VIII, 2).

39. The Historical Inf. is also a feature of Plautine (and still more of Terentian) Latin. It is found in narrative passages written in the style of Tragedy, e.g. Amph. 229 imperator utrimque, hinc et illinc Iovi vota suscipere, ⟨utrimque⟩ hortari exercitum, Trin. 835 imbres fluctusque atque procellae infensae frangere malum, ruere antemnas, scindere vela, Amph. 1110 sqq.; also in less ambitious narrations, e.g. Merc. 46 obiurigare pater haec noctes et dies. It seems to be limited to the Pres. Inf. of Active or Deponent Verbs in Main Sentences (Bacch. 482 is probably not an exception to this rule).

On the use of the Pres. Inf. for the Fut. Inf. in phrases like Curc. 597 nego me dicere 'I refuse to tell,' see above, 12; and on the Perf. Inf. in sentences like Poen. 872 nolito edepol devellisse, above, 19.

On the association of Act. and Pass. Inf., e.g. Most. 959 esse et bibi, see the opening paragraph of this chapter.

40. Of the three Periphrastic formations of the Future mentioned above (**15**), (1) *-urus sum*, (2) *volo* with Inf., (3) *eo* with 1 Sup., the first was utilized for the Fut. Inf. Act.,[f] the third, e.g. Bacch. 1171 ut istuc delictum desistas tantopere ire oppugnatum, for the Fut. Inf. Pass. (On *fore ut*, see below.)

Mil. 1186 sq. may serve as example of the first: arcessito, ut, si itura sit Athenas, eat tecum . . . Nisi eat, te soluturum esse navim. The Inf. of the Substantive Verb (cf. above 8) is often omitted with the Fut. Part. Act. as it is with the Perf. Part. Pass. or with the Gerundive, e.g. Pseud. 566 neque sim facturus quod facturum dixeram.

But the earliest form of the Fut. Inf. Act., which still survives in some lines of Plautus and has probably been removed by scribes from more, shews merely *-urum* (indeclinable) without *esse*, e.g. Cas. 693 altero te occisurum ait 'Casina says she will kill you with one of the two swords.' This points to an Impersonal Fut. Inf. Act., just as we have an Impersonal Fut. Inf. Pass., and just as the Gerund (e.g. agitandum est vigilias) was superseded by the Gerundive (e.g. agitandae sunt vigiliae).

41. The Fut. Inf. Pass. does not often occur in Plautus. In class. Lat. it is Impersonal, e.g. credo hostes victum iri, the Inf. of 'itur[g] victum hostes.' But we find in Rud. 1241 a Personal construction: mihi istaec videtur praeda praedatum irier. In Truc. 886 the corrupt reading of the MSS. seems to preserve a trace of the common Latin practice of writing this Tense as a Compound word: spes etiamst hodie tactuiri militem.

From the colloquial use of *est ut, erit ut*, etc., e.g. Ter. Hec. 501 si est ut velit redducere uxorem 'if it is the case that he wishes,' 'if he wishes,' 558 si est ut dicat velle se, redde; sin est autem ut nolit, recte ego consului meae (cf. Adelph. 514 si est facturus ut sit officium suom, faciat), originated the periphrasis *fore* (Impersonal) *ut*. On Pseud. 1319 hoc ego numquam ratus sum, fore me ut tibi fierem supplex, see II, 42.

42. Supine. The Verbal Noun in *-tus* (4 Decl.) is greatly in evidence in Plautus. We find the Acc. with *eo*, etc., e.g. ire obso-

---

[f] Only *sum* has a real Fut. Inf. Act., viz. *fore*, e.g. Cas. 772 quasi nil sciant fore huius quod futurumst.

[g] Like Virgil's *itur in antiquam silvam*. Had the choice of this form for the Inf. Pass. any connexion with that Attraction to the Passive of *coepi, desino*, etc., with a Pass. Inf., e.g. coeptum est pugnari, desitum est pugnari, &c.? (See above, 6.)

natum 'to go a-marketing,' ire venatum 'to go a-hunting;' the Abl. with *redeo*, e.g. Cas. 719 (Men. 278, 288) obsonatu redire 'to return from marketing;' the Dat. with *habeo*, e.g. Cist. 365 me .. habes perditui et praedatui, and with *sum* (see II, 19), also with some Adjectives, e.g. fabula lepida auditui; with others the Abl. (Loc.?), e.g. celer cursu 'quick in running.' Two of these usages took so firm root in the language that they became part of the Verbal system, the Acc. with *eo*, &c. (called the 'First Supine') and the Abl. (Loc.?) with an Adj. (called the 'Second Supine').

Whether the terms 'First and Second Supine' are applicable to Plautine Latin may be doubted. It would be a truer analysis to distinguish from the real First Supine, two types of the phrase *-tum ire*. Type (1) is Passive or Intransitive, corresponding to a Transitive *-tum dare*. Thus *nuptum ire* (e.g. Cas. 86) bears to *nuptum dare* the same relation as *venum ire* (*venire*) to *venum dare* (*vendere*), (cf. *venum ducere* frag. 89, *venum asportare*, Merc. 353), or as *pessum ire* to *pessum dare*. (See Biese: de obiecto interno apud Plautum et Terentium, Kiel (diss.) 1878, p. 42.) Type (2) is a Periphrastic Fut. with the same sense as *volo* with Inf., or our 'I will do,' e.g. Aul. 736 quamobrem ita faceres meque meosque perditum ires liberos, Cist. 4 qui magis potueris mi honorem ire habitum? Bacch. 565 occiperes tute ⟨eam⟩ amare et mi ires consultum male, Ter. Andr. 134 cur te is perditum? The real function of the First Supine appears rather in lines like Curc. 644 ea me spectatum tulerat, Pseud. 520 servitum tibi me abducito, Cist. 90 mater pompam me spectatum duxit, Bacch. 442 cum patrem adeas postulatum, Poen. 21 neu sessum ducat, Men. 835 quo me in silvam venatum vocas? (cf. the legal formula in Cic. Mur. 26 te ex iure manum consertum voco), Asin. 661 quin tradis huc cruminam pressatum umerum? But it is not always easy (e.g. Capt. 179 roga emptum) to distinguish the province of the 'First Supine' and the Acc. of the Verbal Noun, e.g. Capt. 793 hic homo pugilatum incipit.

43. Gerund and Gerundive. (S. Platner: Notes on the use of Gerund and Gerundive in Plautus and Terence, in the American Journal of Philology, vol. xiv, pp. 483 sqq.)

The use of the Gerundive of a Neuter Verb is a curious phenomenon, Epid. 74 puppis pereundast probe, Trin. 1159 si illa tibi placet, placenda dos quoque est quam dat tibi. Beside the O. Lat. construction (cf. 40) with the Gerund governing the Acc., e.g. Trin.

869 hercle opinor mi advenienti hac noctu agitandumst vigilias, we find the class Lat. construction of the Gerundive, e.g. Trin. 866 apud illas aedis sistendae mihi sunt sycophantiae. And we find also that curious intermediate construction, allowed by Cic. with a Gen. Plur., e.g. Capt. 1008 lucis das tuendi copiam, Capt. 852 nominandi istorum tibi erit magis quam edundi copia, Truc. 370 quia tui (Fem.) videndi copia est, Ter. Heaut. prol. 29 date crescendi copiam (*scil.* iis), novarum qui spectandi faciunt copiam, Hec. 372 eius (Fem.) videndi cupidus. Noteworthy is the Descriptive Gen. of the Gerund in phrases like Capt. 153 edundi exercitus, Poen. prol. 34 sermones fabulandi. On the Gen. and Dat. of Purpose see **II, 5. 20**; on the use of the Inf. and of the Subj. (with *ut*) in the function of the Gerund, see above, **33**; **VIII, 2**).

44. Participle. (Tammelin : de participiis priscae Latinitatis. Helsingfors, 1889.)

The proneness of the Italic family of languages to periphrastic Tense-formation with Auxiliary Verbs is reflected in Plautus' predilection for *sum* with Pres. Part. Act., e.g. *sciens esse* Poen. 1038, Ter. Andr. 508, &c., *dicto audiens esse, (dicto) oboediens esse, obsequens esse (fieri);* Most. 141 postilla obtegere eam neglegens fui (= neglexi), Curc. 292 quos semper videas bibentes esse in thermipolio, Capt. 925 te carens dum hic fui. Similarly with *facio*[h], e.g. Asin. 48 propterea quod me non scientem feceris (cf. Ter. Heaut. 872), Amph. 1030 quem . . . faciam ferventem flagris (cf. *fervefacio*), Pseud. 1041 qui te nunc flentem facit.

45. The use of the Verbal Adj. in *-tus* as a Perf. Part. Pass. and Deponent and the formation of a Perf. Pass. Tense, out of this Adj. with the Auxiliary Verb *sum* (or *fui*) are also more or less peculiar to the Italic languages. In Greek ἀγαπητός ἐστι never came to mean more than φίλος ἐστὶ (cf. however γεγραμμένον ἐστὶ beside γέγραπται). Some traces of the older elasticity of this Participle are to be seen in Plautine Latin. Thus *operatus* has no Past signification, but is like *feriatus* in Mil. 7 quia se iam pridem feriatam gestitem, or *ingeniatus* in Mil. 731 qui lepide ingeniatus esset (cf. *tacitus, maestus, iratus*[1]). Again it takes occasionally Active (or Neuter) signification

---

[h] It has recently been suggested that *calefio*, &c., is merely *calens fio*, &c., on the type of which *calefacio* was formed. Similarly *calē(ns)-bam, calē(ns)-bo*, the second part of the Compound being Auxiliary Verbs of the same root as *fio*. And even *amassim, prohibessim*, etc., as if *amans sim, prohibens sim*.

[1] Plautus uses *iratus sum* for 'I am angry,' *iratus fui* for 'I was angry.'

and plays the part of a Past Part. Act., e.g. *iuratus* (cf. Turpilius 33 A. iurasti? B. non sum iurata; cf. Curc. 458), *pransus*, *potus*, etc., Men. 437 ante solem occasum, Pseud. 996 novi, notis (= eis qui noverunt) praedicas. A Pres. Part. Act. seems to play this part in Poen. 653 adiit ad nos extemplo exiens 'immediately after disembarking.' Noteworthy also is the use of the Neut. *pensum* as a Noun in Truc. 765 (where the despairing lover declares his indifference to dress) nec mi adeost tantillum pensi iam quos capiam calceos. Also the curious phrase in Men. 452 qui homines occupatos occupat (= reddit).

46. The independent use of the Fut. Partic., e.g. moriturus te saluto, is unknown to the early Latin writers. The first certain example appears in a fragment of a speech of C. Gracchus (ap. Gell. 11, 10, 4) qui prodeunt dissuasuri (see Sjögren 'Futurum im altlateinischen' pp. 225 sqq.).

47. The Verbal Adj. in *-bundus* is a feature of O. Lat., e.g. Pseud. 1275 sic haec incessi ludibundus. As examples of Participles with the function of Nouns may be cited *benevolens* 'a well wisher,' *natus nemo* 'not a soul,' e.g. Most. 402; with the function of Adjectives, *insciens*, *indigens* (never 'inscius,' 'indigus' in Plautus and Terence).

VI. THE ADVERB.

(P. Gehlhardt: de Adverbiis ad notionem augendam a Plauto usurpatis, Halle, 1892: with it read Seyffert's review in Bursian's Jahresbericht, 1895, p. 294.)

1. The use of Adv. with *esse* is a well-known feature of colloquial Latin. Notable examples are Merc. 583 pulchre ut simus, Truc. 172 longe aliter est amicus atque amator, Ter. Phorm. 529 hic me huiusmodi scibat esse, ego hunc esse aliter credidi: iste me fefellit, ego isti nihilo sum 'aliter ac fui (cf. Pers. 838 sed ita pars libertinorum est, Trin. 46 si ita es ut ego te volo, sin aliter es), Accius 120 quoniam horum aequiter sententiae fuere; also the common phrase *frustrā esse*, e.g. Capt. 854 ne frustra sis 'make no mistake about it,' 'be assured of that.' It is most frequently Impersonal, e.g. *bene est*[k] (passim), Cist. 59 male mihi est, Men.

---

[k] *Optume est*, e.g. Capt. 10, is Superl. of *bene est*, whereas *optumum est* means 'it is the best course to take,' etc., e.g. Capt. 557 concedi optumum est 'retreat is advisable.'

626 quid tibi aegre est?, Asin. 144 nunc quom est melius 'now things are better,' Bacch. 1181 i hac mecum intro, ubi tibi sit lepide victibus, vino atque unguentis. The difference of *pulchre sum* and *pulchre est mihi* may find its true parallel in the change from an Impersonal to a Personal use of a Verb, e.g. *doleo* for *dolet mihi, lubent* for *lubet illis* (see **V**, 1). Or the origin of the construction may be the identity of sense in *esse* and *se habere;* for with *se habere* the Adv. is appropriate, e.g. Poen. 235 nam quom sedulo munditer nos habemus (cf. **I, 4**). We find a combination of Adj. and Adv. in lines like Capt. 271 proxumum quod sit bono quodque a malo longissime[1] (compare Epid. 409, plane hercle hoc quidem est, with Capt. 564, etc., pol planum id quidem est; and see above, **III, 1**). The same use of the Adv. is found with *fio* and *facio*, e.g. Mil. 1348 ne hoc tandem propalam fiat nimis, Capt. 754 qui mihi hoc fecit palam.

2. The Adv. replaces the Adj. also in various phrases of a Greek type, but probably not Graecisms (**I, 3**), e.g. Pers. 385 non tu nunc hominum mores vides?, Poen. 725 rem adversus populi saepe leges, Mil. 472 mulierem hinc ex proxumo, Ennius trag. 55 V. ubi illa paulo ante sapiens virginalis modestia? They may be compared with phrases like *adulescens de genere summo* (Rud. 1197, etc.), *sine virtute argutum civem* (Truc. 495). (On Bacch. 705 sed nunc quantillum usust auri tibi? see **II, 56**.)

3. To qualify an Adj. or another Adv., Plautus loves to use a significant Adv., instead of the colourless *valde* (O. Lat. *valide*), *multum* (never with Adj. in Ter.; cf. Ital. molto), *multo* (normally with Comparative), etc., e.g. perspicue palam, scite scitus, inepte stultus. Qualifying Adverbs characteristic of the Comedians' Latin are *insanum* (not 'insane'), *nimium, nimio* (normally with Comparative; but cf. Bacch. 770, Truc. 704, Naevius com. 13), *nimis, nimis quam* (e.g. Truc. 468 nimis quam paucae), etc.; characteristic of Early Latin are *oppido* (usually qualifying a Verb in Plautus, but not in Terence), *adprime*, etc.

The use of certain Pronominal Adverbs, e.g. *quo, unde, inde, huc*, as substitutes for Cases of the Pronouns themselves, has already been mentioned (**IV, 20**), e.g. Aul. 489 quo (= quibus) illae nubent?, Most. 547 conveni illum unde (= a quo) hasce aedes emeram (cf. Epid. 80, 115).

---

[1] For examples of *longe esse*, see Redslob in Berliner Philologische Wochenschrift 18, 816.

4. The Positive sense of the Comparative *ocius* is established as early as Plautus, e.g. Most. 679 evocadum aliquem ocius, but the Comparative sense appears in a line like Curc. 154 nec mea gratia commovent se ocius. Of comic Comparison we may take as example *paenissume*, Most. 656 ita mea consilia perturbat paenissume.

5. On the Adverbial use of the Abl. Case, e.g. Mil. 1124 quin si voluntate nolet, vi extrudam foras, see II, 58; of the Acc., II, 36. *Partim* is nothing but the older form of the Acc. of *pars* and is so construed in Ter. Hec. prol. 15 partim sum earum exactus, partim vix steti.

The construction of *abhinc* has been already discussed (II, 37). *Fortasse*, a by-form of which is *fortassis* (e.g. Bacch. 671), sometimes takes Acc. and Inf., e.g. Asin. 37 ubi fit polenta, te fortasse dicere, Truc. 680 A. haben ? B. parasitum te fortasse dicere, frag. inc. 58 fortasse ted amare suspicarier, Poen. 1004 fortasse medicos nos esse arbitrarier 'perhaps he thinks we are doctors,' Ter. Hec. 313 fortasse unum aliquod verbum inter eas iram hanc concivisse. The same construction with the Conjunctions *scilicet* and *videlicet* (VIII, 2), (cf. Lucr. scilicet esse globosa tamen) is perfectly intelligible, since they are clearly Compounds of *scio* and *licet*, *video* and *licet;* just as the Adverb *ilicet* takes the construction of *eo* in a line like Capt. 469 ilicet parasiticae arti maxumam malam crucem 'the jester's profession may go and be hanged' (Cist. 685, actum est, ilicet me infelicem et scelestam, is perhaps Acc. of Exclamation). But the etymology of *fortasse* (-*is*) has not yet been discovered.

VII. THE PREPOSITION.

(Pradel : de praepositionum in prisca Latinitate vi atque usu. Part i, Leipzig, 1901.)

1. The genesis of Prepositions from Adverbs may be illustrated from lines like Cas. 763 omnes festinant intus totis aedibus, Most. 596 an metuis ne quo abeat foras urbe exsulatum ?, where the meaning, already expressed by the Case-forms *aedibus* ' in the house,' *urbe* ' from the city,' is made definite by the addition of the Adverbs *intus* and *foras*. These Adverbs at a much later time came to be used as Prepositions.

The independent existence of Prepositions in Compound Verbs, e.g. *supplico*, which is seen in O. Lat. Tmesis [m], e.g. *sub vos placo* for *supplico vos* (cf. Trin. 833 distraxissent disque tulissent), leaves a trace of itself in Plautus in the retention of the bare Abl. (or Acc.) without a Preposition after Compound Verbs like *abeo* (or *accedo*) (see II, 1).

It is seen, too, in the collocation of the words in lines like Stich. 453 ite hac secundum vos me, Cas. 815 sensim super attolle limen pedes, nova nupta (where some editors read *supera*, i.e. *supra*) and in lines like Merc. 821 uxor. virum si clam domo egressast foras, Cist. 677 loca haec circiter excidit mi. Possibly also in, e.g. amicum erga (Trin. 1126, 1128, etc.), me advorsum (Poen. 400, etc.). But the Postpositon of Prepositions is a feature of all the Italic languages, and must date from a very early time. In class. Lat. it survives in *quocum, mecum, quamobrem*, etc. In Plautus postposition with the Interrog. Pron. is normal, with the Rel. very frequent, e.g. Mil. 1047 qua ab illarum?, Asin. 397 qui (Instr.-Abl.) pro istuc?, Merc. 752 quos inter iudex datu's, Ter. Eun. 542 quo in loco dictumst, parati nihil est; Lucilius 182 Ma. quando in eo numero mansi, quo in maxima non est pars hominum, 1327 quīs in versamur. We find also, e.g. Capt. 406 rebus in dubiis, Most. 30 iuventute ex omni, Ter. Hec. 473 ni te ex ipsā haec magis velim resciscere. In Stich. 71 gratiam per (a patre *P*) si petimus, the reading is not quite certain; more so in Amph. 238 sed fugam in se tamen nemo convortitur 'but however no one turns himself to flight.'

(For fuller details see Studemund in Verhandlungen der philolog. Versammlung in Karlsruhe. Leipzig, 1883, pp. 49, 57, 58; Degering: Beitraege zu hist. Syntax. Erlangen, 1893.)

2. List of noteworthy Prepositions.

a, ab. Of Plautine usages the following call for notice:

> Mil. 154 foris concrepuit hinc a vicino sene, Merc. 699 quisnam hinc a nobis exit? 'from the house of;'
> Pseud. 735 possum a me dare, Capt. 449 viaticum ut dem a trapezita tibi (cf. Horace's scribe decem ab Nerio);
> Poen. 1092 amat ab lenone hic, Pseud. 203 ubi sunt, ubi latent quibus aetas integra est, qui amant ab lenone?;

---

[m] Tmesis appears with other word-groups too, e.g. with *sis* or *si vis* 'please,' Asin. 354 si erum vis Demaenetum, quem ego novi, adduce. On *at-qui, postquam*, etc., see the next chapter.

Syntax of Plautus.

Poen. 618 mulieres ab re divina apparebunt domi (cf. Poen. 405 quom ab re divina rediero);

Asin. 891 da (*sc.* vinum) ab summo, Most. 347 da ab Delphio 'beginning with;'

Men. 1011 ab umero qui tenet 'by the shoulder;'

Rud. 1100 A. dum hic hinc a me sentiat ('thinks with me'). B. atqui nunc abs te stat (to express dissent, *seorsum* is added in Capt. 710 qui abs te sorsum sentio);

'derived from' Curc. 405 inibis a me solidam et grandem gratiam, Capt 279 A. quo honorest illic? B. summo atque ab summis viris; Ter. Andr. 156 ab illo iniuria;

'in respect of' Cist. 60 doleo ab animo, doleo ab oculis, doleo ab aegritudine, Epid. 129 a morbo valui, ab animo aeger fui, Curc. 51 tam a me pudica est quasi soror mea sit, Truc. 241 quando sterilis est amator ab datis (cf. Abl. of Plenty and Want), Mil. 631 si albicapillus hic, videtur neutiquam ab ingenio senex.

The origin of the use of *ab* to indicate the Agent with a Pass. Verb is seen in a line like Men. 783 A. ludibrio habeor. B. unde? A. ab illo. *Ab re* (the opposite of *in rem* and *ex re*) is used even in a positive sentence, Trin. 239 subdole ab re consulit. Un-Plautine is 'servus a manu,' 'a pedibus,' etc.

absque seems to be a survival from an earlier period of the language. For it is found only in one stereotyped phrase, a Conditional protasis with a Pers. Pron. (or Demonstrative) followed by *esset* or *foret*, e.g. Men. 1022 nam absque ted esset, hodie numquam ad solem occasum viverem, Trin. 832 nam absque foret te, sat scio in alto distraxissent disque tulissent satellites tui me, Pers. 836 nam hercle absque me foret et meo praesidio, hic faceret te prostibilem propediem, Ter. Hec. 601 quam fortunatus ceteris sum rebus, absque una hac foret. (On the subsequent disappearance of the word from the language, see Woelfflin in Rheinisches Museum, 37, pp. 96 sqq.)

ad. The Vulgar Latin use of *ad* with Acc. as the equivalent of the Dat. is, as we have seen (II, 22), already exemplified here and there in Plautus, e.g. Epid. 38 si in singulis stipendiis is ad hostes exuvias dabit. Cf. *nuntiare ad aliquem*, e.g. Capt. 360 and *nuntiare alicui*, e.g. Capt. 400. But the phrase *promittere ad aliquem* Stich. 483, 513 is not an example. It is a variation of *promittere ad cenam* (Men. 794, Stich. 596), which is coined on the type of *vocare ad cenam*. Similarly we find *condicere ad aliquem* (cf. Stich. 433), like *condicere ad cenam* (Stich. 433, 447).

Noteworthy uses of *ad* in Plautus are *adfatim*, 'to weariness,' 'quite sufficiently,' *admodum* 'to (full) measure,' 'extremely,' *usque ad mortem mulcare* Mil. 163. Also :

> Trin. 152 nummorum Philippeûm ad tria milia;
> Amph. 669 ad aquam praebendam commodum adveni domum, Asin. 518 ad loquendum atque ad tacendum tute habeas portisculum;
> Mil. 659 non invenies alterum lepidiorem ad omnes res, Truc. 854 quae sapit .. ad rem suam, Cas. 192 nam viri ius suom ad mulieres obtinere haud queunt; Merc. 629 de istac re argutus es . . . ad mandata claudus, caecus, mutus, mancus, debilis;
> Capt. 275 nam ad ('compared with') sapientiam huius nimius nugator fuit (cf. Mil. 968 ad tuam formam illa una dignast);
> Rud. 317 recalvom ad ('in the style of') Silanum senem (cf. Trin. 874 alterum ad istanc capitis albitudinem, Merc. 265 ad hoc exemplum. Also *quemadmodum*);
> Capt. 699 in libertatest ad (= apud) patrem (cf. *ad forum* with Verb of Rest, e.g. Mil. 930, like Cicero's *ad villam*);
> Men. 965 ad noctem saltem, credo, intromittar domum (cf. *ad postremum* Poen. 844).

advorsus, originally Nom. Masc., and *advorsum*, originally Nom. and Acc. Neut. and Acc. Masc., of the Perf. Part. of *advertor* (cf. II, 43), may be illustrated by :

> Cas. 208 nam tu quidem advorsus (= contra) tuam istaec rem loquere;
> Mil. 242 si illic concriminatus sit advorsum (= apud) militem;
> Plaut. frag. inc. 8 stultus est advorsum ('out of keeping with') aetatem et capitis canitudinem.

It is an Adverb (or Participle) in lines like these (with Dat.) :

> Trin. 724 et capturum spolia ibi illum qui meo ero advorsus venerit (cf. *advorsarius*);

Trin. 1047 nam id genus hominum omnibus est advorsum ;
Stich. 89 ferre advorsum homini (*A :* -nem *P*) occupemus osculum ;
Truc. 503 eugae! Astaphium eccam it mi advorsum (cf. *obviam*).

apud. Noteworthy is the Comedians' phrase *sum apud me* 'I am in my right senses.' Also, e.g.:

Stich. 710 non mora erit apud me 'on my part' (cf. Amph. 555 ut tuis nulla apud te fides sit; Mil. 1197 celebre apud nos imperium tuumst) ;
Men. 89 apud mensam ;
Curc. 395 apud Sicyonem ;
Amph. 1012 apud emporium atque in macello ;
Amph. 591 servo bono, apud erum qui vera loquitur (cf. Pseud. 461);

and *apud forum* (passim). (On the occasional variant *ad forum*, see above.)

circum, originally Cognate Acc. of *circus*, e.g. circum ire 'to go a round,' would be originally used only with Verbs of motion. In the Casina prologue v. 26 (post Plautine?) we have it however with *esse :* Alcedonia sunt circum forum (cf. Truc. 66). *Circa* is unknown to Plautus as a Prep. (but cf. *circumcirca* Aul. 468) ; but not *circiter*, which occurs twice in this function (often as an Adverb) :

Cist. 677 loca haec circiter excidit mi : Mil. 350 circiter triennium.

cis in Plautus is used only of time, e.g. Truc. 348 nulla faxim cis dies paucos siet : ' citra ' is post-Plautine.

clam is both Adverb and Prep. (with Acc.) in Plautus, *clanculum* (apparently a Diminutive of *clam*) only Adv. (but Prep. in Ter. Adelph. 52 alii clanculum patres quae faciunt).

contră (not *-rā* in Plaut.) is rarely [n] a Prep. : Poen. 1355 numquid recusas contra me ?, Pers. 13 A. quis illic est qui contra me astat ? B. quis hic est qui sic contra me astat ?, Pseud. 156 adsistite omnes contra me, Ter. Adelph. 44 ille contra haec omnia ruri agere vitam. On its use (as Adv.) with Abl. of Price, e.g. Mil. 658 cedo tres mi

---

[n] Some say 'never in Plautus and Terence,' regarding *me* in Poen. 1355 as governed by *recusas* (Double Acc.) and in Pers. 13, Pseud. 156 by *ad-* of the Compound Verb. In Adelph. 44 they punctuate after *omnia* and supply with *ille contra haec omnia* the verb *fecit*.

homines aurichalco contra, see II, 60. It is Adv. in a line like Rud. 693 (with Dat.) praesidio Veneris malitiae lenonis contra incedam (cf. obviam ire).

coram is only an Adverb in Plautus and Terence.

cum replaces the Abl. of Description in lines like Aul. 41 circumspectatrix cum oculis emissiciis, Rud. 251 sicine hic cum uvida veste grassabimur? (cf. Capt. 203 quia cum catenis sumus, Cas. 524 cum cibo cum quiqui facito ut veniant); the Instrumental Abl. e.g. Rud. 937 sed hic rex cum aceto pransurust; the Abl. of Manner, e.g. Men. 895 magna cum cura ego illum curari volo, Epid. 516 flagitio cum maiore post reddes tamen; Abl. Abs., e.g. Pers. 332 sequere hac, mea gnata, me cum dis volentibus; Abl. of Time, e.g. cum primo luci Cist. 525, cum diluculo abire Amph. 743.

Noteworthy phrases are: *cum cura esse* (= diligens esse) Bacch. 398; *cum eo cum quiqui* 'notwithstanding' Poen. 588 (cf. Men. 666 cum viro cum uxore di vos perdant!, Merc. 988); *nupta esse cum aliquo* (also 'alicui') e.g. Amph. 99; *cavere cum* 'to be careful in dealings with' Most. 1142, Pseud. 909; *orare* (lit. 'to speak') *cum aliquo*, e.g. Asin. 662; *cum animo suo cogitare*, e.g. Most. 702; *osculari cum aliquo*, e.g. Mil. 243; *pignus dare cum aliquo*, e.g. Pers. 188; *iudicem habere cum aliquo*, e.g. Rud. 1380; *tecum habeto* 'keep it to yourself,' Pers. 246.

de, as early as Plautus' time, can readily divest itself of the notion 'down from' and express merely 'from,' 'away from,' e.g. Men. 599 abire de foro, Amph. 215 de suis finibus exercitus deducerent (cf. Aul. 31 hic senex de proxumo 'our aged neighbour'). It acquires ultimately the sense of 'from,' 'in consequence of,' e.g. Cas. 415 de labore pectus tundit, Men. 266 iam abs te metuo de verbis tuis; also 'immediately after,' e.g. Most. 697 non bonust somnus de prandio. Notice the phrases: *mercari de aliquo*, Epid. 495; *discere de* (magistro), Poen. 280, whence *de me doctus* 'self-taught,' Truc. 454 (cf. Rud. 293 nos iam de ornatu propemodum ut locupletes simus scitis); *de audito* 'on hearsay,' Merc. 903 vidisti, an de audito nuntias?; tibi quidem *supplicium .. de nobis detur* e.g. Asin. 482; *de mea pecunia* 'at my expense,' e.g. Bacch. 512; *actum est de me* lit. 'my case has already been tried,' e.g. Pseud. 85; *mereri de aliquo*, e.g. Trin. 339 de mendico male meretur 'it is an ill-service to a beggar;' *de mea sententia* 'at my advice,' Bacch. 1038; *de industria*, e.g. Ter. Andr. 794 paulum interesse censes, ex animo omnia, ut fert natura, facias an de industria?; *de die, de nocte,* e.g. Asin. 516 Rud. 898; *quid de argentost?* 'what about the money?,' Most. 569. On its occasional approximation to the 'partitive' function of the Prep. in Romance languages, e.g. French 'boire du vin,' see **II, 1 n.**

erga, if derived from *ē *rĕgā* 'from a line,' must have had originally a local signification 'directly opposite.' The one instance of this in Plautus is doubtful: Truc. 406 A. tonstricem Suram novisti nostram? B. quaen erga aedem sese habet? (mercedem s.h. *Leo*). In all other occurrences it expresses 'feeling (or conduct) towards,' whether the feeling (or conduct) be good or bad, e.g. Capt. 245 per mei te erga bonitatem patris, Asin. 20 siquid med erga hodie falsum dixeris.

ex is already in Plautus' time confused with *de*, e.g. Rud. 173 desiluit . . e scapha, and *ab* (e.g. abire ex). It indicates change of state in a line like Stich. 138 condicionem ex pessuma primariam; 'in consequence of,' e.g. Poen. 69 conicitur ipse in morbum ex aegritudine, Poen. 1200 nunc hinc sapit, hinc sentit, quidquid sapit, ex meo amore; 'in accordance with,' e.g. Capt. 997 ornatus haud ex suis virtutibus, Trin. 707 hic agit magis ex argumento; 'after' or rather 'henceforth,' of time, e.g. Pers. 479 bonus volo iam ex hoc die esse.

Here are some of Plautus' phrases with *ex : ex factis nosce rem*, e g. Most. 199; (senex, adulescens, etc.) *ex proxumo* 'neighbour' Mil. 969; *statua ex auro*, Bacch. 640; *ex advorso* (cf. the Adv. *exadvorsum*), Merc. 880 caelum ut est splendore plenum nonne ex advorso vides?; *ex animo dolere*, Capt. 928, like *miser ex animo* Stich. 1 (cf. **II,** 32, on Loc. *animi* and Abl. *animo*); *ex audito* 'on hearsay,' Bacch. 469; *e re nata* 'under the circumstances,' Ter. Adelph. 295 (cf. Stich. 620, where the reading is doubtful); *ex sententia* 'as one could wish,' e.g. Men. 1151; *e re mea* 'to my advantage,' e.g. Asin. 539; *ex industria* Poen. 219; *ex hoc loco* 'on the spot' (cf. *extemplo*, from the O. Lat. sense of *templum*), e.g. Truc. 443 iam modo (*v.l.* immo) ex hoc loco iubebo; *ex improviso*, Rud. 1192 (but *improviso* without Prep., v. 1196); *ex nomine*, e.g. Stich. 242 nunc Miccotrogus nomine e vero vocor; *ex antiquo* 'in the old style,' Pseud. 1190.

It will be noticed how often it is exchangeable with *de*, e.g. de industria, de audito, or with the simple Abl. (or *in* with Abl.) e.g. animo, nomine, or with *ab*. In fact Plautus seems to allow metrical convenience to dictate the substitution of one of these Prepositions

for another. Thus beside the normal *auferre ab* we find in Pseud.
1225 auferre de; beside *abire a foro*, in Men. 599 abire de foro;
beside *longe ab*, in Rud. 266, longule ex hoc loco. (For a fuller list
of examples see Pradel, pp. 553 sqq.)

extra. On the analogy of *intro* (Motion), *intra* (Rest), we should
expect to find also **extro*. But *extra* is used in both functions, e.g.
Men. 182 extra numerum es mihi, Aul. 711 nam ego declinavi
paululum me extra viam. It has, occasionally, as in class Lat., the
sense of *praeter*, especially with accompaniment of *unus*, e.g.
Amph. 833 mi extra unum te mortalis nemo corpus corpore contigit,
Ter. Phorm. 98 neque notus neque cognatus extra unam aniculam
quisquam aderat.

fini, (see II, 59), with Abl., Men. 859 osse fini dedolabo assulatim viscera (cf. Cato Agr. cult. 28, 2 postea operito terra radicibus
fini). In a sentence like Cato Agr. cult. 113, 2 amphoras nolito
implere nimium, ansarum infimarum fini, the word is a Noun.

in (Kampmann: de 'in' praepositionis usu Plautino. Breslau,
(progr.), 1845).

The old Prep. *indu* (older *indo, endo*), e.g. Ennius Ann. 238 V.
indu foro lato sanctoque senatu, 576 endo suam do (Homer's δώ),
had been superseded by its rival *in* and was current in the language
of Plautus' time only in Compound Verbs, like *indaudire* (later
inaudire).

Noticeable uses of *in* with Acc. are:

dare in splendorem 'to burnish' (= splendefacere), Asin.
426, etc. (cf. Capt. 962, Pseud. 928);

of a stake or wager, e.g. Curc. 611 si vis tribus bolis
('throws of dice') vel in chlamydem, Epid. 701 ni ergo
matris filia est, in meum nummum, in tuum talentum
pignus da;

in rem meam 'to my advantage;' cf. Most. 122 extollunt,
parant sedulo in firmitatem (= firmitatis causa), Mil.
832 neque illic calidum exbibit in prandium, Truc. 740
unam (*sc.* minam) in obsonatum 'for the purpose of;'

Cist. 601 filiam suam despondit in divitias maxumas, Poen.
904 is in divitias homo adoptavit hunc.

distributive, e.g. Aul. 108 dividere argenti nummos in viros.
Truc. 303 quae in noctes singulas latere fit minor ('the wall
loses a brick every night').

Pseud. 128 in hunc diem a me ut caveant, Stich. 635 (like the Acc. of Duration of Time).

With Abl. :

'in the case of,' e.g. Mil. 673 nam in mala uxore atque inimico siquid sumas, sumptus est, in bono hospite atque amico quaestus est quod sumitur, Most. 1116 exempla edepol faciam ego in te, Mil. 611 facilest imperium in bonis, Ter. Andr. 233 in aliis peccandi ;

in mora esse alicui (like *morae esse alicui ;* cf. C. Mueller in Rhein. Mus. 54, 400), *in quaestione esse alicui* 'to have to be looked for,' e.g. Pseud. 663 sed vide sis ne in quaestione sis, quando arcessam mihi.

like the Abl. of Attendant Circumstances, e.g. Mil. 703 at illa laus est , magno in genere et in divitiis maxumis liberos hominem educare.

like the Abl. of Time, e.g. Pseud. 1304 ebibere in hora una, Poen. 228.

The Acc. is substituted for the Abl. in O. Lat. phrases like *in potestatem esse*. Cf. Amph. 180 numero mihi in mentem fuit (for 'in mentem venit'), Ter. Adelph. 528. The reading is not quite certain in lines like Most. 328, 594, Epid. 191, Poen. 590. Similarly the function of the Adverbial Abl. is played by *in* with Acc. in phrases like Bacch. 355 hic nostra agetur aetas in malacum modum, Most. 32 is nunc in aliam partem palmam possidet.

inter.

This is the reciprocal Prep. in Plautine as in class. Latin, e.g. Stich. 729 haec facetiast, amare inter se rivales duos.

Notice also Cist. 505 inter novam rem verbum usurpabo vetus ; Most. 385 abripite hunc intro actutum inter manus.

intra.

The endings -*rō* and -*rā* differ in this, that -*ro* is appropriate to words of motion, -*ra* to words of rest. But this distinction was soon effaced, e.g. Truc. 43 eaque intra pectus se penetravit potio. For the temporal use of *intra* Curc. 448 is noteworthy: subegit solus intra viginti dies.

ob (K. Reissinger : ueber Bedeutung und Verwendung der Praepositionen 'ob' und 'propter' im aelteren Latein. Part I. (progr.) Landau, 1896).

This Prep. played a greater part in O. Lat. than later. Compounds with *ob* are characteristic of the early language; e.g. *occipio* plays the same part in Plaut. as *incipio* in Cic., *oggero* as *ingero*. The oldest sense is 'to,' 'towards,' 'against,' e.g. Ennius Ann. 297 V. ob Romam noctu legiones ducere coepit; cf. *obicere ob*, e.g. Most. 619 obicere argentum ob os impurae beluae, and the frequent *ob oculos obicere, obstare,* etc.

Noteworthy is the sense 'as payment or equivalent for,' e.g. Asin. 347 ait se ob asinos ferre argentum, Truc. 214 nam fundi et aedes obligatae sunt ob Amoris praedium, Ter. Phorm. 661 ager oppositus pignori ob decem minas est.

Also the frequent *ob industriam* 'intentionally,' 'taking pains,' e.g. Cas. 276 (cf. *de industria*, e.g. Cas. 278, and *ex industria*); *ob rem* like *in rem*, Ter. Phorm. 526 A. non pudet vanitatis? B. minime, dum ob rem.

penes (see Langen ' Beiträge,' p. 153) is only used with Pronouns, e.g. Trin. 733 penes me, Amph. 652 quem penest virtus.

per (R. Obricatis: de 'per' praep. latinae .. usu, qualis obtinuerit ante Ciceronis aetatem. Königsberg (diss.) 1884). Its use to express time should be noticed, e.g. Stich. 179 per annonam caram dixit me natum pater, Curc. 644 per Dionysia; cf. *per tempus* 'opportunely,' the opposite of *post tempus* (venire, etc.).

Also its use with *licet*, e.g. Stich. 611 per hanc tibi cenam incenato, Gelasime, esse hodie licet, Epid. 338 per hanc curam quieto tibi licet esse; cf. Rud. 1165 sit per me quidem, Curc. 554, Merc. 1020. And its Adverbial use, e.g. *per pacem* 'peacefully' Amph. 388, *per silentium* 'in silence' Ter. Heaut. 36, etc.; in Amph. 963 (cf. Poen. 573) we have both *per iocum* and *ioco*, A. me dixisse per iocum. B. an id ioco dixisti? On the arrangement of the words used in attestations, e.g. per ego te tua genua obsecro, see I, 4 n.

pone (for 'pos-ne') and *post* (*pos-te*) are closely connected.

Pone is local, e.g. Curc. 481 pone aedem Castoris; *post* is temporal usually, but local in Epid. 237 duae sic post me fabulari inter sese.

prae. Plautus' use of this Prep. will be seen from these examples:

> Bacch. 623 quod fuit prae manu;
> Amph. 527 ne me uxorem praevortisse dicant prae republica;
> Mil. 989 pithecium haec est prae illa, Curc. 98 nam omnium unguentûm odor prae tuo nautea est;
> Rud. 526 omnia corusca prae tremore fabulor, Amph. 1066 exsurgite, inquit, qui terrore meo occidistis prae metu.

praeter.

'along,' 'past,' e.g. Poen. prol. 19 neu dissignator praeter os obambulet, Stich. 461 exivi foras, mustela murem abstulit praeter pedes. In Naevius com. 41 nam ut ludere laetantes inter se vidimus amnem praeter, editors substitute *propter*.

'beyond,' e.g. Amph. 640 quem ego amo praeter omnes, Ter. Andr. 58 horum ille nihil egregie praeter cetera studebat.

'contrary to,' e.g. Most. 965 puere, praeter speciem stultus es, Epid. 106, Ter. Heaut. 59.

'besides;' e.g. Most. 823 tres minas pro istis duobus praeter vecturam dedi.

pro.

The local use, curiously, does not appear in the Dramatists. We may quote Ennius Ann. 628 V. apud emporium in campo hostium pro moene.

The following uses may be noticed:

(1) 'proportion,' Rud. 1115 tum tu pol pro portione nec vir nec mulier mihi es; Mil. 728 pro virtute ut veneat (cf. 738 tua te ex virtute . . accipiam); Aul. 541 pro re nitorem et gloriam pro copia qui habent (cf. Merc. 506), Stich. 690 pro opibus nostris satis commodule; Amph. 289 meus pater nunc pro ('according to') huius verbis recte et sapienter facit.

(2) 'office,' 'authority,' Capt. 244 pro iure imperitabam meo; cf. *pro imperio* Amph. 21, Poen. 44, Ter. Phorm. 196; pro praefectura Capt. 907;

(3) 'equivalence,' *pro nihilo esse duco*, e.g. Pers. 637;

> Truc. 230 quin, ubi nil det, pro infrequente eum mittat militia domum;
>
> Capt. 542 proque ignoto me aspernari, quasi me nunquam noveris;
>
> Men. 927 haud pro insano ('like a madman') respondit mihi (cf. 945).

(4) 'on behalf of,' e.g. Pseud. 232 ego pro me et pro te curabo (cf. *procurare*).

From one or other of these senses come the following: *pro testimonio dicere*, e.g. Poen. 596;

> Naevius com. 89 qua pro confidentia ausu's?
>
> Trin. 303 pro ingenio ego me liberum esse ratus sum, pro imperio tuo meum animum tibi servitutem servire aequom censui.
>
> Rud. 1410 pro illo dimidio ego Gripum emittam manu.

With Trin. 26 concastigabo pro commerita noxia, compare v. 23 amicum castigare ob meritam noxiam.

propter (K. Reissinger: ueber . . 'ob' und 'propter.' Part I, Landau, 1896) is related to *prope* (e.g. Stich. 330 quisnam hic loquitur tam prope nos?) as *circiter* to *circum*, *subter* to *sub*, etc. Its oldest sense must therefore have been local, 'near,' 'beside,' e.g. Mil. 853 ibi erat bilibris aula sic propter cados. The local and the much more frequent causal senses are combined in this passage. (Rud. 33—36):

illic habitat Daemones
in agro atque villa proxuma propter mare,
senex qui huc Athenis exul venit, haud malus;
neque is adeo propter malitiam patria caret.

secundum from the old Gerundive of *sequor*, lit. 'following' (cf. *secundus ventus* 'a following or favourable wind').

(1) 'behind' (like *pone*), e.g. Mil. 1349 nos secundum ferri nunc per urbem haec omnia, Stich. 453 ite hac secundum vos me, frag. 49 secundum eampse aram aurum abscondidi.

(2) 'along,' e.g. Rud. 149 quid illuc est, Sceparnio, hominum secundum litus?

(3) 'after' (like *post*) possibly of time, Cas. prol. 28 (un-Plautine?) ludis poscunt neminem, secundum ludos reddunt autem nemini; more certainly of order, e.g. Capt. 239 nam secundum patrem tu es pater proxumus.

The class. Lat. sense 'according to,' is found by some in Ter. Eun. 1090 postquam eis mores ostendi tuos et conlaudavi secundum facta et virtutes tuas, impetravi.

super.

The logical sense 'concerning' (like *de*) is very common, e.g. Cas. 254 A. qua de re? B. rogas? super ancilla Casina.

supra is local, Pers. 819 ille qui supra nos habitat (= Juppiter ille).

VIII. The Conjunction.

1. In the Indo-European sentence an enclitic word took, as a rule, the second place. This is therefore the natural place for Enclitic Conjunctions like *autem*, *quoque*, although metrical or other considerations occasionally interfere in lines like Cas. 28 secundum ludos reddunt autem nemini, Pseud. 692 eugae! par pari aliud

autem quod cupiebam contigit. Cf. Pseud. 184 eo vos vostros panticesque adeo madefactatis.

2. I give first an alphabetical list of such Conjunctions as call for notice. A detailed account of certain functions, Temporal, Causal, etc., will follow.

List of noteworthy Conjunctions:

adeo (Langen 'Beiträge,' pp. 139 sqq.; Sydow: zum Gebrauch von 'adeo' bei Plautus. Stettin, (Schulprogr.) 1896).

The addition of Prepositions for the sake of giving precision was not confined to Nouns, e.g. salio de monte, and Verbs, e g. desilio (de) monte (see II, 1) : it is found also with Adverbs. *Adeo* is an example. The Pronominal Adverb *eo* meant 'to that spot or quarter' (see IV, 14) and was often used as a Case of the Demonstrative *is* instead of 'ad eum,' 'ad eam,' 'ad eos,' etc. (see IV, 20). Precision was given to these two uses of the word by the addition of the appropriate Preposition *ad*, e.g. Ter. Phorm. 55 adeo res redit. *Adeo* has two meanings in O. Lat. It means either 'up to that point,' often with *usque*, e.g. Asin. 328 mansero tuo arbitratu, vel adeo usque dum peris, or else 'in addition to that,' 'furthermore,' e.g. Men. 827 tibi aut adeo isti. *Nunc adeo*, with *edico*, etc., peremptorily breaks off a discussion, etc., e.g. Mil. 159 nunc adeo edico omnibus, Pseud. 855 nunc adeo tu, qui meus es, iam edico tibi, Rud. 728.

an (P. Hinze: de 'an' particulae apud priscos scriptores Latinos vi et usu. Halle, 1887). A recent theory, the truth of which is doubtful, makes *at-nĕ* the original form of this Conjunction (i.e. *at* with the Interrogative Particle *ne*). This would become *anne* by the law of Latin Phonetics. Before an initial consonant this would be sounded in rapid discourse without the final *ĕ* as *ann* or *an*, so that *anne* (used by Plautus only when an initial vowel follows) and *an* are doublets (*anne est?*, etc., *an sum?*, etc.) and the use of *an* before an initial vowel (e.g. *ăn est?*), a use found as early as Plautus, is really the misuse of the preconsonantal for the prevocalic form of the word. The common formula of a Disjunctive Interrogation *ne . . . an*, e.g. Men. 198 egone an tu? would, according to this theory, be originally *ne . . . anne*, e.g. Rud. 1069 iurene anne iniuria?, with the same repetition of *ne* as is seen in *ne . . . uecne* (see below). (On the employment of *an* in Interrogations, see below, 7.) *Annon* has not in Plautus' time become a Conjunction (or Conjunctional word-group); for he more frequently repeats the Verb after *non*, e.g. Capt. 846 iuben an non iubes?, Pers. 533 tacen an non taces? (but Rud. 1399 tacen an non?, Curc. 566, etc.), whereas in Terence *annon* is normally the mere correspondent of *an*, e.g. Phorm. 852 sed isne est, quem quaero, annon? (but Eun. 546 is est an non est?).

ast 'furthermore;' usually in Conditional Sentences, e.g. Capt. 683 si ego hic peribo, ast ille, ut dixit, non redit, Trin. 74, Ennius Ann. 561 V.; but not always, e.g. Merc. 246 atque oppido hercle bene velle illi visus sum, ast non habere cui commendarem capram, Accius 260.

at has the force of 'at least,' when preceded by *si*, in lines like Men. 670 si tibi displiceo, patiundum: at placuero huic Erotio, Men. 746 si me derides, at pol illum non potes (cf. Pers. 170 quamquam ego vinum bibo, at mandata non consuevi simul bibere una; for other examples see Seyffert in Bursian's Jahresbericht, 1880, p. 297).

Its use in prayers, curses, etc., may be illustrated by Merc. 793 at te, vicine, di deaeque perduint, and the common *at ita me*, e.g. Capt. 622.

Notice also Merc. 464 A. tu prohibes. B. at me incusato 'oh! of course, blame me.'

at enim 'but indeed' (on the use of *enim* in Plautus, see below) in dialogue is used to oppose a preceding statement of the other speaker, e.g. Most. 922 A. vel mihi denumerato... B. at enim ne quid captioni mihi sit, si dederim tibi. (For other examples of *at enim* see Seyffert in Studemund's Studien 2, p. 426 *n*.)

atque (*ac*) (see E. Ballas: Grammatica Plautina I. de particulis copulativis. Griefswald, 1868) i.e. ad-que 'and in addition,' 'and thereto,' (cf. Pseud. 769), has not yet wholly become a mere Copula (e.g. Aul. 97 fures venisse atque·abstulisse dicito), but often means 'and even,' 'and nevertheless,' e.g. Trin. 941 A. e caelo? B. atque medio quidem, Bacch. 569 A. quid duas? B. atque ambas sorores, Capt. 354 solvite istum nunciam, atque ('and in fact') utrumque, Rud. 121 dabitur opera atque in negotio, Trin. 746 atque ea condicio huic vel primaria est, Pers. 829 ac tu Persa es? 'and so you are the Persian.'

The O. Lat. sense of 'all at once,' 'forthwith,' is very common in Plautus, e.g. Most. 1050 quoniam convocavi, atque illi me ex senatu segregant, Poen. 651 dudum mane ut ad portum processimus, atque istunc e navi exeuntem oneraria videmus.

When used comparatively (= quam) (see E. Lalin: de particularum comparativarum usu apud Terentium. Norrcopiae, 1904), e.g. Mil. 764 haud centensumam partem dixi atque, otium rei si sit, possum exponere, Merc. 897 amicior mihi nullus vivit atque is est, Ter. Andr. 698 non Apollinis magis verum atque hoc responsumst, the leading word is sometimes omitted, e.g. Bacch. 549 quem esse amicum ratus sum atque (= aeque atque) ipsus sum mihi, Amph. 274 neque se luna quoquam mutat atque (= alio atque) uti exorta est semel. In Amph. 583 proinde ac meritus es, editors change *ac* to *ut* (see Langen 'Beitraege,' p. 295).

Corrective *atque* (e.g. Truc. 197 i intro, amabo, vise illam; atque opperimino: iam exibit) is often changed by scribes and by editors to *atqui*, e.g. Stich. 96 atque (-i *alii*) hoc est satis (see below). On the use of *atque* as a Copula, the equivalent of *et* and *-que*, see below, 6.

atqui, or rather *at qui*, a combination of *at* with the Particle *qui* (see below), e.g. Asin. 823 at pol qui dixti rectius, Rud. 946 at pol qui audies post, Merc. 727 A. dic igitur. B. dicam. A. atqui dicundumst tamen, is in Plautus' plays normally accompanied by Fut. or Gerundive, and expresses a strong threat or threatening assertion. Plautus uses *atque* in the sense of Cicero's (and Terence's) *atqui*, e.g. Aul. 287 atque ego istuc, Anthrax, aliovorsum dixeram; Ter. Eun. 451 bene dixti, ac mihi istuc non in mentem venerat, Andr. 524, etc. (For details see Leo in Nachrichten Göttinger Gesellschaft 1895, pp. 421 sqq.)

aut (W. Kohlmann: de 'vel' imperativo, quatenus ab 'aut' particula differat. Marburg, 1898) is commoner than *vel* (see below) in Plautus and Terence. Just as *-ve* (see below) appears as the equivalent of *que* in some phrases, so *aut* and *et* appear in such phrases as sobrie et frugaliter Epid. 565, sobrie aut frugaliter Pers. 449.

autem (see Langen 'Beiträge,' p. 316) is sometimes joined immediately to *et* or *sed*, e.g. Merc. 119 et currendum et pugnandum et autem iurigandum est in via, Poen. 841 et adire lubet hominem et autem nimis eum ausculto lubens, Rud. 472 sed autem, quid si hanc hinc abstulerit quispiam?; but usually has an intervening word, e.g. Mil. 1149 si et illa volt et ille autem cupit, Truc. 838 agite, abite tu domum et tu autem domum.

The repetition in Stich. 733 is a piece of comic Assonance: tecum ubi autem est, mecum ibi autemst.

As example of *autem* in indignant repetition of another's words, we may take Pseud. 305 A. metuo credere. B. credere autem! 'give credit indeed!,' Ter. Adel. 940 A. fac; promisi ego illis. B. promisti autem! de te largitor, puer.

ceterum, the Neut. Sing. (e.g. Pers. 692 numquid ceterum me voltis?, Cas. 94 dehinc conicito ceterum), is often used Adverbially 'for the rest,' e.g. Merc. 267 vosmet videte ceterum quanti siem, Poen. 125 dehinc ceterum valete, adeste. The Neut. Plur. is similar, *cetera*, e.g. Mil. 927 quiescas cetera, Trin. 289 cetera ('for the rest') rape, trahe, fuge, late. The genesis of the Adversative Conjunction is seen in a line like Trin. 994 ceterum ('for the rest,' 'but in short') qui sis, qui non sis, floccum non interduim.

cur (Langen: Analecta Plautina II. Münster (progr.), 1882, p. 3) is appropriate to direct Questions, although not quite unknown in indirect (e.g. Capt. 1007 attat scio cur te patrem esse adsimules, Ter Heaut. 1).

donec. Neither the origin of this word nor the relationship of the three forms *donec*, *donicum* and *donique* (Lucr.) is at all clear. On the use of the Conjunction in temporal sentences, see below, 10.

dum (G. M. Richardson: de 'dum' particulae apud priscos scriptores Latinos usu. Leipzig, 1886), a word of uncertain etymology, is often a mere Particle, appended to Imperatives, e.g. *iubĕdum*, *dic(e)dum agedum*, and other words, e.g. *quĭdum?* 'how so?' (always forming a sentence by itself, e.g. Mil. 325), *ehodum* (used by Terence). In *primumdum* it probably retains its temporal sense, as in *nondum* 'not yet,' *vixdum* (not used by Plautus and only once by Terence, Phorm. 594), *etiamdum* (see below), *interdum*. (On *nedum* 'much less,' see below; the relation of *dudum* to *dum* is uncertain.) It retains its independence in a line like Rud. 778 abi modo; ego dum hoc curabo recte, and in the expression *dum . . dum* 'at one time . . at another,' Merc. 348 dum servi mei perplacet mi consilium, dum rursum haud placet (cf. Accius 395 ita dum interruptum credas nimbum volvier, dum quod sublime ventis expulsum rapi saxum, Afranius 372 dum me morigeram, dum morosam praebeo; whereas Catullus 62, 45 sic virgo, dum intacta manet, dum cara suis est, gives the phrase the sense of *dum . . tamdiu*; in Plaut. Truc. 232 the MSS. offer *dum . . . tum*). On the use of *dum* as a temporal Conjunction 'while' or 'until,' see **6**; on its acquired Conditional sense 'provided that' (cf. *dummodo*), e.g. Accius 203 oderint dum metuant, see **5**. It acquires a Causal sense in a context like Trin. 1149 quid ego ineptus, dum sermonem vereor interrumpere, solus sto?, Ter. Andr. 822 dum studeo obsequi tibi, paene inlusi vitam filiae; a Concessive in a context like Rud. 1261 dum praedam habere se censeret, interim praeda ipsus esset, Curc. 170 ipsus se excruciat qui homo quod amat videt nec potitur dum licet. On its Final sense (with Subj.) see below. The legal word-group *dumtaxat*, literally 'while (or provided that) it touches,' occurs once in Plautus, Truc. 445 iubebo ad istam quinque perferri minas, praeterea opsonari dumtaxat minā.

enim (Langen 'Beiträge,' pp. 263 sqq.) is in the Comedians' Latin normally (cf. W. Clement in Amer. Journ. Phil. 18,402 sqq.) an Asseverative particle, corresponding to *enimvero*, e.g. Most. 551 A. quid tute tecum? B. nihil enim 'nothing at all.'

Etenim in the prologue of the Amphitruo (v. 26) etenim ille, quoius huc iussu venio, Iuppiter non minus quam vostrum quivis formidat malum, is said to be post-Plautine. *At enim* is common in Plautus, but *sed enim* seems not to occur (in Bacch. 1080 the MSS. offer *et enim*, which some editors change to *at enim*, some to *sed enim*), although we have *verum enim* Cist. 80. *Quid enim* appears in Amph. 694 quid enim censes? (On *non enim*, wrongly changed by editors to *noenum*, see below.)

equidem. Mistaken ideas of Plautine Metre formerly induced editors to change *quidem* to *equidem* in a great number of lines (see Skutsch in Hermes 32, p. 95). This created not a few occurrences of *equidem* with other persons than the first. If we are to follow the MSS., one or two still remain, e.g. Pers. 639 ita me di bene ament sapienter! atque equidem miseret tamen (equidem *P*, eo *A*), Mil. 650 o lepidum semisenem, si quas memorat virtutes habet, atque equidem plane educatum in nutricatu Venerio!, Epid. 603 adulescentem equidem dicebant emisse, Poen. 1240 quia annos multos filias meas celavistis clam me, atque equidem ingenuas liberas summoque genere gnatas, Trin. 611 atque equidem ipsus ultro venit Philto oratum filio. Undoubtedly the word is normally associated with the First Person. The popular etymology, from *ego* and *quidem*, is difficult to justify phonetically, though in a line like Epid. 202

A. et ego Apoecides sum. et egoquidem sum Epidicus,

the Compound *egoquidem* may have come fairly near in pronunciation to *equidem*. In Men. 1070 sq. the two words appear in neighbouring lines:

novi equidem hunc; erus est meus.
egoquidem huius servos sum.

These two examples shew that *egoquidem* emphasizes the 1 Pron. far more than *equidem*.

ergo (Langen 'Beiträge,' p. 235). The common etymology ē *rĕgo is supported by the Assonance in Most. 1119 A. aliud te rogo. B. aliud ergo nunc tibi respondeo. This use of *ergo* in impatient correction occurs again in Aul. 323 A. cocum ego, non furem rogo. B. cocum ergo dico, Cist. 608.

As other examples of its Plautine use may be taken these lines: Men. 758 ut aetas mala est! mers mala ergost, Pers. 24 A. satin tu usque valuisti? B. haud probe. A. ergo edepol palles, Most. 972 A. Philolaches . . . tibicinam liberavit. B. Philolachesne ergo? ('really'), Pseud. 1084 A. pol haud mentitust. B. ergo ('therefore') haud iratus fui, Most. 812 A. non tu vides hunc voltu uti tristi est senex? B. video. A. ergo inridere ne videare, Bacch. 866 A. pacisci cum illo paullula pecunia potes. B. pacisce ergo, opsecro, quid tibi lubet (cf. Asin 688, etc.). On the pleonastic phrase *ergo igitur*, e.g. Trin. 756, see below (s.v. 'igitur').

et (see E. Ballas: Grammatica Plautina. I de particulis copulativis. Greifswald, 1868) (cognate with Greek ἔτι 'further,' 'in addition') has sometimes, like *atque*°, (see above) the sense of 'and nevertheless,' 'and further,' e.g. Bacch. 1196 lubet et metuo, Epid. 141 huic homini opust quadraginta minis celeriter calidis, danistae quas resolvat, et cito. The sense of *etiam* it has normally in combination with a Pers. Pron., *et ego*, *et tu*, etc, in lines like Capt. 1009 A. salve Tyndare. B. et tu, Curc. 686 A. heus tu, leno, te volo. B. et ego te volo. But cf. Rud. 8 (if the line be Plautine) et alia signa ('other constellations too') de caelo ad terram accidunt. On the use of *et* as a mere Copula, the equivalent of *-que*, see below, 6; on *et . . quidem* in ironical ejaculations, see s.v. 'quidem.'

etiam, i.e. *et iam*, usually accompanies a Verb in O Lat., while *quoque* usually accompanies a Noun. (For details see Kirk in Amer. Journ. Phil. 18, 36; 21, 303.) The following examples of Plautus' use of the Conjunction may suffice: Trin. 572 quid nunc? etiam ('still') consulis?; Rud. 959 is mihi nihil etiam ('as yet') respondit; Most. 1000 A. numquid processit ad forum hodie novi? B. etiam

---

° As *atque* is changed by editors to *atqui*, so is *et* to *at* in lines like Capt. 888 et nunc Siculus non est, Boius est.

('yes'). In impatient commands it is usually joined with 2 Sing. Pres. Ind. in Plaut. and Ter., e.g. *etiam taces?* 'won't you be quiet?' The addition of *dum* produces the Temporal Conjunction *etiamdum*, normally used in Negative Sentences (for examples, see Richardson 'de dum partic.' p. 8). On the combination of *etiam* with *quoque*, see s.v. 'quoque.'

etsi, i.e. *et si* 'even if.' The origin of the word is shewn in lines like Trin. 474 A. edim *nisi si* ille votet. B. at pol ego *et si* votet, Rud. 1348 sqq.

>   A. illaec advorsum *si* quid peccasso, Venus,
>   veneror te ut omnes miseri lenones sient.
>   B. tamen fiet, *et si* tu fidem servaveris.

On the construction of this Concessive Conjunction, see below, 5.

haud (Sigismund: de 'haud' negationis apud priscos scriptores usu (in Commentationes philologicae Jenenses, Leipzig, 1883). On its use, see below, 8.

idcirco (Pradel 'de praeposit.' p. 498).

igitur 'then' is (like *quoniam*) temporal or logical, e.g. Mil. 772 quando habebo, igitur rationem mearum fabricarum dabo (like 810 ego enim dicam tum quando usus poscet), Most. 637 A. quid eo est argento factum? B. salvum est. A. solvite vosmet igitur, si salvumst. In its temporal sense it is often strengthened by temporal Adverbs like *tum*, e.g. Most. 132 unum ubi emeritumst stipendium, igitur tum specimen cernitur, *demum*, e.g. Most. 380 miserum est opus igitur demum fodere puteum, ubi sitis fauces tenet; in its logical sense, by *ergo*, e.g. Most. 848 ergo intro eo igitur sine perductore.

immo (P. Specht: de 'immo' particulae apud priscos scriptores usu. Jena, 1904) is confirmative, not corrective, in a line like Pers. 721 A. nam te sensi sedulo mihi dare bonam operam. B. tibin ego? immo sedulo (*A*: serio *ut vid. P.*). On *immo si scias*, see below, s.v. 'si' (cf. *immo si audias* Bacch. 698, Epid. 451).

ita (Th. Braune: Observationes .. ad usum 'ita' 'sic' 'tam' ('tamen') 'adeo' particularum Plautinum ac Terentianum. Berlin, 1882) is cognate with the Pron. *is* and stands in the same relation to *sic* as *is* to *hic*[p]. Thus with Verbs of saying, *ita* precedes an Oratio Obliqua, *sic* an Oratio Recta, e.g. Pseud. 596 mi ita dixit erus meus miles, septumas esse aedis a porta (with *ita*), Asin 352 sic hoc

[p] *Ut* is the correlative of *ita* as *qui* of *is*, e.g. *ita ut occepi* Trin. 897, etc., 'as I was saying,' the formula for resuming after an interruption. On *sicut* see below.

respondit mihi: 'ego pol Sauream non novi' (with *sic*). The relationship is clearly shewn in a sentence of the Trinummus, vv. 233 sqq. nisi ('but') hoc sic faciam opinor, ut utramque rem simul exputem, iudex sim reusque ad eam rem. ita (sc. id) faciam, ita placet. *Ita* seems to be wrongly used for *sic* in a line like Bacch. 385, where the exposition follows. *Ita* is, like *etiam*, used for 'yes,' e.g. Mil. 1262 A. militem pol tu aspexisti? B. ita. Presumably this stands for *ita est* (see **V. 8**, on the omission of *est*). We find also *sic* for 'yes,' e.g. Ter. Phorm. 813 A. illa maneat? B. sic; also *sic est*, e.g. Ter. Haut. 242.

Itane? 'actually?' is common in indignant remonstrance and the like, e.g. Poen. 557 itane? temptas an sciamus? Rud. 747 itane, impudens? tune hic, feles virginalis, liberos parentibus sublectos habebis? (see Seyffert in Bursian's Jahresbericht 18, 976).

Terence does not follow Plautus in allowing *ita* with an Adj. or Adv., but only *tam* (Adelph. 984 the better reading). *Ita* (perhaps never 'nam ita;' see Langen 'Beiträge,' p. 232) often introduces the reason for a previous statement, e.g. Bacch. 12 Praenestinum opino esse; ita erat gloriosus, Mil. 158. We find *itaque* with this function in lines like Pers. 505 neque istoc redire his octo possum mensibus, itaque hic est quod me detinet negotium, although this use has been questioned (see Bosscher: de Plauti Curculione. Leyden (diss.), 1903, p. 47). It finds a parallel in *nam* and *namque* (see below).

nam, like *enim*, has an asseverative sense, but is not so far removed from the classical use, (see Spengel's note on Ter. Ad. 15), e.g. Mil. 1325 nam ('indeed') nil miror si lubenter, Philocomasium, hic eras (confirming P.'s previous remark), Men. 537 A. ubi illae armillae sunt, quas una dedi? B. numquam dedisti. A. nam ('true') pol hoc unum dedi.

It often introduces a particular instance of a general statement, e.g. Trin. 25, where it is misinterpreted by Cicero (following the Auctor ad Herennium 2, 35):

> amicum castigare ob meritam noxiam
> immoene est facinus; .. nam ('for instance') ego amicum
>   hodie meum concastigabo.

Cicero in his youthful work on Rhetoric (de Invent. 1, 95) cites this as an example of a false syllogism.

Similarly it follows a threat in lines like Asin. 130 at malo cum tuo ; nam iam ex hoc loco ibo ego ad tresviros.

In his note on Ter. Ad. prol. 15 nam quod isti dicunt malevoli, homines nobilis eum adiutare, where Terence passes on to a new point in his rival's indictment of him, Donatus remarks: 'nam' incipiendi vim habet modo. On *uti-nam*, see below.

nam, the Interrogative Particle, often appears in Tmesis, e.g. Amph. 592 quo id, malum, pacto potest nam?, Mil. 924 num ille te nam novit? The Interrogative and Asseverative uses can hardly be discriminated in lines like Most. 368 A. quid ego ago? B. nam quid tu, malum, me rogitas quid agas? accubas, Aul. 42 sqq. nam cur me miseram verberas ? . . . nam qua me nunc causa extrusisti ex aedibus? On *quia-nam* 'why?' see below; on *ecquidnam*, 7, below.

namque, used only before an initial vowel in the Dramatists (except Ennius Trag. 370 R. namque regnum suppetebat mi), is strengthened by *enim* in Trin. 61 namque enim tu, credo, me imprudentem obrepseris. Like *nam* it confirms a previous remark in lines like Capt. 604 A. istinc loquere, siquid vis, procul. tamen audiam. B. namque edepol, si adbites.propius, os denasabit tibi.

nĕ (on Affirmative -*ne* see M. Warren : On the Enclitic 'ne' in Early Latin, in American Journal of Philology, vol. II) like *nam* is used asseveratively and interrogatively. (On Interrogative -*nĕ*, see below, 7.) Its asseverative use is most frequent in an answer like *tune* 'yes you' to a question like *egone?*, e.g. Stich. 635 A. egone? B. tune. A. mihine? B. tibine, Pers. 220 A. itane est? B. itane est.

If it were confined to such cases, it might be explained as a mere comic repetition, like that of *autem* in Stich. 733 (quoted above, s.v.), or like Pers. 212 A. heia! B. beia!, Pseud. 235 A. at—B. bat!

But it is found in other collocations, e.g. Epid. 541 plane hicinest, Mil. 309 hoccine si miles sciat, credo hercle has sustollat aedes totas atque hunc in crucem, Ter. Heaut. 950 sed Syrum quidem egone, si vivo, adeo exornatum dabo. We must therefore admit the occasional asseverative use of this Particle, although the limits of its use are not easy to define. The Latin Grammarians talk of a 'confirmativa particula *ne*' in lines like Hor. Sat. 1, 10, 21 o seri studiorum quine putetis ; and in Glossaries we find *nĕ* glossed by *ergo*. But *ergo* is also offered as a gloss of *an* in Virg. Ecl. 3, 21 an mihi cantando victus non redderet ille?, a sentence which is unmistakeably a question, so that all that can be meant is that this question is tantamount to an explanatory statement. Since Interrogative *-ně* is often used by Plautus in the sense of *nonne* (see below, 7,) there are many lines of this kind in Plautus; e.g. Merc. 588 sumne ego homo miser?, 'am I not unlucky?,' is of course tantamount to the statement 'well, I am unlucky!' But one is unwilling to recognise here, instead of the familiar Interrogative *-ně*, the unfamiliar Affirmative *-ně*. To substitute *nē* (*nae*) for *-ně* in all examples of the Affirmative use is impossible. Donatus in his note on Ter. Andr. prol. 17 (faciuntne intellegendo ut nihil intellegant?) says: 'NE quidam corripiunt et cum interrogatione pronuntiant: quidam producunt, quorum alii 'ne' pro 'nonne' accipiunt, id est 'non,' alii 'ne' pro 'valde.' But, not to speak of the awkwardness in the postposition of *nē* (*nae*), we often find the reduced form *n*, e.g. Ter. Adelph. 770 tun si meus esses (cf. Haut. 217), which could not be replaced by *nē*. (For statistics of affirmative *-ně*, see Mulvany, Class. Rev. 9, 15.) On negative *ně* of *nequeo* (beside *non queo*, etc.), see below, 8.

nē, in O. Lat. also *nei* (*nī*), e.g. Most. 924 niquid committam tibi. Noticeable is the use of *ne etiam* 'not even,' e.g. Most. 423 ut ne etiam aspicere aedes audeat, *ne* (not 'neve[q]') . . *neve* (*nive*, e.g. Poen. 38), e.g. Trin. 314 sqq., *ne non*, e.g. Cas. 575 metuo ne non sit surda atque haec audiverit. *Neque* . . *neque* (see below) can play the part of *ne* . . *neu*, e.g. Ter. Heaut. 975 nec tu aram tibi nec precatorem pararis. Beside *ut ne*, we find *qui ne*, e.g. incert. com. 47 haud facilest defensu qui ne comburantur proximae, (more likely *quī nē* than *quī ně*, i.e. *quin*).

nedum 'much less' is unknown to Plautus (cf. Amph. 330 vix incedo inanis, ne ire posse cum onere existumes), who however appends the Particle *dum* to *ne* in lines like Mil. 431 ne dum quispiam nos vicinorum imprudentis aliquis immutaverit. Terence's Comedies offer one instance, Heaut. 454 satrapa si siet amator, numquam sufferre eius sumptus queat; nedum tu possis.

neque, *nec*. On the O. Lat. use of *nec* for *non*, e.g. *nec recte dicere*, see 8. The Copula sometimes unites clauses which are not strictly connected in sense, so that it is hardly distinguishable from this O. Lat. use, e.g. Rud. 359 O Neptune lepide, salve! nec te aleator nullus est sapientior, Aul. 206 (see Leo's note for more examples). We find *neque* for *neu*, especially when preceded by another *neque*, e.g.

[q] Editors correct Trin. 293 ne[u] colas neve inbuas ingenium.

Syntax of Plautus.

Bacch. 476 neque amat nec tu creduas, Men. 221? neque defiat neque supersit. The classical use of *neque* . . *et* is also Plautine, e.g. Rud. 1083 hoc neque isti usust et illi miserae suppetias feret, Cist. 691. On the Double Negative *neque* . . *haud*, etc., see below, 8.

In *necne*, the Indirect Disjunctive Interrogative, the O. Lat. use of *nec* for *non* survives (cf. *annon*). The first member of the sentence has either no Interrogative Particle or else *-ně*, e.g. Capt. 713 emitteresne necne eum servum manu? (like the more frequent *annon*, e.g. Capt. 846 iuben an non iubes?)

nempe becomes before an initial consonant *nemp*. For instances of *nempe ergo*, e.g. Ter. Andr. 195, see Skutsch 'Plautinische Forschungen' I, p. 38.

nimirum. The genesis of this Conjunction is revealed in the pages of Plautus. He uses various phrases with *mirum est* (usually without *est*) or *mira sunt* (see below, under 'si'), especially (1) with *si* in Negative and Interrogative Sentences (but also Cas. 191), e.g. Truc. 305 nil mirum—vetus est maceria—lateres si veteres ruunt, (2) with *nisi* or *ni*, in Affirmative Sentences, e.g. Amph. 319 mirum ni hic me quasi murenam exdorsuare cogitat. Of these Terence recognises only *mirum* (1) with *si* (but also Andr. 651), (2) with *ni*, e.g. Andr. 598 A. ubi nunc est ipsus? B. mirum ni domist. A variation of the expression appears occasionally in Plautus, once *nisi mirumst* (Pseud. 1213 tu, nisi mirumst, leno, plane perdidisti mulierem), once *ni mirum* (Aul. 393 ni mirum, occidor nisi ego intro huc propere propero currere. Terence recognizes only *ni mirum* or, as we may believe him to have written, *nimirum*, a single word, Eun. 508 nimirum dabit haec Thais mihi magnum malum, 268, 784. The omission of *est* is affected also by *mirum* when joined with *quin*. *Mirum quin* (with Subj.) is ironical, e.g. Trin. 495 mirum quin tu illo tecum divitias feras 'you could hardly take your wealth with you to the grave,' Rud 1393 (see Sonnenschein's note).

nisi (older *ně-si*, like ně-queo, ně-fas, etc.) and *ni* (older *nei*; see O. Brugmann: über den Gebrauch des condicionalem 'ni' in der älteren Latinität. Leipzig, 1887) are usually interchangeable. But in wagers (see below, 5) only *ni* is found; on the other hand, only *nisi* in that curious O. Lat. use of the word in the sense of 'sed.' This use seems to have originated in the phrase *nihil scio nisi hoc (scio)*, e.g. Rud. 750 quae patria sit profecto nescio, nisi scio probiorem hanc esse, for the Apodosis normally consists of *nescio* or some similar Negative Verb in 1 Sing. Pres. Ind., Cist. 676

ubi ea sit nescio, nisi, ut opinor, loca haec circiter mi excidit. Extensions of this normal use are, e.g. Aul. 364 quos pol ut ego hodie servem cura maxumast : nisi unum hoc faciam, ut in puteo cenam coquant, Epid. 265 mihi istic nec seritur nec metitur : nisi ea quae tu vis volo, Mil. 24 me sibi habeto, ego me mancupio dabo : nisi unum ('but there's one consideration'): epityra estur insanum bene (cf. Most. 278 quid olant nescias, nisi id unum, ut male olere intellegas.) The class. Lat. use of *nisi* for *praeter* is as old as Plautus, e.g. Rud. 970 dominus huic, ne frustra sis, nisi ego nemo natust. For the ironical *nisi forte* (e.g. Most. 941 nisi forte factu's praefectus novus) we sometimes find *nisi* alone, e.g. Amph. 901 sic est, vera praedico : nisi etiam hoc falso dici insimulaturus es, and *nisi si*, e g. Most. 769 nec mi umbra hic usquamst, nisi si in puteo quaepiamst. The pleonastic formation *nisi si* (cf. *quasi si, nemo homo*, IV. 21) conveys, like the similar Greek formation εἰ μὴ εἰ, an additional suggestion of uncertainty. It is formed on the type of *nisi ut*, (e.g. Pseud. 1102 A. sed quis hic homo est chlamydatus ? B. non edepol scio, nisi ut observemus quo eat aut quam rem gerat), *nisi quod* (e.g. Pers. 517 ego tantundem scio quantum tu, nisi quod pellegi prior), and the more frequent *nisi quia* (e.g. Pers. 545 iuxta tecum aeque scio, nisi quia specie quidem edepol liberalist, quisquis est). The substitution of *si* for *ut* or *quod* or *quia* adds a fresh element of doubt. (For additional examples of *nisi quod, nisi quia* see Schmalz in Berliner Philologische Wochenschrift 25, 557.) On *quidni, quippini*, see below.

non (older *noenum*; see 8, below).

nonne (cf. *anne*, above) is appropriate before an initial vowel, while *non* (cf. *an*) is used interrogatively before consonant or vowel, e.g. Amph. 407 non loquor, non vigilo, nonne hic homo modo me pugnis contudit ? (See below, 7).

num (see 7).

postquam and *priusquam*. (On their use in Temporal Sentences, see 10, below.)

postquam (often in Tmesis, e.g. Truc. 647 post illuc quam veni) is more or less of a Causal Conjunction in lines like Capt. 487 abeo ab illis postquam video me sic ludificarier, Ter. Phorm. prol. 1 postquam poeta vetus poetam non potest retrahere a studio . . maledictis deterrere . . parat.

priusquam, the opposite of *posterius quam* (Asin. 63 posterius istuc dicis quam credo tibi), often in Tmesis, e.g. Rud. 626, Mil.

1096, Most. 326, is the Plautine Conjunction for 'before.' *Antequam* is once found in Terence (Hec. 146), but not in Plautus. In Cato's prose both *priusquam* and *antequam* are in equal use.

praequam is formed like *prae quod*, Stich. 362 immo res omnes relictas habeo, prae quod tu velis. Cf. also *advorsum quam*, Trin. 176 utrum indicare me ei thensaurum aequom fuit, advorsum quam eius me obsecravisset pater? 'contrary to his father's entreaties.' Its use may be illustrated from Most. 982 nihil hoc quidem est, triginta minae, praequam alios dapsiles sumptus facit, 1146 iam minoris omnia alia facio, prae quam quibus modis me ludificatust. In Merc. 23 (from the prologue, and therefore possibly post-Plautine) it is used in the sense of *praeterquam* (see below) :

nec pol profecto quisquam sine grandi malo
praequam res patitur studuit elegantiae.

Similar is *praeut*, e.g. Mil. 20 nihil hercle hoc quidemst praeut alia dicam—quae tu numquam feceris, Amph. 374 A. perii ! B. parum etiam, praeut futurum est, praedicas, Men. 376.

praeterquam (Lalin : de particularum comparativarum usu apud Terentium. Norrcopiae, 1894) had not yet become crystallized into a single word at the time of the Dramatists, as we see from, e.g. Ter. Heaut. 59 quod mihi videre praeter aetatem tuam facere et praeter quam res te adhortatur tua, Plaut. Pers. 366 quae praeter sapiet quam placet parentibus. We have *praeter quam quod* in Ter. Heaut. 399 nam dum abs te absum, omnes mihi labores fuere quos cepi leves, praeter quam tui carendum quod erat.

proin, proinde. The theory is wrong, that these two words had different functions, *proin* being used in commands, e.g. *proin tu hoc audi,* and *proinde* in comparisons, e.g. *proinde atque hoc.* The two words are really the same ; *proin* is the preconsonantal, *proinde* the prevocalic doublet (like our 'a' and 'an'). An example of *proinde* in a command, when prevocalic, is Asin. 27 proinde actutum . . eloquere. (See Skutsch 'Forschungen' I, 82.)

propterea (see Reissinger : die Präpositionem 'ob' und 'propter.' Part. I, Landau, 1897, p. 75).

qua—qua (see below, 6).

quam is sometimes enclitically appended in Adverbial sense, e.g. *nimis quam* (Most. 511 etc.), *admodum quam* (Amph. 541 etc.), *perquam*. Comparative *quam* often lacks the leading word, e.g. Men. 726 non, inquam, patiar praeterhac, quin vidua vivam quam (*i.e.* potius quam) tuos mores perferam (cf. Cas. 256, Poen. 747), Rud. 1114 eo tacent, quia tacita bonast mulier semper quam loquens, Rud. 943 non edepol pisces expeto quam (*i.e.* tam quam) tui sermonis sum indigens. It is omitted after *plus*, *minus*, etc., in phrases like Pers. 21 plusculum annum 'for rather more than a year,' Trin. 402 minus quindecim dies sunt 'it is less than a fortnight,' Stich. 160 plus annos decem 'for over ten years.' On the Pleonasm *ut . . quam* in Exclamations, e.g. Stich. 570 ut apologum fecit quam fabre!, see below, s.v. 'ut.'

quamobrem or rather *quam ob rem*, with the same arrangement as *qua de re*, e.g. Poen. 317, etc., is hardly yet crystallized into a Conjunction (see Reissinger: die Präpositionem 'ob' und 'propter.' Part I. Landau, 1897, p. 22). To the redundancy of colloquial speech (cf. I, 11) we may ascribe the abnormal expression in Ter. Andr. 382 invenerit aliquam causam quam ob rem eiciat. Or we may recognize in it a symptom that the phrase was becoming a mere equivalent of *cur*. Cf. *quare* (below).

quamquam and *quamvis* (see 4).

quando. (P. Scherer: de particulae 'quando' apud vetustissimos scriptores Latinos vi et usu, in vol. II. of Studemund's 'Studien auf dem Gebiete des archäischen Lateins.' Berlin, 1891.) The Temporal (see 10) and Causal (see 3) senses may be illustrated from a passage of the Persa, 638 sq. tanquam hominem, quando animam efflavit, quid eum quaeras qui fuit? . . . dico equidem: quando hic servio, haec patriast mea. As an Interrogative, or with *expecto*, etc., the word is seldom used by Plautus and Terence, e.g. Curc. 212 quando ego te videbo?, Ter. Eun. 697. They prefer *quam mox*, e.g. Truc. 208 quam mox te huc recipis?, Mil. 1406 quam mox seco?, Mil. 304 insidias dabo quam mox . . . recipiat se, Ter. Phorm. 161 dum expecto quam mox veniat, Ennius Ann. 86 V. omnes avidi exspectant ad carceris oras, quam mox emittat pictis e faucibus currus. (For details see Seyffert in Berliner Philologische Wochenschrift, 18, p. 1350. The Present, not the Future, is used with *quam mox*.) Like *siquando* is *ubi quando* in Capt. 290 genio suo ubi quando sacruficat, . . Samiis vasis utitur. The addition of *quidem* forms the Causal Conjunction *quandŏquidem*, e.g. Stich. 483, Merc. 180, Ter. Andr. 487.

quapropter, sometimes in Tmesis, e.g. Amph. 815 quid ego feci qua istaec propter dicta dicantur mihi?, is like our 'where-for(e)' an example of the addition of a Preposition to a Particle, in order to give it definiteness and precision (see above, s.v. 'adeo').

quare, or rather *qua re*, is, like *quoi rei* (Poen. 479), found in Plautus only once, Epid. 597 A. quibus de signis agnoscebas? B. nullis. A. qua re filiam credidisti nostram?

quasi (Lalin : de particularum comparativarum usu apud Terentium. Norrcopiae, 1894) is apparently a similar shortening of *quam si*[1] as *siquidem* of *si quidem*. Plautus uses *quăsi* and *quam si* indiscriminately, e.g. Amph. 1078 nec secus est quasi si ab Accherunte veniam, Capt. 273 nec mihi secus erat quam si essem familiaris filius. He does not restrict the Conjunction to imaginary comparisons; thus we find, e.g. Capt. 80 quasi, quom caletur, cocleae in occulto latent, Asin. 178 quasi piscis, itidemst amator lenae : nequam est, nisi recens, Pseud. 199 quasi Dircam olim, Rud. 1008 itidem quasi peniculus novus exurgeri solet.

In these comparisons of fact it is the equivalent of *quemadmodum*, and takes the Ind., the Mood of fact. It has the sense of *fere* in lines like Capt. 20 quasi una aetas erat 'they were of about the same age,' 286 videlicet propter divitias inditum id nomen quasi est, Most. 623 quasi quadraginta minas.

The usual Sequence of Tenses with *quasi* ' as if' is departed from in lines like Ter. Phorm. 382 proinde expiscare quasi non nosses (cf. Phorm. 388, Heaut. 527).

Quasi si (e.g. Cas. 46 quasi si esset ex se nata, non multo secus), *quasi quom* (e.g. Ter. Adelph. 739 ita vitast hominum quasi quom ludas tesseris), *quasi ubi* (e.g. Ter. Eun. 406 quasi ubi illam exspueret miseriam ex animo) may also be mentioned. *Quasi si* may be compared with *nisi si* (see above).

-que (see below, 6) may be appended to a word ending in *-ĕ*, e.g. Trin. 76 ut te videre audireque aegroti sient.

quemadmodum, or rather *quem ad modum* (cf. quemnam ad modum? Bacch. 190), illustrates the common arrangement of Relative, Preposition, Noun (cf. quod ad exemplum est? Trin. 921, *quamobrem*, etc.). It is an equivalent of *quomodo*, e.g. Mil. 884 tibi dixi miles quem ad modum potesset deasciari, Pers. 35, and exhibits that use of *ad* to denote comparisons or similitude (see **VII, 2**) seen in phrases like Merc. 428 ad illam faciem 'of that appearance;' cf. ad eundem modum Ter. Adelph. 424, ad istunc modum Bacch. 749, ad exemplum Ter. Hec. 163, and the like.

---

[1] Cf. *tamquam si* Asin. 427 tamquam si claudus sim, cum fustist ambulandum, beside *tam quasi* Men. 1101 tam quasi me emeris argento, liber servibo tibi.

qui (O. Kienitz : de ' quî ' localis, modalis apud priscos scriptores Latinos usu, Leipzig, 1879), if really the old Instrumental Case, retains its original force in a line like Bacch. 84 mihi dicito ' dato qui bene sit :' ego ubi bene sit tibi locum lepidum dabo (qui ' the means,' ubi ' the place '). On its use as a Rel. Pron., see **IV, 6.** As a Conjunction it plays the part of *quomodo, quare*, e.g. Poen. 169 qui id facturu's? (cf. class. Lat. *qui fit ut* . . ?), often answered by *quia* (see below); of *utinam*, e.g. qui illum di perdant! (passim); of *ut*, e.g. Trin. 688 nolo ego mihi te tam prospicere qui meam egestatem leves, sed ut inops infamis ne sim, Amph. 339. It sinks to a mere Particle, like *quidem*, in such phrases as hercle qui, pol qui, etc. On *at qui, quippe qui*, see s.v. ' at,' s.v. ' quippe.' *Quidum* ' how so ? ' always forms a sentence by itself (see p. 96). ' Alioqui ' and ' ceteroqui ' are not found in O. Lat. writers.

quia, the 3 Decl. Neut. Plur., as *quid* is the 3 Decl. Neut. Sing. and *quod* is the 2 Decl. Neut Sing., has the sense of *quod* in a line like Pseud. 107 atque id futurum unde unde dicam nescio, nisi quia futurum est. It shews the Interrogative sense of *quid ?* in the Compound *quianam ?* (cf. *quidnam ?*) 'why?' used by Ennius and the Tragedians (cf. Virg. Aen. 10. 6), but not by the Comedians (see Langen ' Beiträge,' p. 325).

Although *quia* is normal after verbs of emotion, e.g. Capt. 203 at nos pudet quia cum catenis sumus, it is doubtful whether it is used after 'Verba Sentiendi et Declarandi,' for *nisi quia* in Pseud. 568 admits of another explanation (see below, s.v. ' quod'). On the use of *quia* as a Causal Conjunction, see below, 3.

quidem may be joined to *et* without an intervening word, e.g. Mil. 259 A. abeo. B. et quidem ego ibo domum. As illustrations of its ironical use take Bacch. 221 A. nam iam huc adveniet miles. B. et miles quidem !, Ter. Heaut. 606 A. mille nummum poscit. B. et poscit quidem ! (On *equidem* and *ego quidem*, see above.)

quidni, in which phrase (as in *quippini;* see below) *ni*[a] has the O. Lat. sense of *nē* or rather *non*, stands normally in Tmesis, e.g. Mil. 1120 A. itan tu censes? B. quid ego ni ita censeam?, Ter. Heaut. 529 A. scis esse factum ut dico? B. quid ego ni sciam?; but not, e.g. Mil. 923 populi odium quidni noverim, magnidicum, cincinnatum?, Ter. Phorm. 64 A. nostin? B. quidni?, 813 etc. Its

---

[a] Festus cites *quid nisi?* from Afranius 129,
A. me auctore, mater, abstinebis. B. quid nisi ?,
but does not say in what sense the phrase is used.

equivalent, *cur non*, is also frequent, e.g. Most. 209 A. . . quae istuc cures . . B. cur, obsecro, non curem?, Most. 454 A. eho! an tu tetigisti has aedis? B. cur non tangerem? *Quid*, as the equivalent of *cur*, e.g. Most. 419 sed quid tu egredere?, is merely an instance of that use of the Acc. Neut. Pron. with various verbs (e.g. Most. 786 quod me miseras ' the business on which you sent me ') discussed above, II, 35. The fuller phrase *quid est quod* is frequent, e.g. Most. 69 quid est quod tu me nunc obtuere, furcifer?, Men. 677 scin quid est quod ego ad te venio? (for other examples see Dittmar 'Moduslehre,' pp. 11 sqq.). The other uses of *quid* in Interrogations and Exclamations may be illustrated by Curc. 458 quid quod iuratus sum?, Ter. Phorm. 754 quid? duasne uxores habet?, Rud. 736 A. esse oportet liberas. B. quid, 'liberas'! (for more details see Seyffert in Berliner Philologische Wochenschrift, 1896, p. 816); and the combinations of *quid* with other Particles, by *quid ita?*, *quid iam?* (e.g. Mil. 473). On *quid si* see below, 5. On *quid istic?* see IV, 13.

quin (O. Kienitz: de 'quin' particulae apud priscos scriptores Latinos usu. Carlsruhe, 1878). The literal sense, quĭ-ne 'how not?' 'why not?,' appears clearly in lines like Trin. 291 quin prius me ad plures penetravi? 'why did I not make my way to the majority (i.e. the dead) before?' With 2 Sing., Plur. Pres. Ind. it has the force of a command, e.g. *quin taces?* And in this sense the Imperative was, by a laxity of usage, substituted for the Ind. in colloquial Latin, e.g. *quin tace*. Sometimes the two Moods stand side by side, e.g. Asin. 254 quin tu abs te socordiam omnem reice et segnitiem amove atque ad ingenium vetus vorsutum te recipis tuum?, Pseud. 891 quin tu is accubitum et convivas cedo, Most. 815 quin tu is intro atque otiose perspecta ut lubet. With 1 Sing. it has the force of an exhortation, e.g. *quin taceo?, quin tacemus?* Sometimes it takes the Dubitative Subj. e.g. Mil. 426 A. me rogas, homo, qui sim? B. quin ego hoc rogem, quod nesciam?

From this last it is but a step to the Conjunction expressing hindrance. For a sentence like *numquae causa est quin rogem?* might be expressed in Parataxis thus: *quin rogem? numquae causa est?* Amph. 559 tamen quin loquar haec, uti facta sunt hic, numquam ullo modo me potes deterrere, might be expressed with this punctuation :

    tamen quin loquar haec, uti facta sunt hic?
    numquam ullo modo me potes deterrere.

Of Plautus' use of this Conjunction of hindrance the following examples are noteworthy :

> Curc. 164 adsum ; nam si absim, haud recusem quin mihi male sit.
> Men. 725 non, inquam, patiar praeterhac, quin vidua vivam quam (*i.e.* potius quam) tuos mores perferam (cf. Ter. Heaut. 763).
> Amph. 1106 non metuo quin meae uxori latae suppetiae sient.
> Most. 329 si cades, non cades quin cadam tecum.
> Mil. 1194 triduom servire numquam te quin liber sis sinam.
> Bacch. 1012 nihil est illorum quin (= quod non) ego illi dixerim.

In the corroborative use also of *quin* the literal sense 'how not?' is clearly apparent, e.g. Capt. 1017 A. quid tu ais? adduxtin illum huius captivum filium? B. quin, inquam, intus hic est 'why! I tell you, he's inside here.' In this use *quin* is often strengthened by a Particle like *etiam, edepol, hercle,* e.g. Poen. 706 quin hercle accipere tu non mavis quam ego dare.

Editors change *hercle quin* of the MSS. in Men. 428 (cf. Men. 1092, Trin. 464) to *hercle qui* and *atquin* of the MSS. in Rud. 760 to *atqui*, probably rightly. On *quin(e)* for 'isne qui' (cf. Hor. Sat. 2, 10, 20, o seri studiorum, quine putetis, etc.), e.g. Trin. 360 quin comedit, quod fuit, quod non fuit? 'what! the man who devoured?', Most. 738 A. ventus navem nostram deseruit... B. quaen subducta erat tuto in terra?, see IV, 6.

quippe. From Cicero's *quippe qui*[†] (Nom. Sing.), used normally with Subj., we must distinguish Plautus' *quippe qui* (cf. above, s.v. 'qui'), e.g. Amph. 745 quippe qui audivi (said by Alcmena), Aul. 348 horum tibi istic nihil eveniet, quippe qui ubi quid subripias nihil est. We have also *quippe quando*, e.g. Capt. 886 A. vae aetati— B. tuae; quippe quando mihi nil credis, *quippe quom*, e.g. Rud. 979 quippe quom extemplo in macellum pisces prolati sient, nemo emat, as well as *quippe qui* (in various cases), e.g. Epid. 618 A. habe bonum animum. B. quippe ego quoi libertas in mundo sitast (cf. Pseud. 1275).

Quippini (like *quidni;* see above) 'why not?,' e.g. Men. 948 A. itane censes? B. quippini?, is as rare with a Verb (e.g. Pseud. 917

[†] On Plautus' *qui quidem* with Subj. in the function of *quippe qui*, see V, 30 *n.*

A. nimis tandem ego abs te contemnor. B. quippe ego te ni contemnam?) as *quidni* is rare without a Verb (e.g. Truc. 726 A. nostin tu hunc Strabacem? B. quidni?).

quo and *quominus*:

quo for *ut* is normal in class. Lat. when there is a Comparative in the sentence (cf. *quominus* with *minus* for *non*, as in Mil. 876 minus si tenetis, 603 si minus cum cura aut cautela locus loquendi lectus est).

In Plautus both *quo* and *quī*, the Abl. and Instr. Cases, are unrestricted in this function, e.g. Epid. 289 quo illum ab illa prohibeas. And *ut* is freely used with a Comparative, e.g. Cist. 636 quae mihi dedit, parentes te ut cognoscant facilius (cf. v. 714 qui suos Selenium parentes facilius posset noscere, Aul. 33 quo .. facilius), Capt. 33, Accius 598 ut curentur diligentius, Aul. 595 quasi pueri qui nare discunt scirpea induitur ratis, qui laborent minus, facilius ut nent et moveant manus.

From *quominus* (in Tmesis, e.g. Amph. 84 quive quo placeret alter fecisset minus) we must distinguish *quo minus*, e.g. in the phrase *quo dixi minus* 'as I omitted to say' (Capt. 430; cf. Amph. 479, Merc. 24), Stich. 162 quo minus laboris cepisse illam existumo (see I, 1).

quoad, i.e. *quo-ad* (with the same postposition of the Prep., as in *quapropter*, etc.; see VII, 1) appears in Afranius as *adquo* 278 ut scire possis adquo te expediat loqui, 248 ni tantum amarem talem tam merito patrem, iratus essem adquo liceret. It is the Relative equivalent of *adeo* 'to that point,' 'to that extent,' and has hardly yet become a Temporal Conjunction in Plautus' time, Asin. 296 quoad vires valent ('to the full extent of my power'), Men. 769 verum est modus tamen quoad pati uxorem oportet, Pseud. 623 nam olim, quom abiit, argento haec dies praestitutast, quoad referret nobis, neque dum rettulit. The view that *quŏd* of *quod possum*, *quod potui*, etc., was pronounced *quōd* and was a contraction of *quoad* is now generally abandoned.

quod. The passage of the Neut. Sing. Pron. into a Conj. may be illustrated by these lines:

>   Epid. 131 empta ancillast, quod ('as') tutĕ ad me litteras
>   missiculabas.
>   Pseud. 639 ut id agam quod missus huc sum (see II, 35).
>   Rud. 1258 illuc est quod ('why') nos nequam servis utimur

(cf. Cas. 460; *quid istuc est quod*, Capt. 541; and often *hoc est (erat) quod* 'this is the reason (the meaning) of,' e.g. Merc. 711 pol hoc est ire quod rus meus vir noluit, Cas. 531, Men. 1135, Asin. 863).

Merc. 502 quin tibi quidem quod rideas magis est quam ut lamentere (cf. Aul. 203).

Capt. 586 filium tuum quod ('whereas,' 'that') redimere se ait, id ne utiquam mihi placet.

Capt. 996 quod male feci crucior.

Aul. 91 quod ('if') quispiam ignem quaerat, extingui volo (cf. Mil. 162).

Capt. 670 quod (= quantum, quoad) in te uno fuit (cf. Mil. 1160 quod ego potero).

Most. 303 certe ego, quod te amo ('in loving you'), operam nusquam melius potui ponere.

Capt. 621 neque mi esse ullum morbum, nisi quod servio. (On *nisi quod*, see above, s.v.)

Ter. Eun. 926 nam ut mittam quod ('the fact that') . . eam confeci sine molestia.

Ter. Phorm. 168 ut ne addam quod sine sumptu ingenuam, liberalem nactus es.

That the later use of *quod* with Finite Verb, instead of Acc. and Inf., is found in Plautus is very doubtful. The apparent instances are: Mil. 893 dum nescientes quod bonum faciamus, ne formida (quod = aliquod?), Asin. 52 equidem scio iam filius quod amet meus (*v.l.* quid, *v.l.* amat. Plautus uses *quod amat* = *amica*), and to these some add Truc. 383, Poen. 1374, Most. 691, Bacch. 1009, Poen. 547 (see Thulin 'de coniunctivo Plautino' p. 138; Schmalz in Berliner Philologische Wochenschrift 25, 557).

Quod, used as in Aul. 91, Mil. 162 (just quoted), approaches the sense of 'although' in lines like Rud. 1150 si hercle tantillum peccassis, quod posterius postules te ad verum convorti, nugas, mulier, magnas egeris, Ter. Eun. 1063 miles, edico tibi, si te in platea offendero hac post unquam, quod dicas mihi 'alium quaerebam, iter hac habui,' periisti, Andr. 395 nam quod tu speres (*v.l.* speras) 'propulsabo facile uxorem his moribus, dabit nemo,' inveniet inopem potius quam te corrumpi sinat.

Quodsi is found in Terence (e.g. Andr. 258 quod si ego rescivissem id prius, Eun. 924 quod si astu rem tractavit), but probably not in Plautus (for *quod* may be the Relative in Cist. 152 quod si tacuisset, tamen ego eram dicturus).

quom is generally regarded as an old Neut. Sing. of the Relative. It plays the same part as *quod* in sentences like the formula for congratulating a slave after manumission, *quom tu es liber gaudeo* (Epid. 711, Men. 1031, 1149), Bacch. 338 (with *istuc* as antecedent) istuc sapienter saltem fecit filius, quom (quod *alii*) diviti homini id aurum servandum dedit. On Causal *quom*, see below, 3; on Temporal *quom*, 10; on Concessive *quom*, 4.

quomodo, or rather *quo modo*, like *quo pacto, qua arte*, etc., has hardly yet crystallized into a mere Conjunction. (For details, see Ladyzynski: de quibusdam priscorum poetarum scaenicorum locutionibus, Leopoli, 1895; and see above on *quemadmodum*.)

quoniam (i.e. *quom iam;* like *etiam, nunciam*, etc.). On its Causal and Temporal uses, see below (3, 10).

quŏque, a word of uncertain etymology, is the equivalent of *etiam* (see above). The combination of these two Conjunctions produces (1) *quoque etiam*, emphasizing the preceding word, e.g. Amph. 717 et te quoque etiam, Sosia, Men. 1160 venibit uxor quoque etiam, (2) *etiam—quoque*, e.g. Most. 1110 immo etiam cerebrum quoque omne e capite emunxisti meo. In Asin. 184 *et quoque* is suspected by editors.

scilicet, a Compound of *scio*, in some form or other, with *licet*, retains the old construction of Acc. and Inf. (cf. *videlicet*, below) in lines like Asin. 787 ita scilicet facturam, Ter. Heaut. 856 scilicet daturum, 892 continuo iniecisse verba tibi Dromonem scilicet; but is also used parenthetically, e.g. Rud. 1098 continuo hunc novisse dicent scilicet, Asin. 490 A. tam ego homo sum quam tu. B. scilicet ('of course'): ita res est, Capt. 283 id Orcum scire oportet scilicet ('I suppose'), Ter. Eun. 346 comites secuti scilicet sunt virginem.

sed. Noteworthy is the use of this Particle to indicate a surprising discovery, e.g. *sed estne hic* . . .? (for examples, see Kaempf 'Pronomina Personalia,' p. 44), *sed eccum* (see Bach in Studemund's Studien, 2, 389), and similar phrases.

si. The use of this Conjunction as a Conditional 'if' is fully treated below, 5.

Si plays the part of *quod* or *quom* after verbs like *gaudeo, miror*, etc., and naturally takes the Ind. Mood. (By the time of Terence, *miror si* can be used like *miror an*, e.g. Ter. Andr. 175 mirabar hoc si sic abiret.) But there is always a different nuance with *si*, e.g. Poen. 1326 sqq. gaudeo et volup est mihi, si quid (*v.l.* quidem) lenoni obtigit magni mali, quomque e virtute vobis fortuna obtigit, where the *si*-clause is stated from information, the *quom*-clause from personal knowledge.

The Protasis of *mira sunt* (not used by Terence, though in Eun. 288 he uses *mira* for *mirum*, mira vero militi quae placeant) or *mirum* (rarely *mirum est*) is in the Ind., e.g. Pseud. 1216 mira sunt ni Pseudolust, Cas. 191 mira sunt vera si praedicas, Cas. 554 atque edepol mirum ni subolet iam hoc huic vicinae meae, Mil. 1041 ecastor haud mirum si te habes carum, Ter. Andr. 755 mirum vero, impudenter mulier si facit meretrix?, 598 mirum ni domist; similarly with *non miror*, etc., e.g. Amph. 29 mirari non est aequom, sibi si praetimet, Merc. 784 non miror, si quid damni facis aut flagiti, Pseud. 442 idne tu mirare, si patrissat filius? *Satis est, satis habeo*, etc., also have Ind. in the Protasis, e.g. Bacch. 911 satin est, si plura ex me audiet hodie mala?, Capt. 446 satin habes, mandata quae sunt facta si refero? Not unlike this is the use (with Ind. Mood) of *si*, 'if it is really the case that,' in lines like Most. 772 A. (aedes) inspicere volt. B. inspiciat, si lubet, Most. 636 A. salvomst. B. solvite vosmet igitur, si salvomst, Merc. 606 si neque hic neque Accherunti sum, ubi sum?, Truc. 748 si volebas participare, auferres dimidium domum. The causal force of this *si* is seen in the frequent use of *ergo, eo, igitur* in the Apodosis.

Si plays the part of *ut* (Final) after verbs like *exspecto*, and naturally takes the Subj. Mood, e.g. Trin. 98 exspecto si quid dicas (cf. Trin. 148 ausculto si quid dicas). *Si*, 'in the hope of,' is accompanied by *posse* in Subj. (except that 1 Sing. Ind. is used when present time is referred to), e.g. Mil. 1207 nam si possem ullo modo impetrare ut abiret nec te abduceret operam dedi, Men. 417 adsentabor, quidquid dicet, mulieri, si possum hospitium nancisci, Trin. 531 em istic oportet obseri mores malos, si in obserendo possint interfieri, Most. 837 at tu isto ad vos obtuere, quoniam cornicem nequis conspicari, si volturios forte possis contui. *Si* 'in case' takes Ind. in phrases like Pers. 611 adduco hanc, siquid vis ex hac percontarier. On *si* 'although' (cf *etsi*) in lines like Merc. 694 decem si vocasset summos ad cenam viros, nimium obsonavit, see below, 4. The phrase *si maxume*, an emphatic form of *si* (as *quom maxume* is of *quom*), is accompanied by the Ind. (e.g. Bacch. 1001 non dabis, si sapies; verum si das maxume, nae ille alium gerulum quaerat, si sapiet, sibi, Ter. Phorm. 295 verum si cognatast maxume, non fuit necesse habere) or the Subj. (e.g. Bacch. 1004 nam ego non laturus sum, si iubeas maxume, Ter. Adelph. 340 tum si maxumê fateatur, . . non est utile hanc illi dari) (see Seyffert in Berliner Philologische Wochenschrift 24, 140).

Si plays the part of *an* after verbs like *video, viso*, etc., and takes the Ind., just as Indirect Questions often do in Plautine Latin (cf. V, 28), e.g. Pers. 825 vide vero, si tibi satis placet, Cas. 591 viso huc, amator si a foro rediit domum.

Si, in the sense of 'si modo' (cf. *modo si* Amph. 646, Capt. 996), takes the Subj. (but Ind. in Poen. 915 proba materies datast, si probum adhibes fabrum), e.g. Capt. 850 scis bene esse, si sit unde, Curc. 299 recte hic monstrat, si imperare possit, Poen. 550 omnia istaec scimus iam nos, si hi spectatores sciant. In the Apodosis we often find *possum*, e.g. Cist. 308 adhinnire equolam possum ego hanc, si detur sola soli, Poen. 351 si sapias, curam hanc facere compendi potes. The Apodosis (cf. Mil. 1429 magis dicas, si scias, quod ego scio, Ter. Eun. 355) is suppressed with the phrase *immo si scias*, e.g. Cas. 668 immo si scias dicta quae dixit hodie!

Quid si takes the Ind. in a request for information, the Subj. in an exhortation to action, e.g. Asin. 537 quid si hic animus occupatust, mater, quid faciam? mone, Poen. 330 A. quid si adeamus? B. adeas.

On *quid nisi*, see above, s.v. 'quidni.'

Si—sive (seu) is the usual formula in Plaut. and Ter., e.g. Ter. Andr. 216 si ista uxor, sive amicast, not, as in classical Latin, 'sive (seu)—sive (seu).' Sometimes we find *si—si*, e.g. Rud. 1257 at ego deos quaeso ut, quidquid in illo vidulost, si aurum, si argentum est, omne id ut fiat cinis, Capt. 114.

Of the other associates of this Particle, *quodsi* and *ast* have been treated above; *sin* may be illustrated by Ter. Andr. 210 si illum relinquo, eius vitae timeo, sin opitulor, huius minas.

sic. (Th. Braune: Observationes . . . ad usum 'ita,' 'sic,' 'tam' ('tamen'), 'adeo' particularum Plautinum ac Terentianum. Berlin, 1882.) The O. Lat. alliterative (and etymological?) phrase *sic sinere* 'to let be' is frequent in Plautus, e.g. Pseud. 477, 1301, Aul. 524. But the use of *sic* in oaths, followed by *ut*, occurs only once, Poen. 869 Diespiter me sic amabit . . . ut ego hanc familiam interire cupio (cf. Ter. Heaut. 463), the usual phrase being *ita me di ament, ut*. On the distinction between *sic* and *ita* see above, s.v. 'ita.' *Sic* is associated with *hic, ita* with *is*, e.g. Merc. 268 nunc hoc profecto sic est (then follows the explanation), Cist. 147 haec sic res gesta est, Asin. 127 sicine hoc fit? foras aedibus me eici? Contrast Trin. 107 id ita esse ut credas (referring to a preceding statement), Ter. Eun. prol. 29 peccatum imprudentiast . . . id ita esse vos iam iudicare poteritis. But it would be dangerous to assert that in the colloquial Latin of the Dramatists *sic* and *ita* (like *hic* and *is*) were never under any circumstances interchanged (e.g. Rud. 399, Ter. Phorm. 536). On *sic* and *ita* in the sense of 'yes,' see above, s.v. 'ita.'

sicut, i.e. *sic ut* (cf. *ita ut*, s.v. 'ita,' above), often gives a particular instance or proof of a statement, e.g. Poen. 503 sqq. tardo amico nihil est quicquam nequius . . . sicut ego hos duco advocatos, homines spissigradissumos, and acquires the sense of 'seeing that,' 'since,' e.g. Mil. 974 quin tu illam iube abs te abire quo lubet; sicut soror eius huc gemina vēnit Ephesum et mater, accersuntque eam. (For other examples, see Langen 'Beiträge,' p. 249.)

simulac. Just as the Adj. *similis* is followed by *atque* or *ac* (e.g. Ter. Phorm. 31 ne simili utamur fortuna atque usi sumus), so the Adv. *simul* is followed by *atque* or *ac*, a combination found as early as Liv. Andr. (see below, 10). The rare use of *simul* alone, e.g. Ter. Phorm. 823 hic simul argentum repperit, cura sese expedivit, is due to Parataxis. For *simul ut* may be cited Titinius 50 simul ut pueras hac (*v.l.* has) nocte suspirare crevi.

tam. (Th. Braune: Observationes . . . ad usum 'ita,' 'sic,' 'tam' ('tamen'), 'adeo' particularum Plautinum ac Terentianum. Berlin, 1882.) The following examples are noteworthy:

>Mil. 457 tam east quam potis nostra erilis concubina.
>Stich. 295 tam gaudium grande adfero.
>Pers. 533 numquam ego te tam esse matulam credidi.
>Mil. 741 nam hospes nullus tam in amici hospitium devorti potest
>>quin, ubi triduum continuum fuerit, iam odiosus siet.
>Mil. 901 quis hic, amabo, est qui tam pro nota nominat me?
>Mil. 1246 tam mulier se ut amaret.

Also the use of *non tam—quam* in the comparison of ideas or actions, e.g. Cas. 429 atque id non tam aegrest iam, vicisse vilicum, quam id expetivisse opere tam magno senem; sometimes *non tam—sed*, e.g. Mil. 851 non hercle tam istoc ('on that account') valide cassabant cadi, sed in cella erat paulum nimis loculi lubrici.

In Mil. 11 we should read (with the MSS.) tum bellatorem—Mars haud ausit dicere neque aequiperare suas virtutes ad tuas, not (with Bothe) 'tam b. M. se h.'

In *tametsi* (also *tamenetsi*) *tam* seems to play the part of *tamen*; and the same may perhaps be said of Merc. 33 :

> quae nihil attingunt ad rem nec sunt usui,
> tam amator profert saepe advorso tempore.

(cf. Festus 360 M. antiqui 'tam' pro 'tamen' usi sunt, with examples from Naevius, Ennius and Titinius, e.g. Titin. 157 quamquam estis nihili, tam ecastor simul vobis consului, where it is put in antithesis to *quamquam* 'although'.)

Similarly *tamendem* is used by Plautus, as well as *tandem*, in lines like Mil. 585 verum tamendem, quidquid est, ibo hinc domum, Merc. 595 sed tamendem, si podagrosis pedibus esset Eutychus, iam a portu rediisse potuit. We may add Ter. Andr. 520 postremo id mihi da negoti, tu tamendem (tamen idem *MSS.*) has nuptias perge facere (cf. Titinius 58). *Tam gratiast*, 'much obliged to you all the same,' the polite formula used in declining an offer (e.g. Stich. 472), is by some explained as 'tamen gratia est,' by others on the pattern of Hor. Epp. 1, 7, 18 tam teneor dono quam si dimittar onustus.

tamen (H. Karsten: de particulae 'tamen' significatione antiquissima ad Ciceronis fere tempora in latinitate conservata, in Mnemosyne 18, pp. 307 sqq.; read with it Seyffert's review in Bursian's Jahresbericht, 1895, p, 318).

Plautus' use of *tamen* does not differ from Cicero's. Noteworthy is his predilection for putting the word at the end of the line, e.g. Mil. 306 si indicium facio, interii; interii, si taceo, tamen, Epid. 516 abiero : flagitio cum maiore post reddes tamen.

tamquam (Lalin: de particularum comparativarum usu apud Terentium. Norrcopiae, 1894), i.e. *tam quam*, e.g. Trin. 913 A. vide modo ut hominem noveris! B. tamquam me, Epid. 504 A. sed tu novisti fidicinam Acropolistidem? B. tam facile quam me. On *tam quasi* for *tamquam si*, see above, s.v. 'quasi.'

ubi. On its use in Temporal Clauses, see below, 10.

ut (fuller form *uti*) (H. Schnoor: zum Gebrauch von 'ut' bei Plautus. Neumünster, (progr.) 1885).

To express wishes the Conjunction is strengthened by *nam* in class. Lat., *utinam* (cf. *quisnam* beside *quis*), but we find in O. Lat. the simple Conjunction also, e.g. Aul. 785 ut' illum di immortales omnes deaeque quantumst perduint, beside Capt. 537 utinam te di prius perderent. Another Particle used in this function is *qui*, e.g. Men. 451 qui illum di omnes perduint (see above, s.v.).

Along with Optative *ut*, we have Jussive *ut* (often, for the sake of impressiveness, in the full form *uti*), e.g. Capt. 114 sed uti adserventur magna diligentia, a line in which the longer form is not due to the requirements of the metre. Indignant questions are expressed either by Acc. and Inf. (see **V, 38**) or by *ut* and Subj., e.g. Curc. 616 meane ancilla libera ut sit, quam ego numquam emisi manu?, Ter. Phorm. 304 egone illam cum illo ut patiar nuptam unum diem? (For a list of examples with *egone ut* see Dittmar: Studien zur lateinischen Moduslehre. Leipzig, 1897, p. 82.) And *ut* (often omitted) with Subj. is, in other expressions too, the equivalent of the Inf. (e.g. *iubeo ut facias* is equally used with *iubeo te facere*, e.g. Poen. 4 audire iubet vos imperator histricus, bonoque ut animo sedeant, *volo ut facias* with *volo te facere*, e.g. Mil. 1274 A. quid ⟨est quod⟩ volt me facere? B. ad se ut eas), both being equivalents of a Verbal Noun; cf. Pseud. 665 A. numquid vis? B. dormitum ut abeas (= abitionem), Cas. 701 cur non ego id perpetrem quod coëpi, ut nubat mihi?, Pseud. 940 (etc.) potin ut taceas? As the Inf. (for the Gerund) is used with *occasio*, etc. (see **V, 33**), so is *ut* with Subj., e.g. Mil. 977 hercle occasionem lepidam, ut mulierem excludam foras! The laxity of colloquial diction often allows the repetition of *ut* in the course of a long sentence, e.g. Aul. 791 te obtestor, Euclio, ut, siquid ego erga te imprudens peccavi aut gnatam tuam, ut mi ignoscas (cf. Rud. 1256, Trin. 140, Ter. Phorm. 154, etc.). These uses too are noteworthy: *modo ut* 'if only,' e.g. Ter. Andr. 409 modo ut possim 'if I only could,' Pers. 575 modo uti sciam 'if I only knew' (with Negative *modo ne*, e.g. Ter. Adelph. 835 ne nimium modo .. nos .. subvortat). On *ut ne*, e.g. Mil. 200, Trin. 105, see above, s.v. 'ne.'

Ut 'how' in Exclamations is sometimes combined with its equivalent *quam* (cf. Cic. Brut. 10, 39), e.g. Mil. 401, ut ad id exemplum somnium quam simile somniavit!, Asin. 581 ut adsimulabat Sauream med esse quam facete!, Stich. 570. Similarly *ut* and *quot* are pleonastically combined in Cist. 537 ut illaec hodie quot modis moderatrix linguae fuit! (see **I, 11**).

On *ut* 'when,' see below, 10. *Ut* 'as' (see Lalin: de particularum comparativarum usu apud Terentium. Norrcopiae, 1894) is as frequent in Early as in Classical Latin. The construction of *ut opinor* with Acc. and Inf. has been mentioned already (I, 10). The Conjunction acquires a quasi-Causal sense in phrases like Ter. Phorm. 774 haud scio hercle, ut homost, an mutet animum, Phorm. 638 ut est ille bonus vir, tria non commutabitis verba hodie apud vos. Like class. Lat. *qua est audacia* 'with his usual effrontery' (see IV, 5) is Ter. Eun. 525 hanc se intendit esse, ut est audacia; cf. Adelph. 389 A. eho an domist habiturus? B. credo, ut est dementia.

On *praeut, sicut*, see above, s.vv.

In *utqui*, lit. 'as how,' the Rel. is in the Instr. case as in *quippe qui* (see above), e.g. Asin. 506 an ita tu es animata utqui expers matris imperio sies?

But not in *utpote* ('as is possible') *qui* (with Subj.), Mil. 530 pro di immortales! similiorem mulierem, magisque eandem, ut pote quae non sit eadem, non reor deos facere posse, Rud. 462, Bacch. 511.

On *utut* 'however,' which normally has the Ind. of *esse* as its Verb, e.g. Ter. Phorm. 468 nam, utut erant alia, illi certe . . consuleres, see above, IV. 4.

utrum. The use of a Neuter Pronoun in anticipatory apposition to a whole sentence has already been mentioned (IV, 18) as a feature of early Latin, e.g. Men. 536 istuc, ubi illae armillae sunt quas una dedi?, Poen. 840 nam id quidem, illi, ut meditatur, verba facit emortuo. From this anticipatory use of the Neuter of *uter* has arisen the Disjunctive Interrogative *utrum.* We might put a comma after *utrum* in lines like Pseud. 709 dic utrum Spemne an Salutem te salutem, Pseudole (cf. Men. 1119 uter eratis, tun an ille maior?). Some editors punctuate Rud. 104 sed utrum tu? masne an femina's? (cf. Capt. 270 quid tu? servusne esse an liber mavelis?).

-ve. See 6, below.

vel (W. Kohlmann: de 'vel' imperativo quatenus ab 'aut' particula differat. Marburg, 1898), originally 2 Sing. Imperat. of *volo*, preserves a trace of its origin in such uses as:

> Mil. 59 amant ted omnes mulieres . . . vel ('for example') illae quae heri pallio me reprehenderunt.
> Trin. 655 scio, vel ('if you like') exsignavero (cf. Most. 300, Amph. 917).

verum, equivalent of *sed*, is to be distinguished from the Adverb *vero* 'in truth,' 'indeed' (see Langen 'Beiträge,' p. 113).

vidēlicet (also *-ē-*?) a Compound of *video*, in some form or other, and *licet* (as *scilicet* of *scio* and *licet*) takes (like *scilicet*; see above) Acc. and Inf., e.g. Asin. 599 nunc enim esse negotiosum interdius vidēlicet Solonem (vidēl. int. *alii*), or is used parenthetically, e.g. Most. 980 patris amicu's videlicet ('presumably,' apparently').

3. **Causal.** (Zimmermann: Gebrauch der Conjunctionen quod' und 'quia' im älteren Latein. Posen, 1880.)

Quando, properly Temporal (see 10), has sometimes in Plautus and always in Terence (except perhaps Adelph. 206) a Causal sense (like *quandoquidem*), e.g. Men. 202 cape tibi hanc, quando una vivis meis morigera moribus, Trin. 573 quando ita vis, .. spondeo, Capt. 886 quippe quando mihi nil credis, Curc. 527 quando bene gessi ('I have managed') rem, volo hic in fano supplicare. A fuller list of examples is given by Scherer (see p. 106, above.)

Quia was apparently an I-stem Neut. Pl, as *quod* an O-stem Neut. Sing. of the Pronoun. The two Conjunctions thus differ as *mira sunt* and *mirum (est)* (see 2, s.v. 'si'). In Plautus *quia* is more frequent than *quod* (whereas in class. Lat. *quod* attains the supremacy), and is always selected for answering such questions as begin with an Interrogative, e.g. Capt. 174 A. sed quid tu id quaeris? B. quia mi est natalis dies, Capt. 704 A. cur es ausus mentiri mihi? B. quia vera obessent illi quoi operam dabam. Examples of the equivalence of *quod* and *quia* are:

 Capt. 996 quod male feci crucior.
 Amph. 958 nam quia vos tranquillos video, gaudeo et volup-est mihi.
 Asin. 582 hospitem inclamavit, quod sese absente mihi fidem habere noluisset.
 Mil. 1035 me inclamato, quia sic te volgo volgem.

Quia is often strengthened by the Particle *enim* (see above, 2, s.v.), e.g. Capt. 884 A. quid tu per barbaricas urbes iuras? B. quia enim .. asperae sunt.

Quom, as has been already mentioned, is the equivalent of *quod* in sentences like *quom tu es liber gaudeo*. We cannot assign a definite Mood to O. Lat. *quom*, as we can assign the Subj. to Causal *quom* in class. Lat. It follows the variable course of the Relative *qui*, which is found now with Ind., e.g. Bacch. 464 stultus es, qui illi male aegre patere dici, now with Subjunctive, e.g. Mil. 370 ego stulta et mora multum, quae cum hoc insano fabuler, according to the nuance of the sentence in which it stands. (On the nuance of Subj. and Ind. see **V, 24-31**.)

But since it is generally an actual fact which is assigned as cause, the Ind. is greatly predominant with Causal *quom*. Examples of Subj. are :

    Capt. 146 alienus quom eius incommodum tam aegre feras,
        quid me patrem par facere est, quoi ille est unicus?
    Ter. Hec. 658 nunc quom eius alienum esse animum a me
        sentiam,
    . . quam ob rem redducam? (In Phorm. 202
    istaec quom ita sint, the best MS. has *sunt*).

On *quippe qui*, see above, s.v. The line between the Temporal and the Causal use of a Conjunction is not always distinct. See above (s.v.) on *postquam* with a half Causal sense, e.g. Ter. Adelph. prol. 1 postquam poeta sensit scripturam suam ab iniquis observari, . . indicio de se ipse erit, vos eritis iudices. *Quoniam* (i.e. *quom iam*) is never (or hardly ever) Temporal after Plautus (see below 10), and in many of his lines it stands on the border-line between the two senses, e.g. Capt. 930 quid nunc, quoniam tecum servavi fidem?, Most. 64 agite, porro pergite, quoniam occepistis (cf. Accius 120 ad populum intellego referundum, quoniam horum aequiter sententiae fuere).

4. Concessive. (Kriege: de enuntiatis concessivis apud Plautum et Terentium. Halle, 1884.)

Plautine Latin is far removed from class. Lat. in its treatment of Concessive Sentences. The usual Conjunctions are *etsi* and *quamquam*, and both retain their literal sense ' even if,' ' howsoever,' so that the Ind. is normally used.

Si ' if ' acquires a Concessive sense from the context in lines like Trin. 962 quoi si capitis res sit, nummum numquam credam plumbeum, Capt. 529 neque iam Salus servare, si volt, me potest; and the choice of the Subj. or Ind. follows the usage of Conditional *si* (see **10**, below). This Concessive sense is strengthened by the addition of *et* ' even,' e.g. Trin. 474 A. edim, nisi si ille vetet. B. at pol ego, *et si* vetet,

    Rud. 1348 sqq. A. illaec advorsum si quid peccasso, Venus,
        veneror te ut omnes miseri lenones sient.
        B. tamen fiet, *et si* tu fidem servaveris.

In these lines the construction of *et si* with *vetet* Subj., *servaveris* Fut. Perf. is naturally the same as that of the preceding *si* (with *vetet* Subj., *peccasso* 'Fut. Perf.'). The Conjunction *etsi*, hardly to be distinguished from *et si* in Plautus, normally takes Ind. in Plautus (always in Ter.), because the thing is normally spoken of as an actual fact, e.g. Most. 666 (=609) calidum hoc est: etsi procul abest, urit male, Bacch. 1191 age iam, utut est, etsist dedecori, patiar. Indeed *etsi* often has the sense of Greek καίτοι, e.g. Capt. 744 vale atque salve; etsi aliter ut dicam mêres (the speaker corrects himself). *Etiamsi* (Epid. 518?) is rare.

Tametsi similarly, is normally found with Ind., since an express fact is normally stated, e.g. Capt. 321 ne patri, tametsi unicus sum, decere videatur magis 'in spite of the fact that I am his only son.' The Subj. in Trin. 679 datur ignis, tametsi ab inimico petas is the Subj. of the Indefinite 2 Pers. Sing. (cf. **V, 31**). The Ind. too is found in all the occurrences of *tamenetsi*, which should be written *tamen etsi*, e.g. Most. 1167 A. verberibus, lutum, caedere pendens. B. tamen etsi pudet?, Ter. Andr. 864 A. ego iam te commotum reddam. B. tamen etsi hoc verumst? A. tamen. On *si maxume*, see **2, s.v.**

Quamquam, a double *quam* with the same generalized sense (see above, **IV, 4**) as double *ut* (e.g. Amph. 1100 gaudeo, utut me erga meritast 'howsoever she has deserved'), e.g. Truc. 923 quamquam es bella, malo tu tuo (*sc.* es), naturally takes the Ind., since it is a fact which is stated. Sometimes it has the sense of Greek καίτοι (not in Terence), e.g. Capt. 272 quamquam non multum fuit molesta servitus. It never appears without a finite Verb. (in Pseud. 1049 read *homo's*).

Quamvis, i.e. *quam vis* 'as you wish,' in its literal sense (the sense of class. Lat. *quantumvis*) is very frequent. It is only used with Adj. or Adv., e.g. Trin. 797 quamvis sermones possunt longi (*i.e.* quam longi vis) texier, Men. 318 quam vis ridiculus est, ubi uxor non adest. We find *quam velis* (cf. **V, 26**, on *volo* and *velim*) in Pseud. 1175 quam velis pernix homost, for which was substituted in a later version 'quamvis pernix hic est homo.' It can hardly be said to have the sense of 'although' in Plautus, unless possibly in the punning misapprehension of Trin. 554 A. quamvis malam (*i.e.* quam malam vis) rem quaeras, illic reperias. B. at tu hercle et illi et alibi (*scil.* malam rem = malum 'trouble,' 'punishment'); hardly in Bacch. 82 locus hic apud nos, quamvis subito (= quam subito vis) venias, semper liber est. The word does not appear to be ever used by Terence.

Licet comes near (but only near) to the sense of 'although' in Asin. 718 licet laudem Fortunam, tamen ut ne Salutem culpem. 'Quamlibet' is not found in Plautus or Terence.

Like the Conditional Conjunction *si*, the Temporal Conjunction *quom* sometimes acquires from the context a Concessive sense, e.g. Aul. 113 nam nunc, quom celo sedulo omnes ne sciant, omnes videntur scire. The Ind. is normally found with this concessive *quom* in Plautus, but sometimes (and in Terence normally) the Subj., e.g. Capt. 892 ain tu? dubium habebis etiam, sancte quom ego iurem tibi?, Rud. 1124 vidi petere miluom, etiam quom nihil auferret tamen. For a similar use of *quod*, see above, 2, s.v.

5. Conditional. (C. Lindskog: de enuntiatis apud Plautum et Terentium condicionalibus. Lund, 1895.)

The Conditional Conjunctions, *si*, *nisi* (and *ni*) follow in class. Lat. more strict laws than in the time of Plautus. We do not find in his plays that monotony of type which is taught in our School Grammars: (1) si habeo, do, (2) si habebo, dabo, (3) si habeam, dem, (4) si haberem, darem, (5) si habuissem, dedissem. There is not so clear a line of division separating a Conditional Protasis from other kinds of Dependent Sentence, or even between the treatment of a Verb in a Dependent Sentence and in a Main Sentence. In Plautine Latin we cannot separate *si habebo (habeo, habeam), dabo* from *quod habebo (habeo, habeam), dabo*, or *quom habebo (habeo, habeam), dabo;* nor is the O. Lat. quasi-Future use of the 1 Sing. Pres. Subj. (see **V, 26**) in a Main Sentence like sed maneam etiam opinor, 'but I think I will wait,' 'I had better wait,' to be distinguished from its use in a Protasis like *si habeam*. The Indefinite use of the 2 Sing. Subj. (see **V, 31**) is used by Plautus as freely in a Conditional Protasis as elsewhere; and such a Protasis is quite uninfluenced by the Mood of the Apodosis, e.g. Trin. 349 de magnis divitiis si quid demas, plus fit an minus?; Trin. 409 non hercle minus divorse distrahitur cito, quam si tu obicias formicis papaverem, Trin. 414 non tibi illud apparere, si sumas, potest, Trin. 1050 si quoi mutuom quid dederis, fit pro proprio perditum. The elasticity of Plautine Conditionals may be illustrated by these three varieties of the expression of a threat:

> Pers. 827 malum ego vobis dabo, ni abitis, (the normal type; see below).
> Mil. 450 nisi voluntate ibis, rapiam te domum.
> Bacch. 1172 ni abeas . . . malum tibi magnum dabo iam.

And since the Comedies reflect the colloquial Latin of everyday life, we find in them a number of imperfect types of Conditional sentence, which, though not strictly logical nor expressed in the normal form, are easily referred to this or that suppressed thought in the mind of the speaker. Examples of these imperfect Conditionals are:

> Amph. 336 non edepol nunc ubi terrarum sim scio, siquis roget.
> Stich. 171 nunc si ridiculum quaerat (*v.l.* -et) hominem quispiam,
> venalis ego sum cum ornamentis omnibus.
> Merc. 841 ibi quidem si regnum detur, non cupitast civitas.
> Epid. 730 invitus do hanc veniam tibi, nisi necessitate cogar.

Still, although it is not the same laws as in class. Lat. that rule Plautus' expression of Conditions, he obeys other laws; and although the carelessness of colloquial speech permits occasional divergence, there are certain normal types which we can clearly perceive.

In sentences of the form *siquid* $\genfrac{}{}{0pt}{}{haberem}{habuissem}$ $\genfrac{}{}{0pt}{}{darem}{dedissem}$ Plautus follows this rule with regard to the Tense of the Protasis. The Imperf. Subj. is used if the Protasis refers to the same time as the Apodosis; the Pluperf., if it refers to a previous time, e.g. Men. 241 nam invenissemus iam diu, si viveret (cf. Accius 13 quod si ut decuit, stares mecum aut meus maestaret dolor, iam diu inflammari Atridae naves vidissent suas), Men 460 si id ita esset, non ego hodie perdidissem prandium, Aul. 742 ni vellent, non fieret, scio, Aul. 828 quid faceres, si repperissem? Bacch. 217 ni nanctus Venerem essem, hanc Iunonem dicerem, Capt. 871 igitur olim si advenissem, magis tu tum istuc diceres, Mil. 1320 si non mecum aetatem egisset, hodie stulta viveret, Trin. 568 si ante voluisses, esses: nunc sero cupis, Aul. 669 ni subvenisset corvus, periissem miser, Trin. 927 si appellasses, respondisset nomini. So that Plautus does not normally say *siquid habuissem, dedissem*, that is if the 'having' and the 'giving' are thought of as contemporaneous. There are only two examples of this abnormal assimilation of the Protasis to the Apodosis, viz. Rud. 899 pol magis sapisset, si dormivisset domi, Most. 241 edepol si summo Iovi probo argento sacruficassem, pro illius capite quod dedi, numquam aeque id bene locassem. And the Protasis shews an abnormal Pluperf. also in Curc. 700 nam si is valuisset, iam pridem quoquo posset mitteret. As regards the Apodosis of this type of sentence, the Imperf. and Plup. Subj. are apparently used promiscuously by Plautus; sometimes *volui* with Inf. is used, e.g: Cas. 440 volui Charinum, si domi esset, mittere, Mil. 1356. The substitution of the Plup. Ind. for the Plup. Subj. (e.g. Hor. sustulerat nisi . . levasset) shews some traces of itself even in early Latin, e.g. Mil. 52 ubi tu quingentos simul, ni hebes machaera foret, uno ictu occideras (*v.l.* -res).

The type *si habeam, dem* is common in Plautus, e.g. Mil. 1371 nam si honeste censeam te facere posse, suadeam; and we find occasionally 'mixed' forms like Aul. 523 compellarem ego illum, ni metuam ne desinat, Stich. 510 vocem ego te ad me ad cenam, frater tuus ni dixisset mihi te apud se cenaturum esse hodie.

Plautus' expression of threats follows strict laws, which however are not the laws of class. Lat. With *nisi* (*ni*) the Pres. Ind. is used, with *si* the Fut. Perf. Examples are :

(1) with *nisi*, Asin. 670 atqui pol hodie non feres, ni genua confricantur.
   Amph. 358 faciam ego hodie te superbum, nisi hinc abis.
   Aul. 644 atque id quoque iam fiet, nisi fatere.
   Mil. 828 periisti iam, nisi verum scio.

(2) with *si*, Curc. 726 si tu me irritaveris, placidum te hodie reddam.
   Most. 239 si quid tu in illum bene voles loqui, id loqui licebit : (an affirmation)
   nec recte si illi dixeris, iam ecastor vapulabis: (a threat).
   Men. 416 periisti, si intrassis intra limen.

The origin of this curious distinction, *nisi facis* and *si feceris*, has been very plausibly referred to the distinction between command and prohibition, *da* and *ne dederis*. Thus *da—nisi das, vapulabis*, and *ne dederis—si dederis, vapulabis* would be the full forms of the two types of sentence. The exceptions to the law are mainly lines like Stich. 62 iam quidem in suo quicque loco nisi *erit* mihi situm supellectilis, quom ego revortar, vos monumentis commonefaciam bubulis, Cas. 123 quae nisi *erunt* semper plena, ego te implebo flagris, where the addition of the words *quom ego revortar* and *semper* necessitates the use of a Future Tense. A love of variety [u] may explain the abnormal Tenses in Epid. 724 sqq. numquam hercle hodie, nisi supplicium mihi das, me solvi sinam . . . numquam hercle hodie, nisi me *orassis*, solves, Pseud. 143 nunc adeo hanc edictionem nisi animum *advortetis* omnes, nisi somnum socordiamque ex pectore oculisque exmovetis, ita ego vostra latera loris faciam, ut valide varia sint. And *si pergis* with Inf. occasionally takes the place of *si* with Fut. Perf., e.g. Bacch. 570 postremo, si pergis parvam mihi fidem arbitrarier, tollam ego ted in collum atque intro hinc auferam. The Pres. Ind. (1 Pers.) is also found with *nisi* in a sentence like Ter. Heaut. 730 faciet, nisi caveo, which might be called a threat to oneself; cf. Capt. 538 occisast haec res, nisi reperio atrocem mi aliquam astutiam, Men. 847 ni occupo aliquod mihi consilium, hi domum me ad se auferent. Similarly the Fut. Perf. Ind. (1 Pers.) not only with *si*, but also with *nisi* in sentences like Cist. 497 di me perdant . . . si illam uxorem duxero unquam, Capt. 896 nam hercle nisi mantiscinatus probe ero, fusti pectito.

In other types of Conditionals it is more difficult to lay down rules for the use of the Ind. and Subj., the Pres. and the Fut. Colloquial Latin naturally substitutes the Pres. for the Fut., and so a type like this is very common (but not invariable) in Plautus:

>   Mil. 1213 divitias dabo, si impetras.
>   Capt. 331 eum si reddis mihi . . . et te et hunc amittam hinc.
>   Men. 1093 liber esto, si invenis hunc meum fratrem esse.

Both *si vivo* and *si vivam* are found (with Fut., never Fut. Perf., in Apodosis), e.g. Bacch. 766 vorsabo ego illunc hodie, si vivo, probe, Most. 4 ego pol te ruri, si vivam, ulciscar probe. Beside *si sapis* (i.e. if you are a wise man), we also find occasionally *si sapies* (on Poen. 351 see below), the Apodosis shewing Fut. or Imperat., e.g. Men. 121 malo cavebis, si sapis, Amph. 311 proin tu istam cenam, largire, si sapis, esurientibus, Rud. 1391 si sapies, tacebis.

In wagers (with *ni*, never 'nisi') there is a puzzling variety of

---

[u] It is not true to say that, where there are two Protases, the first always exhibits the Fut., the second the Pres., e.g. Capt. 683 si ego hic peribo, ast (=porro si) ille, ut dixit, non redit, at erit, etc. All that can be said is that Plautus often varies the Tense, e.g. Asin. 405 siquidem hercle Aeacidinis minis animisque expletus cedit, si med iratus tetigerit, iratus vapulabit, where the first Protasis has the Pres., the second the Fut. Perf.

Ind. and Subj., the Subj. being perhaps to be explained as a kind of Oratio Obliqua[1], e.g. Pers. 186 da hercle pignus, ni omnia memini et scio, Poen. 1242 da pignus, ni nunc perieres, in savium, uter utri det.

Dum, properly 'while,' 'so long as' (see 2, s.v.) acquires a Conditional sense in a context like Pers. 387 dum dos sit, nullum vitium vitio vortitur, whence arose *dum* (negatively *dum ne*) 'provided that' with the Subj. e.g. Capt. 682 dum ne ob malefacta peream, parvi existumo. Sometimes the Verb is omitted, e.g., Stich. 426 A. ducam hodie amicam. B. vel decem. dum de tuo, Ter. Phorm. 526 A. non pudet vanitatis? B. minime, dum ob rem. In this Conditional sense *dum* was often accompanied by a Particle, such as *quidem*, e.g. Aul. 211 dum quidem nequid perconteris, or *modo*, e.g. Amph. 644 absit, dum modo laude parta domum recipiat se, Ter. Heaut. 641 quidvis satis est, dum vivat modo. Hence *dummodo* of class. Lat.

On *ast*, see above, 2, s.v.

6. **Copulative.** (Sjögren: de particulis copulativis apud Plautum et Terentium. Upsala, 1900.)

Asyndeton is common in Early Latin, e.g. *aequom bonum* Men. 580 (but elsewhere with Copula, e.g. Curc. 65, Ter. Heaut. 788 istuc, Chremes, aequi bonique facio); often in alliterative phrases, e.g. vi violentia Rud. 839 oro obsecro Rud. 882, Ter. Ad. 472 (cf. Cic. Epist.). In Terence it is restricted to certain formulas, e.g. *ancillas servos*. Two Pronouns never stand in Asyndeton in the Dramatists; we find a Copula always employed, e.g. *ego et tu, me atque te*, etc. Two Prepositions rarely, e.g. Cas. 664 sub arcis, sub tectis latentes (but normally *cum . . . cum*, etc., e.g. Most. 392, cum hac cum istac, Curc. 289 cum libris cum sportulis). With some phrases in Plautus we find that this or that Copula has associated itself; thus *atque (ac)* is normally found with *abi ac suspende te*, with *aurum atque argentum*, with *di atque homines*, with *vale atque salve ; que* normally with *Juppiter dique omnes*, with *di deaeque* 'gods and goddesses;' *et* normally joins *sanus* and *salvus*, etc., e.g. sana et salva (Amph. 730, etc.), salvom et servatum (Trin. 1076, etc.); similarly *oro et*

---

[1] Just as in Mil. 1415, iuro per Iovem et Mavortem me nociturum nemini, quod ego hic hodie vapularim, the Subj. is due to the repetition by the soldier of the form of oath dictated to him in v. 1411: iura te non nociturum esse homini de hac re nemini, quod tu hodie hic verberatu's.

quaeso, Curc. 432, etc.; *memini et scio* Curc. 384, etc.; also Numerals, whether the smaller or the larger one precedes, e.g. Merc. 673 octoginta et quattuor (but Most. 630 quattuor quadraginta). Both *que* and *et* appear in Pronominal phrases like *me meosque, me et meos*, etc., while *atque* is usual in *me atque hos*, etc.; both *atque* and *et* in Commands like *i (abi) atque (et) fac*, etc., although Asyndeton, *i (abi) fac*, is more usual (on *abi ac suspende te*, see above); and two Imperatives normally stand in Asyndeton, when the second has the Particle *ne*, e.g. Asin. 638 bono animo es, ne formida, Rud. 1254 abi intro, ne molestu's, Poen. 261 sine amem, ne obturba. *Atque* is the favourite Copula for Prepositions which begin with a Vowel, e.g. Aul. 221 abs te atque abs tuis, Amph. 259 in dicionem atque in arbitratum.

Ve is the Copula used, as in classical Latin, with *nē, si* (see 2 on *sive*), with avoidance of 'nēque,' 'sique'; also with *ni* 'unless,' e.g. Rud. 1420 ad cenam vocem, ni daturus nihil sim . . nive adeo vocatos credam vos esse ad cenam foras. 'Utque' is also avoided, perhaps through fear of confusion with *utique;* and although *quique* is found (e.g. Pseud. 1086 qui nili faciat quique infitias non eat), still *quive* seems to take its place in a line like Poen. 451 qui . . immolarit quive ullum turis granum sacruficaverit. (For other examples see Langen 'Beiträge,' p. 96.) The phrases *plus minusque* and *plus minusve, malum damnumque* and *malum damnumve*, and the like are practically equivalent.

Noteworthy combinations of Copulas are *et—et—et*, e.g. Truc. 45 extemplo et ipsus periit et res et fides, Ter. Andr. 49, *que—que—que*, e.g. Aul. 218 quae res recte vortat mihique tibique tuaeque filiae, Ter. Adelph. 301.

Among the Plautine Copulas must be included *qua—qua*, e.g. Mil. 1392 qua viri qua mulieres, Trin. 1044 mores autem rapere properant qua sacrum qua publicum. On special uses of *atque* and *et*, see 2, s.vv.

7. **Interrogative.** (E. Morris: On the Sentence-Question in Plautus and Terence. Baltimore, 1890.)

-ne, which Plautus (but seldom Terence) sometimes puts late in the sentence, e.g. Curc. 17 et heri cenavistine?, often plays the part of *nonne*, e.g. Pseud. 977 scivin ego?, Amph. 526 facitne ut dixi?, Ter. Andr. prol. 17 faciuntne intellegendo ut nihil intellegant?, (see above, 2). It is often omitted in colloquial Latin, e.g. *rogas?* (see Abraham 'Studia Plautina,' p. 233); and since scribes had a habit

of ignoring a final *n*, it is often hard to tell whether e.g. *novisti* or *novistin* was what Plautus wrote. Apparently *vin* is appropriate to the beginning, *vis* to the middle of a sentence; and the same may hold of *novistin* and *novisti*, etc. (but cf. Curc. 18, etc.).

Nonne is not common in Plautus, but is undoubtedly in use, e.g. Amph. 407 non loquor?, non vigilo? nonne hic homo modo me pugnis contudit? (For a full list of examples, see Schrader : de particularum '-ne,' 'anne,' 'nonne' apud Plautum prosodia. Strasburg, 1885, pp. 42 sqq.) It is only found before a word beginning with a Vowel (i.e. it is never a disyllable in Prosody), while *non* (as in the line just quoted) takes its place before an initial consonant. But we are not justified in writing *non* in these cases as '*nonn*' (like *tun, egon, hicin*, etc.), for *non* is often found before an initial vowel. The relation of *nonne* to *non* is precisely that of *anne* (before initial vowel only) to *an* (before initial cons. or vow., e.g. ăn est)[1]. The form enlarged by the addition of *-ne* pleased the ear of Plautus when a vowel followed, but he did not choose to give it trochaic scansion (cf. *hisce, illisce* before vowel, *his, illis* before consonant or vowel).

Num (cf. *numquid*) and *numnam*, e.g. Aul. 242 sed, pro Iuppiter, num ego disperii?, Most. 1031 A. perii, interii ! B. numquid Tranio turbavit?, Amph. 1073 A. numnam hunc percussit Iuppiter? B. credo edepol (occasionally in indirect questions, e.g. Pers. 78, Poen. 1008, Ter. Andr. 235), apparently do not necessarily expect a Negative answer, e.g. Bacch. 1110 Ter. Haut. 429. *Num non* occurs in the phrase *num non vis* (Aul. 161, Most. 336, Poen. 1079). The existence of 'numne' (see Lease, Classical Review, xi, 348) in the Dramatists' Latin is doubtful. *Numquid aliud me vis?*, usually shortened to *numquid me vis?* or *numquid vis?* or *numquid aliud?* was the formula of polite leave-taking (cf. Donatus' note on Ter. Eun. II. iii. 50: recte abituri, ne id dure facerent, 'numquid vis?' dicebant iis quibuscum constitissent).

An does not necessarily express an alternative question in O. Lat. e.g. Pseud. 309 A. te vivum vellem. B. eho! an iam mortuust? But the alternative use is also frequent, e.g. Amph. 343 servusne an

---

[1] Cf. *iam* and *iamne* in Pomponius 157 R. iamne abierunt? iam non tundunt? iamne ego in tuto satis? If the theory mentioned above (2) be right, that *an* (e.g. an sum?, ăn est?) had originally the form *anne*, then we should be justified in regarding *non* in questions as a mere apocopated form of *nonne*. Still Plautus seems so often to append or withhold *-ne* at caprice (e.g. *iam* and *iamne*) that it seems more likely that *non* in questions and *nonne* are two distinct forms.

liber?, Bacch. 162 tibi ego an tu mihi servus es?, Amph. 56 utrum sit an non voltis?, Epid. 223 quid erat induta? an regillam induculam an mendiculam?

The Neuter of *ecquis* often plays the part of an Interrogative Conjunction in Plautus, e.g. *ecquid audis?* And the same is true of *numquid, satin* (e.g. Trin. 925; cf. Capt. 638 A. satin istuc mihi exquisitumst . . .? B. tam satis quam . . ., Ter. Phorm. 682 A. satin est id? B. nescio hercle, tantum iussus sum), *etiam* and similar words. We may add *ēn* of *en umquam*, e.g. Trin. 589 o pater, enumquam aspiciam te? (see below, IX). On the Indirect Interrogatives *utrum, necne, annon*, see 2, s.vv.

8. Negative. (A. Habich: observationes de negationum aliquot usu Plautino. Halle, 1893; read with it Seyffert's review in Bursian's Jahresbericht, 1895, p. 319.)

The prefix *nĕ-* of *nequeo, nescio, nefas, nisi* (older *nesi*), *numquam* (= nĕ-umquam), *neutiquam* (scanned *n'ŭtiquam*, and by some editors[2] printed *ne utiquam*), *nullus* (= nĕ-ullus), is the first element of *nolo* (= nĕ-volo), with 2, 3 Sing. *nĕvis, nĕvolt* still surviving beside the more usual *nonvis, nonvolt* in Plautine Latin. The same Particle is the second element of *quin* (2), e.g. quin sciret for 'qui nĕ sciret.' But its independent use in the time of Plautus is not proved by the variant reading *ne multa* (*P*: non multa *A*) in Trin. 364 eo non multa quae nevolt eveniunt, nisi fictor malust, which some refer to a marginal correction of *nisi* to the older spelling *nesi*. (In Truc. 877 read *refacere*, Most. 124 *reparcunt*. *Nē*, not *nĕ*, is the word used in Pseud. 437, 633). (On the affirmative Particle *nē*, see 2.)

The O. Lat. *nec* (e.g. res nec mancipi; cf. Festus 162 M.), replaced by *non* in Class. Lat., still survives in Plautine Latin (see 2), especially in the phrase *nec recte dicere*, e.g. Most. 240 nec recte si illi dixeris. Like 'necuter' (later) may be *necullus* of Trin. 282 neque in via neque in foro necullum sermonem exsequi (neque u. *A*, ullum *P*), but other examples, such as *nec quoquam* (*v.l.* nēquoquam) Most. 562, are still less free from suspicion. Cf. Asin. 704, Rud. 359 (p. 102), Curc. 547; also Poen. 489, Truc. 231. Editors change *nec—quidem* in Most. 595 to *ne—quidem*. (On Copulative *nec, neque*, see 2.)

Of the O. Lat. form *noenum* (*nĕ-oenum* 'not one') there is only

[2] Donatus' remark 'una pars est orationis' may imply that *ne* and *utiquam* were written separately.

one certain example in Plautus, Aul. 67 noenum mecastor quid ego ero dicam meo, just as of the form *oenus* for *unus* (viz. Truc. 102). Editors have sometimes wrongly substituted it for *non enim* 'indeed not' (cf. 2 'enim'), e.g. in Mil. 648, Aul. 594, Trin. 705.

Haud (*hau*, a form found only before a word beginning with a consonant) is not used in questions, commands, conditional, consecutive and final clauses. *Non* is not subject to these restrictions. *Haud* is especially used with Adj. or Adv., and generally stands immediately before the negated word.

A double Negative usually merely strengthens the Negation (but cf. *nonnullus, haud nolo*), e.g. *neque—haud* (normally separated by a word), Bacch. 1037 neque ego haud committam, Men. 371, Epid. 664, Bacch. frag. 9, Ter. Andr. 205 (the only example in Terence) neque tu haud dices tibi non praedictum, etc., *neque— numquam*, Pseud. 136 neque ego homines, magis asinos numquam vidi, Men. 1027, etc., *neque—nullus* Rud. 359 nec te aleator nullus est sapientior. Cf. Epid. 532, Curc. 579, Mil. 1411. The class. Lat. use of *neque . . . neque* after a Negative is found in Capt. 76 quos numquam quisquam neque vocat neque invocat, Epid. 110, Trin. 281, etc.

On the Pronominal equivalents of *non*, such as *nihil, nullum, nullus*, see **IV, 28**. To these may be added *numquam* e.g. Pers. 628, Ter. Andr. 384 numquam faciam (Donatus' note is : 'numquam' plus habet negationis, quam 'non'), often strengthened by the addition of *hodie*[a] (like Virgil's *numquam hodie effugies*) e.g. Trin. 971, Ter. Phorm. 805 nunquamne hodie concedes mihi?, Naev. trag. 15. Cf. Men. 217 neque hodie . . meream. On *numquam quisquam*, see **IV, 28**. On *minus* (cf. *quominus*), see p. 111.

9. Prohibitive. (H. Elmer : a Discussion of the Latin Prohibitive, based upon a complete collection of the instances from the earliest times to the end of the Augustan period. Reprinted from the American Journal of Philology, vol. XV., Parts ii and iii. Ithaca, N.Y., 1894 ; read with it Seyffert's review in Bursian's Jahresbericht, 1895, p. 338). The use of the Subjunctive as an Imperative has been already mentioned (**V, 25**). In O. Lat. a Prohibition is as often expressed by *ne* with Subj. (Pres more often than Perf.) as by *ne* with Imper. e.g. *ne me moneas* or *ne me mone*. It is often difficult

---

[a] Donatus remarks on Ter. Adelph. 215 : 'hodie' non tempus significat, sed iracundam eloquentiam ac stomachum. (Cf. Hor. Sat. 2, 7, 21 non dices hodie?)

to distinguish between *ne*, the Prohibitive, and *ne*, the Final Conjunction, in lines like Cist. 558 illaec tibi nutrix est, ne matrem censeas ('I say this lest you should think'), Mil. 1274 viri quoque armati idem istuc faciunt, ne tu mirere mulieres (cf. class. Lat. *nedum* 'much less'; see 2). Whether it is possible to detect a different nuance of meaning in *ne-* Prohibitions with Pres. Subj. and with Perf. Subj. is matter of controversy. We find the latter Tense often with other than Prohibitive *ne*, e.g. Bacch. 37 pol magis metuo ne defuerit mihi in monendo oratio, and the same interchange of Tenses with *cave*, e.g. Epid. 437 cave praeteribitas ullas aedes . . . incertus tuom cave ad me rettuleris pedem, where a difference of nuance is very unlikely.

As a circumlocution, *cave* plays the same part in early Lat. as *noli* (e.g. Capt. 840) in class. Lat. It normally takes the Tense in *-sim* (S.-Aorist Optative) or the Perfect Subjunctive, e.g. *cave faxis*, *cave feceris*, and is not often found with the Pres. Subj., except when *cave ne* is used or some other part of *caveo* than the Imper. (For details, see Studemund in Versammlung zu Karlsruhe, p. 54.) On O. Lat. *ne . . neve* for class. Lat. *neve . . neve* and on *neque . . neque* in the same function, see above, 2, s.vv.

10. **Temporal.** (Schubert: zum Gebrauch der Temporalconjunktionen bei Plautus, Leipzig, 1880.)

For Plautine Latin we must discard the hard-and-fast rules of our School grammars, that '*quom* takes the Pluperf. Subj., *ubi* the Perf. Ind.', and so on. The various Temporal Conjunctions (except perhaps *quoniam*, as is explained below) all receive the same treatment. And the Tense used is merely the ordinary Tense of Independent Sentences in narration. The Perf. Ind. is, of course, pre-eminently the narrative Tense, e.g. *heri veni*, and so Plautus more often says *quom veni, ubi veni*, etc., than anything else. But the Historical Present (see V, 11) is also a narrative Tense, and so Plautus can also say *quom venio, ubi venio*, etc. (especially when the main Verb is also Hist. Pres.). If the priority of the one action to the other is insisted on, the Pluperf. becomes appropriate, e.g. *quom veneram, ubi veneram*, and so on. Just as we found in discussing the Subjunctive Mood (V, 28, sqq.), that Plautine Latin makes no sharp distinction between main and dependent clauses, so we find in Plautus' treatment of Temporal Sentences. The use of the Subj. often implies purpose (for examples, see below), but it may be due to a number of other nuances, to as many, in fact, as those which condition the use of the Subj. in other Dependent Sentences or in Main Sentences. These general remarks must be borne in mind, while we consider the details of Plautus' use of the Temporal Conjunctions.

With *postquam* and *priusquam* we might regard the Pluperf. as the natural Tense. But we must remember that in Plautine Latin the expression is rather *post veni quam feci, prius veni quam feci* (see above, 2, s.vv.), so that the ordinary Tense of narration is as suitable with them as with the others.

Priusquam (*antequam* is not found at all in Plautus and only once in Ter., although frequent in Cato) takes the Subj. (just as in class. Lat.) when Purpose is implied, e.g. Amph. 533 exire ex urbe priusquam lucescat volo (contrast Mil. 708 priusquam lucet, adsunt, a mere statement of the time of their arrival), or when the sense is that of *potius quam*, e.g. Amph. 240 animam omittunt priusquam loco demigrent. Often the choice of Subj. or Ind. seems arbitrary, e.g. Rud. 494 utinam te prius quam . . . vidissem . . . cruciatu in Sicilia perbiteres (with Subj.), Capt. 537 utinam te di prius perderent quam periisti e patria tua (with Ind.); Merc. 601 prius quam recipias anhelitum, uno verbo eloquere (with Subj.), Asin. 940 da savium etiam prius quam abitis (with Ind.). In general the Subj. attached itself more and more to *priusquam* after the time of Plautus. The Historical Pres. Ind. is used in Curc. 637 is prius quam moritur, mihi dedit tanquam suo. (For full details and examples see Hullihen: 'Antequam' and 'Priusquam.' Baltimore, 1903.)

Postquam is most often found with Perf. Ind., e.g. Men. 34 postquam puerum perdidit, animum despondit, Truc. 647 post illoc quam veni; never with Pluperf. in Plautus (but in Terence, e.g. Andr. 177 qui postquam audierat; cf. Caecilius 44). It takes Pres. Ind. especially when it has the sense of 'since,' e.g. Most. 925 tibi umquam quicquam, postquam tuus sum, verborum dedi? But it is also found in the sense of 'after' with the Historical Present, especially when the Main Verb is in the same Tense, e.g. Capt. 24 postquam belligerant Aetoli cum Aleis . . . capitur alter filius; (with *iam* Men. 24 postquam iam pueri septuennes sunt, pater oneravit navim magnam multis mercibus), Afranius 207.

Dum is associated with the Present Tense. In the sense of 'while' it usually takes the Historical Pres. Ind. (see 2, s.v.), e.g. Bacch. 279 forte ut adsedi in stega, dum circumspecto, atque ego lembum conspicor; but is also found with other Tenses of the Ind., e.g.

Amph. 599 ordine omne, uti quidque actum est, dum apud hostes sedimus, edissertavit, Truc. 217 dum fuit, dedit, Truc. 164 te, dum vivebas, noveram, Rud. 558 tibi quidem edepol copiast, dum lingua vivet, qui rem solvas omnibus, Bacch. 443 noster esto, dum te poteris defensare iniuria, Turpilius 173 dum ego conixi somno, hic sibi prospexit vigilans virginem. When it refers to future time the Fut. Ind. is used, e.g. Men. 728 vivito vel usque dum regnum obtinebit Iuppiter. The Subj. in Truc. 103 is due to the idea of Purpose: oenus eorum aliqui osculum amicae usque oggerit, dum illi agant ceteri cleptae 'in order that they may act meanwhile.' This idea of Purpose is also present when *dum* 'until' takes the Subj., e.g. Amph. 697 paulisper mane, dum edormiscat unum somnum, Trin. 170 lupus observavit dum dormitarent canes (but not apparently in Bacch. 932 lubet lamentari dum exeat); and absent when it takes the Ind. (usually Pres.), e.g. Ter. Eun. 206 exspectabo dum venit, Amph. 472 erroris .. ego illos .. complebo .. adeo usque satietatem dum capiet pater illius quam amat, Pers. 52 usque ero domi, dum excoxero lenoni malam rem aliquam. On *dum* (*dummodo*) 'provided that' (with the Subj., e.g. Capt. 694 dum pereas, nihil interdico aiant vivere) see 5, above. (For full details see G. M. Richardson: de ' dum' particulae apud priscos scriptores Latinos usu. Leipzig, 1886; J. Schmalz 'Donec und Dum' in Archiv lat. Lexikographie, 11, 333 sqq.)

Donec (older *donicum*) 'until' differs from *dum* 'until' in being used of past time. In this use it normally takes Perf. Ind. and is rarely found with Historical Pres. Ind. (Cist. 583 ⟨non hercle⟩ hoc longe destiti instare usque adeo donec se adiurat anus iam mihi monstrare). Usually however it refers to the future and takes Fut. Perf., e.g. Vidul. frag. 5, neutri reddibo, donicum res diiudicata erit haec (but Fut., e.g. Liv. Andr. Odyss. donicum videbis). Quite exceptional is Rud. 812 ni istunc istis (*scil.* clavis) invitassitis usque adeo donec qua domum abeat nesciat, periistis ambo. (For fuller details see J. Schmalz.' Donec und Dum' in Archiv Lat. Lexikographie, 11, 333 sqq.)

On *quoad*, see 2, above.

Ut, like *postquam*, is chiefly associated with the Perf. Ind., e.g. Epid. 14 nam ut apud portum te conspexi, curriculo occepi sequi. The use of the Pluperf. implies that the action is previous to the action of the Main Verb, e.g. Curc. 646 postquam illo ventumst, iam, ut me collocaverat, exoritur ventus turbo, Most. 484 ut foris cenaverat tuos gnatus, postquam rediit a cena domum, abimus omnes cubitum. The Imperf. sometimes occurs, e.g. Asin. 343 verum in tonstrina ut sedebam, me infit percontarier. Rarely the Historical Pres., e.g. Merc. 100 discubitum noctu ut imus, ecce ad me advĕnit.

Ubi, when used of past time, commonly takes the Perf. Ind., e.g., Amph. 216 haec ubi legati pertulere, Amphitruo castris ilico producit omnem exercitum, Capt. 1002 nam ubi illo adveni . . . haec mihi advenienti upupa qui me delectem datast. It can also take the Historical Pres., e.g. Amph. 1061 ubi parturit and (with *iam*) Capt. 234 (quoted below), Ennius trag. 83 nam ubi introducta est puerumque ut laverent locant in clupeo. For the Pluperf. may be cited Aquilius 10 ubi primum accensus clamarat meridiem.

Quando (see 3, above) signifies indefinite time, e.g. Novius 25 quando (indefinite) ludos vēnit ('has come'), alii cum (definite) tacent, totum diem argutatur quasi cicada. So in the few instances in which it refers to the past, it takes Imperf. or Pluperf., Pseud. 1180 noctu in vigiliam quando ibat miles, quom tu ibas simul, conveniebatne in vaginam tuam machaera militis?, Epid. 433 quom militabam, pugnis memorandis meis eradicabam hominum aures, quando occeperam.

Quoniam is nothing but *quom iam*. The addition of *iam* [b] makes the Pres. the appropriate Tense (or the Perfect of completed action e.g. Most. 1050), e.g. Bacch. 292 quoniam vident nos stare, occeperunt ratem tardare, Aul. 9 is quoniam moritur, ita avido ingenio fuit, numquam indicare id filio voluit suo, Trin. 149 quoniam hinc est profecturus peregre Charmides, thensaurum demonstravit mihi in hisce aedibus. Similarly *ubi iam*, Capt. 234 sed id ubi iam penes sese habent, *postquam iam*, Men. 24 postquam iam pueri septuennes sunt, pater oneravit navem, take the Pres. Like *nemo homo*, with pleonastic addition of *homo* (see IV, 21), we find once *quoniam iam* Truc. 402 quoniam iam decumus mensis adventat prope. After Plautus' time the Conjunction dropped its Temporal and retained its Causal sense (see above 3). Already in Cato the Temporal function is played by *cum* (*quom*) *iam*, not by *quoniam* (if our MSS. are to be trusted on this point), Agr. Cult. 161, 3 post annos octo, cum iam est vetus, digerito (like *ubi iam* 158, 1 ubi iam coctum incipit esse, eo addito). Cf. Merc. 552 demum igitur quom

---

[b] Compare the use of the Historical Pres. in all periods of Latin with *iamdudum, iam pridem, iam diu*.

sis iam senex, tum in otium te conloces. But *quoniam* is Temporal in Accius praet. 17 quoniam quieti corpus nocturno impetu dedi, . . visum est in somnis pastorem ad me adpellere pecus, Pacuvius 393 quoniam ille interit, imperium Cephalo transmissum est.

Quom. A few examples will suffice to shew the freedom of its construction :

> Ter. Andr. 517 quom intellexeras id consilium capere, cur non dixti extemplo Pamphilo?
> Aul. 178 praesagibat mi animus frustra me ire, quom exibam domo.
> Ennius Ann. 227 V. tonsam ante tenentes parerent, observarent, portisculu' signum quom dare coepisset.
> Amph. 668 gravidam ego illanc hic reliqui, quom abeo, Ter. Eun. 792 quom tibi do istam virginem, dixtin hos dies mihi soli dare te?, Eun. 345 huc quom advenio, nulla erat.
> Trin. 194 posticulum hoc recepit quom aedes vendidit, Ennius Ann. 35 V. et cita (*v.l.* excita) cum tremulis anus attulit artubu' lumen, talia tum memorat.
> Ter. Andr. 856 quom faciem videas, videtur esse quantivis preti.
> Most. 470 quia septem menses sunt quom in hasce aedes pedem nemo intro tetulit.
> Truc. 163 O Astaphium, haud istoc modo solita es me ante appellare,
> > sed blande, quom illuc quod apud vos nunc est apud med haberem.

'As soon as' is in Plautus expressed usually by *quom extemplo* (e.g. Most. 101 aedes quom extemplo sunt paratae . . laudant fabrum), a phrase which fell into disuse after his time; also by *ubi primum* (e.g. Mil. 109 ubi primum evēnit militi huic occasio) and once by *simulac* (cf. above, 2), Asin. 479 ut vapules, Demaenetum simul ac conspexero hodie. But *quom primum* has always the literal sense 'when for the first time' (cf. *ut primum* Epid. 600), e.g. Asin. 890 pater, iube dari vinum : iam dudum factum est, quom primum bibi. (For fuller details see J. C. Jones in Archiv Lat. Lexikographie 14, pp. 89 sqq., 233 sqq.). *Quom maxume* is as early as Plautus, e.g. Amph. 427 legiones quom pugnabant maxume, Mil. 1153 nunc quom maxume opust dolis. The Vulgar

Lat. *iam ut* (Subj.) appears in Ter. Hec. 378 iam ut limen exirem, ad genua accidit 'at the moment of going out.' (On Curc. 646, see p. 134.)

Examples of the Iterative type of Temporal (and Conditional) Sentences are:

>Bacch. 424 sqq. ante solem exorientem nisi in palaestram veneras,
>gymnasi profecto haud mediocres poenas penderes.
>id quoi (quom *alii*) obtigerat, hoc etiam ad malum accersebatur malum:
>et discipulus et magister perhibebantur improbi.
>... inde de hippodromo et palaestra ubi revenisses domum,
>cincticulo praecinctus in sella apud magistrum adsideres:
>quom librum legeres, si unam peccavisses syllabam,
>fieret corium tam maculosum quam est nutricis pallium.

Turpilius 21 antehac si flabat Aquilo aut Auster, inopia tum erat piscati.

Aquilius 6 nam me puero venter erat solarium:
>ubi is te monebat, esses, nisi quom nil erat.

IX. THE INTERJECTION.

(P. Richter: de usu particularum exclamativarum apud priscos scriptores Latinos, vol. I, Part ii of Studemund's Studien auf dem Gebiet des archäischen Lateins, Berlin, 1890; F. W. Nicolson: the use of 'hercle' ('mehercle'), 'edepol' ('pol'), 'ecastor' ('mecastor') by Plautus and Terence, in vol. IV of Harvard Studies in Classical Philology, Boston, 1893.)

Details regarding Plautus' use of Interjections belong mostly to the domain of Accidence, not of Syntax. The Acc. of Exclamation (often accompanied by an Interjection) has been already mentioned, II, 47. *Em* naturally takes an Acc., since it is nothing but the Imperative of *emo*, 'I take'; e.g. Capt. 859 A. cedo manum. B. em manum. (The Bembine Scholiast remarks on Ter. Phorm. 52: 'em,' hoc cum gestu offerentis dicitur.)

En is with Plautus and Terence merely used in rhetorical questions in the collocation *en unquam*, etc., e.g. Men. 925 dic mihi: en unquam intestina tibi crepant?

Eccum, -am, etc. (for *ecce-hum*, an old form of *hunc*), and *eccillum, -am*, etc. (whence, according to a probable account, Romance Pronouns like Fr. celui) are characteristic of the Old Comedians' language. When a noun without a verb follows *eccum* it is normally put in the Acc., e.g. Mil. 1216 eccum praesto militem, Bacch. 568 duas ergo hic intus eccas Bacchides. A similar Compound is *ellum* (cf. Ital. ello) for *em-illum*. For the phrase *pro deûm fidem* (e.g. Ter. Andr. 237) we find in Caecil. 212 pro deûm . . . imploro fidem, which shews that *pro* does not govern an Acc. Case (cf. *pro di immortales*, e.g. Ter. Adelph. 447). On the use of *O* with Vocatives, see above, II, 52; and on the construction of the Dative with *vae* (but *vae te!* Asin. 481), *ei* (e.g. *ei mihi!*), see II, 24. *Malum!*, 'curse you!' interjected as an Enclitic after an Interrogative, e.g. Rud. 945 quid tu, malum, nam me retrahis?, Men. 390 cui, malum, parasito?, Most. 6 quid tibi, malum, hic ante aedes clamitatiost?, is an elliptic expression of *malum tibi sit*.

PRINTED BY JAMES PARKER AND CO.,
CROWN YARD, OXFORD.